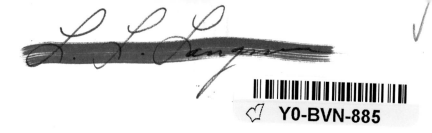
THEY LOVE ME,
THEY LOVE ME NOT

*A Worldwide Study of the Effects of
Parental Acceptance and Rejection*

RONALD P. ROHNER

HRAF PRESS

1975

ABOUT THE AUTHOR

RONALD P. ROHNER received his B.S. degree in Psychology from the University of Oregon and his M.A. and Ph.D. degrees in Anthropology at Stanford University. He is currently Visiting Professor of Anthropology and Human Development and Senior Research Scientist, Boys Town Center for the Study of Youth Development, at Catholic University of America. Prior to June 1975, he was Associate Professor of Anthropology and Human Development in the Department of Biocultural Anthropology at the University of Connecticut, with a joint appointment in the Department of Child Development and Family Relations. He also served as a member of the University's Program Faculty, Social Science and Health Service Training Program. He has done fieldwork in Turkey and among the Kwakiutl Indians in British Columbia and has served as a Research Assistant at Oregon State Hospital, a Research Consultant to the State of Connecticut, and as Director of the Rejection-Acceptance Project. He is the author of numerous journal articles and reviews and of three previous books.

INTERNATIONAL STANDARD BOOK NUMBER: 0-87536-332-6
LIBRARY OF CONGRESS CATALOG CARD NUMBER: 75-17092
© COPYRIGHT 1975
HUMAN RELATIONS AREA FILES, INC.
ALL RIGHTS RESERVED
PRINTED IN THE UNITED STATES OF AMERICA

To Olga A. G. Little, M.D.

WITH AFFECTION

FOR SHOWING THAT MANY OF THE EFFECTS

OF REJECTION

CAN BE OVERCOME

Contents

List of Figures

List of Tables

LIST OF TABLES—*continued*

Preface

This book is the product of nearly fifteen years' research on two complementary problems. The first and conceptually larger question is one that has fascinated and disturbed me since childhood: "What does it mean to be a human being? How are we all alike and how are we different?" Questions like these sent me into the field of psychology as an undergraduate and then into anthropology for my Ph.D. These experiences have since become consolidated into an interdisciplinary perspective on the boundary between psychological anthropology and cross-cultural psychology—especially as they relate to the second topic of this book, human development in species and cultural perspective. More specifically, the book addresses a series of questions about the worldwide causes and consequences of parental acceptance-rejection. It asks, "Do humans everywhere respond uniformly to the withdrawal of parental warmth and affection? Do similar psychological, social, and environmental conditions induce parents the world over to behave toward their children in parallel ways? How is it possible, methodologically, to determine if these things are true?"

These questions anticipate my dual purpose in writing this book, namely (a) to introduce a conceptual and methodological perspective called the "universalist approach," and (b) to use this approach in exploring the pancultural antecedents and effects of parental acceptance-rejection. I also hope to arouse behavioral scientists' and students' interest and participation in the "universalist question," that is in questions about the "nature of human nature." Moreover my hope is that the epistemological commitment and requirements of the universalist approach will induce behavioral scientists to work toward a cumulative "science of man"—in distinction to the now laterally spreading, noncumulative, and insular behavioral science disciplines. The goal of the universalist approach is to establish "principles" of human behavior, i.e. to establish scientifically derived generalizations about human behavior that are specieswide in their applicability. Research efforts that aspire to establishing "principles" of behavior are more likely to produce a cumulative science of man than the more restrictive and conventional objectives of behavioral science.

This is not intended as a technical research monograph. Rather, the book is addressed to a wide audience—students and professionals alike—in all the behavioral sciences, with the work itself lying on an interface between anthropology and psychology, especially human development.

The volume includes six chapters. Chapter One lays out the general characteristics of the universalist approach, its assumptions, and its requirements. It discusses why, historically, behavioral science, especially anthropology, has avoided a search for "principles" of human behavior, and it discusses instances of a widely diffused, recent, and mounting interest in making specieswide generalizations. Finally it lays out a general research strategy for establishing generalizations about human behavior. Chapter Two draws heavily from worldwide ethnographic descriptions of parental behavior and children's responses as a way of helping to introduce the "phylogenetic perspective" and the "anthropological perspective" described in Chapter One. Chapter Two also discusses the nature and the predictable causes and consequences of parental acceptance-rejection.

Drawing from the evidence provided by psychologists and psychiatrists regarding the effects of parental rejection, mainly in the United States, Chapter Three focuses on five major topics: (a) developmental problems created by "maternal" deprivation in humans as well as in monkeys; (b) child abuse; (c) personality disturbances arising in children and in adults as a consequence of parental rejection; (d) behavior disorders and conduct problems; and (e) mental illness. Chapter Four reviews crosscultural statistical (i.e. holocultural) evidence regarding the causes and effects of acceptance-rejection, especially the relation between acceptance-rejection and (1) societal maintenance systems (e.g. household type, forms of subsistence economy, political organization, etc.); (2) institutionalized expressive systems (including the religious beliefs of a people, their art, mythology, medical beliefs, etc.); and (3) the natural environment. The chapter also looks at the worldwide effects of rejection-acceptance on (4) personality development and functioning. Chapter Five compares socialization practices and personality functioning in two nonindustrial societies. By our criteria, children in one society, the Alorese, are rejected, but in the other, the Papago, they are accepted. The objective of this chapter is to show how the rejection-acceptance process and its outcome, as described throughout the book, are related in expectable ways to the total social and emotional environment wherein children are raised. Finally, Chapter Six reviews the argument and the data of the entire volume, ties the various pieces together, and states my position about the species-wide antecedents and effects of parental acceptance-rejection. Readers who want more methodological detail about the procedures used in the research, especially in the holocultural component of the Rejection-Acceptance Project (RAP), are invited to refer to the Appendixes.

Individual chapters have profited from the critical reading of many colleagues and students. Too many individuals have given help and encouragement to acknowledge by name. My gratitude goes to all those students and research assistants who worked so hard with me over the years in the RAP. My debt to them is so great that I use the plural pronoun "we" throughout the text. Several persons must be singled out for individual recognition. First and foremost, I credit the work of Evelyn C. Rohner (Ph.D. candidate in psychology), with whom I coauthored Chapter Three, but whose imprint is conspicuous more broadly throughout. She helped edit the entire volume, chapter by chapter, and she typed the entire manuscript at least once. I am fond of the title to this book, THEY LOVE ME, THEY LOVE ME NOT, but I can take no credit for it. I thank Harry F. Wolcott and Norman Delue for sharing their inspiration with me.

I also want to acknowledge the four grants given me by the University of Connecticut Research Foundation to pursue different facets of this work. Most of the computerized portion of the work was done in the University of Connecticut

Computer Center under NSF grant GJ-9. I also acknowledge with gratitude a National Science Foundation Postdoctoral Fellowship at the University of Pittsburgh in the summer of 1966. Work under the Fellowship was a significant impetus to the cross-cultural survey component of the Project. In 1971, the University of Washington generously provided me with research space while I was there as a Visiting Scholar. I thank all these institutions and agencies for their part in bringing this and other work in the Rejection-Acceptance Project to fruition.

RONALD P. ROHNER

After all there is but one race—humanity.

G. MOORE

CHAPTER ONE

The Universalist Approach to Behavioral Science

The phrase "universalist approach" refers to an orientation toward behavioral science that has as its objective the establishment of scientifically derived generalizations about human behavior, generalizations that are specieswide in their applicability.[1] Contributors to this orientation are committed to the search for at least two classes of verifiable generalizations or principles of human behavior: (1) "context free" generalizations, i.e. generalizations that hold true across our species regardless of culture, physical type, sex, geographic region, or other limiting conditions, and (2) "context dependent" generalizations—generalizations that hold true within certain contexts or under certain conditions *wherever they occur*, for example in all cultural systems of a certain "type" or in a specific kind of environment, within a certain age grouping or sex, or under other limiting conditions.

Generalizations within each of these classes may take the form either of universal causal-functional relationships or of universally valid descriptive statements. The latter form of generalization is not concerned simply with the theoretically bland cultural universals that anthropologists describe in every introductory textbook—for example "all societies have a form of subsistence economy," "the family in one form or another is universal," "an incest taboo is found everywhere," or "all people have some form of religious belief."

1

Even though true, such universal categories of culture as currently described within most of anthropology are scientifically trivial. Rather, the universalist approach is more interested in comprehending the mechanisms or processes that create specific universals—e.g. *Why* is an incest taboo universal? Within this level of generalization, the universalist approach asks not simply "What are the major descriptive facts of human life?" but "Why are these descriptive facts true?"

Universal causal-functional relationships, the second level of generalization, deal with a somewhat different though not necessarily more complex issue. Here the concern is with worldwide (universal) *relationships* among phenomena. These relationships may be causal, in the sense that one variable produces a commensurate change in a second variable, or they may be functional, in the sense that a change in one variable is associated—perhaps only indirectly—with a commensurate change in the second variable. In all forms of the universalist approach, however, scholars want to be sure that the discovered relationships are valid for all mankind—either within all human populations or among all populations where certain limiting conditions exist. We must be assured that these relationships are not simply an artifact or special circumstance of the unique setting (e.g. specific culture, gene pool, local region) in which the relationship was discovered.

The universalist approach comprises two complementary facets—a conceptual facet and a methodological facet. Conceptually, and at the highest level of abstraction, the universalist approach asks the philosophically based question, "What does it mean to be a human being?" The universalist approach asks about the nature of human nature, or, more specifically, about researchable features of "human nature." From this point of view, then, it should be clear that the universalist approach is not interested simply in the behavior of middle-income White Americans, Black Americans, Kwakiutl Indians, or Turkish peasants, or even about a comparison between any two or more of these groupings, but rather in mankind as a whole. In order to do universalist research, scholars must make basic assumptions about the nature of man. Principally, they must make a supposition comparable to the one anthropologists call the psychic unity of man. They must assume that all normal (i.e. nonpathological) humans are subject to the same developmental tendencies and, additionally, that at birth all normal humans share the same general capacities for thought, feeling, and action. It seems to us that any research on man's "nature" must contain at least implicitly these two assumptions.

This emphasis on universals does not mean that the universalist approach disregards significant cognitive, emotional, or other behavioral differences among human populations. Indeed, an interest in human variability is but the complement of the search for universals. For example, the thought processes of young children may prove to be qualitatively different in some respects from the cognitive processes of adults, but the cognitive functioning of children at a certain age may turn out to be more or less invariant throughout our species (see the discussion of Piaget, later in this chapter). If this is true, these developmental likenesses and differences would be especially interesting to the universalist approach. Unlike the idiographic or particularistic orientation described later, which often focuses on superficial local differences (e.g. local "cultural" differences), the universalist interest in variability relates to significant differences in the behavior repertoires of subpopulations within our total species.

Methodologically, the universalist approach does not dictate any given procedure or class of research techniques. Quite different methods are appropriate for asking different kinds of questions. The universalist approach does presume, however, the presence of at least the minimum standards of scientific inquiry. The generalizations that are to be elevated to the level of universalist principles must be able to withstand scientific scrutiny: they must be supported by empirical evidence collected in an intersubjective (i.e. objective) and impersonal manner, and the procedures used must be open to public review and replication, thereby assuring that the purported principles are capable of verification or falsification by independent investigators. In addition, investigators must employ only variables that are transculturally equivalent, thus providing assurance that the variables can be measured directly by the same procedures in different societies *and* that the measurements can be compared (see Sears 1961, Brislin, Lonner, and Thorndike 1973: 13-14, 24-29). These minimal requirements are needed in order to distinguish appealing but nonetheless speculative specieswide generalizations from scientifically derived generalizations. Toward the end of this chapter (as an illustration of the universalist approach) we describe a productive multimethod research strategy for pursuing issues described throughout this book.

One additional point regarding the methodological and conceptual mix comprising the universalist approach is the need for comparative research, at least at some point in the inquiry. Insofar as behavioral scientists are interested in establishing valid, specieswide generalizations about man, then their research design must consider relevant variations found throughout the species, or perhaps simply discover if any variation exists with respect to the behavior in question. In either case, the investigator will be led to something like a comparative, worldwide sampling design in his research. The rationale here is that if behavioral scientists want to be confident in the specieswide generalizability of their principles, they are obligated to show that the principles can indeed be generalized beyond the population or cognate populations from which they were originally derived or discovered. This point has been emphatically repeated in anthropology and cross-cultural psychology (see, for example, Brislin, Lonner, and Thorndike 1973: 143-44; Dawson 1971: 291; DeVos and Hippler 1969: 324; Jahoda 1970: 2-3, 1975).

The comparative emphasis in the universalist approach sometimes extends across species to the other primates or even to other members of the mammalian class. Cross-species research may be notably productive for many issues that have a suspected biological or evolutionary base.

This emphasis on worldwide or sometimes cross-species

comparative research points out that no matter how carefully or elegantly the relevant variables have been controlled, it is definitely not sufficient to claim that a universalist principle has been established, as is so often implicitly done, after successfully testing an hypothesis within a single country or even comparatively between samples in two different national groups. The generalizations from these tests may in fact form universalist principles, but these presumptions cannot be accepted until the propositions have survived some form of worldwide testing.

Many exciting questions that are amenable to the universalist approach appear on the interface between established disciplines, between psychology and anthropology, for example, or between social anthropology and human biology. There is little doubt, therefore, that productive contributors to the universalist approach will continue to involve themselves in interdisciplinary or multidisciplinary research.

To sum up so far, we are describing a new paradigm for the science of man, an orientation that has fascinated curious minds for centuries. But only recently have behavioral scientists been bold enough to suggest that a serious part of the research agenda in the behavioral sciences should include the search for "principles" or verified generalizations about human behavior. To this mounting interest we attach the label "universalist approach" and specify its several characteristics, which include the demand for comparative, nomothetic (i.e. generalizing) research based on acceptable standards of scientific inquiry. In addition, but as a matter of nonessential fact, many contributors to the universalist approach also tend to engage in interdisciplinary research. Viewed in this way, the universalist approach becomes a paradigm for assessing the adequacy of the generalizations that professionals and laymen alike continually make about man and man's creations; the approach includes a methodological and conceptual orientation for determining whether our beliefs or hunches about man's "nature" and man's productions are cross-culturally valid.[2] From this point of view, it is surprising that so many serious scholars have been critical of attempts to formulate scientifically derived nomothetic statements. Puzzling as it is, it is nonetheless true. Przeworski and Teune (1970: 5) seem to recognize this point when they write that: "Historians argued whether their approach should be idiographic or nomothetic; anthropologists discussed whether functionally integrated systems must be treated only in toto or whether traits can be abstracted and compared; sociologists continue to disagree about the importance of the 'postulate of indispensability'— whether every existing structure is functional for the system; economists argued whether a universal definition of their discipline can be constructed; and political scientists debated the value of generalizations confined to a specific set of institutions."

A good deal of the controversy originates in a disagreement over the relative importance of idiographic (i.e. particularistic) vs. nomothetic (i.e. generalizing) research. The controversy has a somewhat different natural history in each of the behavioral sciences. The dispute as it is expressed in social anthropology serves to illustrate the problem. A great part of the writing in social anthropology is specifically idiographic; it focuses on a specialized problem among a particular people in a localized community (or perhaps within a specific region), in a fixed time period. This idiographic or historicist orientation—a concentration on the concrete and particular—has an honored position within anthropology. In fact, one readily gets the impression that for many anthropologists this orientation is as far as anthropology needs to go; some would say it is as far as anthropology *should* go—that the special and proper mission of the anthropologist is to describe completely "my people," "my community," or "my tribe."

By its very nature, the idiographic approach emphasizes man's diversity and variability—the unique in man's behavior, the idiosyncratic, the specific, the unusual, or the spectacular. In this way, however, we lose sight of the equally important commonalities in human behavior that all men share; we lose sight of the relative homogeneity in the behavior potential among men throughout our species—a homogeneity created by several million years of common biological ancestry.

Several anthropologists have commented on this state of the field. Manners and Kaplan highlight the argument when they write:

> A sizeable body of field research has been undertaken not with a self-conscious interest in contributing to generalization and theory formation, but rather with the intention of documenting the differences, the great variety in the patterns of human behavior. While it is true . . . that such documentation may provide others with the materials out of which theory can be constructed, the results have tended in these instances to the creation of books and articles closer in plan and execution to natural history . . . or to literature and art than to what we would characterize as science. In their concern for what is unique these authors have, implicitly or explicitly, deflected attention from the recurrent or the repetitive patterns of cultural behavior and social institutions to the particularities of the societies they have studied [Manners and Kaplan 1968: 2].

Comparing anthropology with literature, Eric Wolf (1964: 89-90) punctuates the same point: "In this emphasis on the particular—indeed, on the characteristics of the individual case as an ultimate touchstone against which theory must be tested—anthropology resembles literature. For literature, too, focuses on the particular as ultima ratio. Good literature is not written by constructing frames of universal applicability; these frames must first be filled with the vibrancy of particular life, *in order* to become universally meaningful. So anthropology, too, seeks this vibrancy of particular life."

Several beliefs and assumptions underlie and pervade the idiographic orientation of anthropology. Anthropologists unanimously deplore "ethnocentrism" and endorse a conception of "cultural relativity"—the notion that behavior in one society can be evaluated only from the point of view of the members of that society and not from an outsider's culture-bound, ethnocentric viewpoint. The doctrine of cultural relativity emphasizes the dignity of all lifeways and bodies of custom. Some scholars have escalated the concept of cultural relativity into "radical relativism" or "cultural particularism"—the claim that every cultural system is different (as indeed they are), and that because of this uniqueness it is impossible to compare one "culture" with another (a conclusion which does not necessarily follow from the premise, as we show below). The following paragraph from Manners and Kaplan (1968) attends to this point:

> The extreme particularists, pluralists, humanists, or radical relativists have insisted on the uniqueness of each culture—either by referring to its genius, flavor, configuration, style, pattern and so forth, or by emphasizing the self evident, "that no two cultures are exactly alike." Because they were right, in the sense that no two anythings are exactly alike, their opposition to generalizations, speculations about cross-cultural regularities, or cause-and-effect statements applied comparatively carried enough weight to discourage free theory formation in anthropology. It always turned out that "My people don't do it that way." And because the speaker had done extensive field work among "his people" and therefore had a firsthand familiarity with their lifeways, his observation could not be easily dismissed [Manners and Kaplan 1968: 4].

Related to the doctrine of radical relativism is the "extreme functionalist" viewpoint, the belief that behavior in one society cannot be compared with the same class of behavior in another society, because customs or institutions in any given social system are understandable only within the context of the whole system. Thus, the argument goes, we do violence to an element of culture when we abstract it from its cultural matrix for the purpose of comparing it with the same form of behavior in a second social system.

Both radical relativism and its offshoot, extreme functionalism, make a nomothetic science of man impossible, because they deny the credibility of comparisons and generalizations across cultural boundaries. Both positions are in excess of the truth. In this regard we fully agree with Kaplan and Manners (1972), who write:

> The comparativist knows just as well as the relativist that no two cultures are exactly alike. But he departs from the committed and the practicing relativist in at least two important respects: (1) while he accepts, at least in general, the dictum that all parts of a culture are somehow functionally interrelated . . . he adds the Orwellian modifier that some parts are

more interrelated than others; and (2) he believes that comparison following abstraction is not only nonrapacious but is methodologically legitimate, heuristically suggestive, and scientifically fruitful. The comparativist, having accepted more seriously than the relativist the premise of the psychic unity of mankind is therefore more prepared also to accept the similarities revealed by observation and comparative empirical research. The relativist is concerned overwhelmingly with the differences. The comparativist is interested in the similarities as well as the differences. For the relativist each culture is demonstrably unique. For the comparativist, each culture's demonstrable uniqueness as a whole may be overshadowed by the demonstrable similarity of many of its parts to those of other cultures. The narrow relativist tends to be esthetically offended by comparison, for comparison must inevitably play down or blur some of the distinctions that give each culture its pure flavor. The comparativist, on the other hand, tends to be "scientifically" offended at the relativist's insistence on the differences. For while he knows that no two objects or events in nature are exactly alike, taxonomies, typologies, and processes are defined and ordered through selection and abstraction, by a process in which the relevant is separated from the less relevant and irrelevant [Kaplan and Manners 1972: 6].

In criticizing the ideology of "radical relativism," we do not intend to deprecate the significance of the underlying concept of cultural relativity. The latter concept is an indispensable reminder to cross-cultural and universalist researchers that we must not confuse our own cultural values with a sense of the "natural," or with inalienable truth or objectivity.

Emphasis on ethnographic fieldwork has contributed more than any other single factor to the particularistic bias in anthropology. This emphasis emerged in American anthropology before the turn of the century and has evolved today into an informal professional ethic, whereby fledgling anthropologists are not recognized by their seniors as being fully credentialed until they have completed a period of fieldwork, preferably in some remote location for an extended period of time. Fieldwork has become an institutionalized rite-of-passage in anthropology, and the resulting ethnographies contribute to and validate anthropology's idiographic foundation in that—by their very nature—ethnographies concentrate on the way of life of a particular people in a particular place at a particular time. Thus an emphasis on ethnography supports and encourages the particularistic "my people" view in anthropology.

This stress on fieldwork emerged in American anthropology before 1900. Its origin is traced to the pervasive influence of Franz Boas, the "father of American anthropology," but it became immutably fixed in the 1920s through the writing and teaching of the British anthropologist, Bronislaw Malinowski. Anthropologists often credit Malinowski as being the founder of "modern" fieldwork. He is credited for developing "participant-observation" research, where ethnographers live for extended periods of time in native communities, learn the native language, and observe and participate in most aspects of daily life there.[3] Writing about participant observation in 1922, Malinowski (1961: 25) constructed his now famous phrase regarding the essence of participant observation research: "to grasp the native's point of view, his relation to life, to realize *his* vision of *his* world."

This dictum has come to be identified as part of the *emic* approach in anthropological inquiry—another factor contributing to the idiographic basis of anthropology. The emic approach requires the fieldworker to achieve an insider's (i.e. the "native's") view about the native's world, to describe the culture in terms of the native's own conceptual categories, rather than the categories of the investigator (i.e. the categories of anthropology). Description of behavior from the point of view of the outsider, the investigator, or the academic anthropologist is known as the *etic* approach. The linguist Kenneth Pike, originator of these constructs, describes them as follows:

> The etic viewpoint studies behavior as from outside of a particular system, and as an essential initial approach to an alien system. The emic viewpoint results from studying behavior from inside the system.
>
> The etic approach treats all cultures or languages—or selected groups of them—at one time. It might well be called "comparative." . . . The emic approach is, on the contrary, culturally specific, applied to one language or culture at a time.

. . . emic systems and emic units of these systems are in some sense to be discovered by the analyst, not created by him. . . . Etic systems, on the other hand, are assumed to be classifications created by the analyst—constructs for the handling of comparative data, or for the handling of data before its emic ordering can be ascertained [Pike 1967: 37, 55].

In the past decade, the emic approach has become identified with "cognitive anthropology," an omnibus term covering several related interests, including ethnosemantics, ethnoscience, ethnographic semantics, folk science, formal semantic analysis, componential analysis, folk taxonomy, and the "new ethnography." All of these interests draw on linguistics as the major conceptual and methodological stimulus. Culture is viewed as a code, or as a set of rules comparable to the grammar of a language. As in linguistic analyses, cognitive anthropologists are not interested in describing or predicting actual behavior, but in discovering the mental rules underlying behavior (Tyler 1969: 13). Thus culture is viewed as being entirely a cognitive phenomenon (hence the term *cognitive* anthropology). Cognitive anthropologists work with trained key informants for substantial periods of time with the objective of eliciting (i.e. discovering), in the informant's own language, the conceptual principles that underlly the informant's behavior. An ideal but only theoretically attainable ethnography using this method would describe completely all aspects of the significant cognitive systems of a particular people localized in a particular place and time. For many cognitive anthropologists, worldwide comparative research as the term is currently understood is not only improper but impossible. In the work of many of these scholars we see anthropology's idiographic bias taken to its methodological limits. (Later in this chapter, however, we discuss an innovative strand of cognitive anthropology—or more specifically of ethnosemantics —that strives toward establishing universalistic generalizations.)

We do not disclaim the emic stance to worldwide, nomothetic research. To the contrary, we believe that most successful cross-cultural research will probably always incorporate at least a partially relativistic, comparative, or emic perspective—a special perspective that comes from deep immersion in anthropological materials or from an extended period of "Malinowski-like" fieldwork. It is probably true that any effort to understand human life must at some point take human life into account from its own point of view. This does not mean, however, as some claim, that it is improper for the analyst to use objective—i.e. etic—concepts or measures. Indeed an emic/etic blend will probably best facilitate cross-cultural, comparative, generalizing research (see Pelto 1970: 85).

The reluctance of many anthropologists to generalize is supported by the dialectical history of American anthropology. Suspicion against cross-cultural generalizing goes back to the turn of the century, when Franz Boas and his later students energetically fought the nonempirical, grand theorizing (i.e. speculations) of many nineteenth-century cultural evolutionists, who had attempted to reconstruct the history of culture or parts of culture by arbitrarily picking-and-choosing from among the world's societies or customs and then ordering these societies and customs in a purported evolutionary sequence. Once ordered, the tautological claim was made that the arrangement itself proved that culture (or an aspect of culture) had indeed evolved as the scheme specified. This ethnocentric and often naive use of the comparative method rankled Boas; he regarded this kind of thinking as mere conjectural history, a form of scholarship he deplored.

In addition to questioning the deductive reasoning behind theories of cultural evolution and arguing against the perceived abuse of the comparative method, Boas and his students also devoted considerable energy to combating uninformed, ethnocentric generalizations about "human nature"—ideas such as "adolescence is always a time of storm and stress" and "children are more imaginative than adults." Herskovits describes anthropology's refutation of these generalities:

> Human nature was that chameleon-like force in man that was variously held to cause him to seek profits, or to be a monogamist or to have polygamous tendencies, or to strive to better

his standard of living or to do any of those things that seemed obviously basic to students of Euroamerican society. The anthropologist, however, beginning, "But, in Kamchatka . . ." or in Senegal or Ecuador or Pukapuka—would proceed to give instance where men and women, presumably activated by this same "human nature" eschewed profits, or were polygamist or monogamist, or seemed to be content with their lot. It can, indeed, be said that the philosophy of cultural relativism, that has come to dominate most anthropological thought and, indeed, social science in general, had its beginnings in the refutations of "human nature" that mark the literature of cultural anthropology [Herskovits 1956: 617-18].

Addressing the same point, Margaret Mead has written:

It was a simple—a very simple—point to which our materials were organized in the 1920s, merely the documentation over and over of the fact that human nature is not rigid and unyielding . . . but that it is extraordinarily adaptable, that cultural rhythms are stronger and more compelling than the physiological rhythms which they overlay and distort. . . .

The battle [against naive theories of human nature] which we once had to fight with the whole battery at our command, with the most fantastic and startling examples that we could muster is now won. [It is true, however, that some people] still believe in their heart of hearts that all men, Samoan, Manus, Mundugumor, Eskimo and Bantu, are really all made in their own image, with a few non-essential trappings of feathers and cowrie shells to obscure the all-important similarities. But nevertheless the trends towards a deeper appreciation of the malleability of the human being is marked enough so that students of primitive societies and their significance can go on to other questions [Mead 1939: x-xi].

Thus in reacting to ethnocentric views about human nature and other overreaching generalizations, anthropologists earlier in the century became distrustful of most forms of cross-cultural generalizing, and, as we will point out shortly, this distrust later evolved into an antagonism toward any kind of worldwide generalization.

Unlike many European and some American ethnologists of the 1800s, Boas believed strongly in the value of empirical, inductive fieldwork. Also unlike many of his evolutionist colleagues, Boas recognized the importance of diffusion in the process of culture change. Guided by these beliefs, he recommended that ethnologists should "explore in detail the customs and traits of a single tribe—to collect and minutely describe every detail, every aspect of culture including such disparate activities as canoe building and food preparation" (Rohner and Rohner 1969: xxi). When this was done among a number of tribes within a circumscribed region, it would then be possible to try to trace the geographic distribution of culture traits within that region, and thereby trace the diffusion and ultimately discover the origin of individual traits and trait complexes. This interest in diffusion and the limited reconstruction of culture history has come to be known as the historicalist school of American anthropology. Interest in diffusion led historicalists to develop an atomistic view of culture, wherein culture came to be viewed as a composite of discrete and often unrelated traits and trait complexes. This "shreds and patches" view of culture made yet another contribution to the particularistic foundations of anthropology, especially since its practitioners tended to be suspicious of any cultural comparisons or generalizations that exceeded the bounds of, at most, a single culture area or delimited geographic region. Some scholars disagreed with these views, however, thereby precipitating a debate as to whether anthropology is or should be history (idiographic) or science (nomothetic). Boas, Kroeber, and Radcliffe-Brown loomed prominently as discussants in the controversy. Herskovits summarized the debate when he wrote that the "distinction between science and history has long figured in discussions of anthropological theory, turning largely on the question whether anthropology is an historical or a scientific discipline. Such a formulation at once raises the problem whether the aims of anthropological study should be to recover the story of the development of human culture and of given cultures, or whether the ends of research should be to disclose broad principles of forms and structures and interrelationships that will lead to the enunciation of valid 'laws' of culture" (Herskovits 1956: 610).

The historicalist paradigm lost ground dramatically in the 1920s, as scholars became increasingly disillusioned with this sterile, atomistic approach toward culture. This disaffection was precipitated and fanned largely by the teaching and writing of two British anthropologists, Radcliffe-Brown and Malinowski, and by the writing of the American anthropologist, Ruth Benedict. These scholars criticized historicalism in its various forms. For them, but especially for Malinowski, the concept of a culture trait was an anathema; cultures were now to be studied as functionally integrated wholes. This view, too, eventually contributed to the idiographic bias of anthropology in the form of extreme functionalism, most notably in Benedict's configurationalist viewpoint. For Benedict, as Murdock (1965: 146) has written, "every culture is a unique configuration and can be understood only in its totality. She strongly implied that the abstraction of elements for comparison with those of other cultures is illegitimate." Moreover, she argued that an element of culture has no meaning except in its context: by itself it is meaningless. Murdock reaches the same conclusion we do regarding the scientific merit of this extreme functionalist viewpoint. He (Murdock 1965: 146) writes: "I submit that this is nonsense. Specific functions, of course, are discoverable only in context. Scientific laws or propositions, however, can be arrived at, in anthropology, as in any other science, only by abstracting and comparing features observable in many phenomena as they occur in nature." This description of the development of the idiographic bias in anthropology does not by any means exhaust all the factors operating to produce this bias, but we have identified the most salient forces contributing to the particularistic foundations of the discipline.

Even though for years the anthropological zeitgeist has been suspicious, even antagonistic, toward pancultural generalizing, during the past decade or so behavioral science—including psychology, sociology, political science, linguistics, ethology, human biology, as well as anthropology—has witnessed a dramatically mounting interest in worldwide or specieswide generalizations. Many of these generalizations are speculative, much like the arguments of some nineteenth-century evolutionists. Others, however, approach the standards of scientific credibility and are thus consistent with at least this requirement of the universalist approach. We turn now to a brief review of some of the most conspicuous generalizing interests.

Man has probably wondered about the nature of "human nature" for as long as he has had the capacity for introspection. In modern times, men such as Sigmund Freud, C. G. Jung, G. S. Hall, and, among the contemporary expositors, Jean Piaget, Claude Lévi-Strauss, and John Bowlby have been among the most influential international contributors to the universalist question. As diverse as their views may be, all these men (except Lévi-Strauss) share a common Darwinian or evolutionist perspective, and they all postulate a biological substrate to complex forms of human behavior.

Freud, for example, presumed the universality of the Oedipus complex, universal stages of psychosexual development, and several innate, specieswide drives, including the instinctual basis of aggression (Death Instinct). Biological and evolutionary processes are clearly implicated in these and other features of Freud's psychoanalytic system. Little in Freudian theory as it is commonly employed, however, is consistent with the requirements of the universalist approach, not because it is not generalizing in scope or because it has not been used comparatively (i.e. cross-culturally), but because it is so resistant to objective testing—or, stated another way, because many of its supporters have so zealously protected the theory from scientific criticism that it has come to be regarded by many scientists as mere (i.e. unscientific) ideological cant.

Jung, a one-time student of Freud, was also imbued with an evolutionary and a universalist perspective. His analytical psychology speaks of the collective unconscious—the realm of the psyche that is common to all mankind. Archetypes or Primordial Images—a part of the collective unconscious—are central to Jung's theory. They refer to ancient patterns of human experience and feeling, which have been perpetuated throughout all ages and in all societies. Another feature of Jung's analytical theory that was purported to have its roots in man's primordial animal archetype is the Shadow, which is said to consist of man's animal instincts transmitted phylogenetically from infrahumans. As with much of Freud's work, little in Jung's theory is consistent with the requirements of the universalist approach. In fact Jung is often accused of having abandoned medicine (psychiatry) for mysticism.

Unlike Freud or Jung, G. Stanley Hall was not a personality theorist. Hall's chief significance lies in his contributions to child development studies in the 1880s and 1890s. Like Freud and Jung, however, he was strongly influenced by Darwinism, and he was a thorough-going universalist in his theoretical perspective (although his work, like that of the others, falls outside the perimeter of the universalist approach). Hall is best known for his thesis regarding the universality of adolescent stress, which states that adolescence is invariably and universally a period of storm and stress, resulting from the genetically induced physiological changes that occur at puberty. Hall saw the emotional life of adolescents oscillating between exuberant gaiety and euphoria on the one hand and depressive gloom and melancholy on the other. Conceit, vanity, and egoism vie with bashfulness and humiliation; apathy and inertia vascillate with energetic curiosity. We know today that adolescence is not universally stressful. Margaret Mead first ruptured this myth in her book *Coming of Age in Samoa* (1928). Hall also believed that the development of the child's mind recapitulated the evolutionary development of the species *Homo sapiens*. Moreover, he took seriously the dictum of "ontogeny recapitulates phylogeny," or, in more popular terms, that the development of the human embryo repeats in compressed form the evolutionary development of the species —a position shared today by the brilliant and controversial Swiss psychologist, Jean Piaget.

Piaget has been working for over half a century on a universalist theory of the development and structure of human cognitive processes. Like the other men described in this section, his thinking and that of his associates is infused with genetic and evolutionary perspectives. Piaget makes no attempt to evaluate his theory on a worldwide comparative

basis, but many other scholars have put Piagetian propositions to the test. Over a hundred cross-cultural studies have
supported, for the most part, Piaget's ideas about the postulated stages of cognitive development, but certain other
features of his system have not fared as well (Dasen 1972).[4]
Overall, though, Piagetian studies of man's cognitive development approximate the requirements of the universalist
approach.

The distinguished if enigmatic and sometimes mystical
French anthropologist Claude Lévi-Strauss (see, for example, Lévi-Strauss 1966, 1969, 1971) shares much in
common with Piaget. Together these scholars form a significant nucleus of the "structuralist movement." Other points
of comparison aside, both men are interested in the nature
of the human mind, not as a physical structure, but in terms
of universal logical operations; both men regard the human
mind as working in the same way throughout our species.
Lévi-Strauss is concerned with universal principles of human
thought or mental processes. In effect, he asks the question:
"What is the mind like when it is thinking, especially in a
nonscientific mode?" Unlike Piaget, Lévi-Strauss does not
seem to draw from evolutionary theory or from biology to
explain these processes, except perhaps by remote implication. Much of his writing is characterized by an obscurity of
method and an ambiguity in style. He is not concerned with
data in the "real word," but with deductively constructing
or abstracting models of the "world." For example he attempts to discover the mental substratum of cultural institutions and myths. His work is essentially nonempirical and
nontestable, and it lies outside the perimeter of adequate scientific theory. Still, Lévi-Strauss's "French structuralism"
has international appeal, not so much among scholars who
face toward science, but among the many readers who respond to the arts, to the humanities, and to speculative
philosophy—and also among those who enjoy games of logic.

The evolutionary-biological-ethological perspective anticipated above has gained enormous appeal in universalist
writings during the past decade. In fact, most universalist or
specieswide generalizations have a definite evolutionary

bent, and many have an explicitly ethological and biological or genetic orientation as well. Some of this writing, however, is nothing more than compelling fiction cloaked as scholarly judgment. A variety of issues and only somewhat interrelated themes are represented in these publications. Some of the principal issues include the evolution of hominid social bonds, the purported instinctual basis of human aggression, the evolution of sex differences in behavior, the evolution of a universal culture pattern, and a universalist-evolutionary orientation to ethnosemantics and to linguistics. All of these issues have in common an interest in the evolution of human social, emotional, or cognitive *behavior* (rather than human morphology). Not all universalist research, however, as we point out later, is construed from an evolutionary, biological, or ethological point of view, although it is probably true that at some point in all such research the facts of biology, genetics, or evolution have to be recognized.

John Bowlby, an internationally eminent psychoanalyst, has produced an influential theory regarding the evolution of social bonds—specifically of infant-mother attachment behavior, a theme of substantial concern to this book. Bowlby is admittedly influenced by the renowned Austrian ethologist Konrad Lorenz and by Piaget, as well as other ethologists. His perspective is a creative blend of ethology, control-systems theory, psychoanalysis, and evolutionary theory. Bowlby's book, *Attachment* (1969), is concerned with the child's tie to his mother. The infant's smiling response is viewed as an adaptive, phylogenetically evolved, species-specific, and universal trait that through the process of natural selection ensures the infant's survival by releasing the mother's genetically "programmed" response of love. The infant's smile and the mother's love response form the beginning of the attachment bond that is essential for both the survival of the infant and perpetuation of the species (see Ainsworth 1973, Bowlby 1958, Freeman 1966, Freedman 1968). Bowlby (1958) makes a comparable argument for sucking, clinging, following, crying, and possibly cooing and babbling as evolved responses, in the Darwinian sense.

All these responses enhance the parent-child bond. Thus, infant-mother attachment is viewed as being instinctive. (A similar argument is made by Hamburg 1963, 1968). Bowlby's influence has been substantial. Drawing stimulation explicitly from him, the anthropologist Jerome Barkow recently called for a Darwinian approach to "biosocial psychological anthropology." For Barkow, such a perspective "means moving our emphasis from the distinctive characteristics of each social group to the transcultural behavioral components and processes which all human groups share and which distinguish them from the social groups of other species" (Barkow 1973: 376).

In a spate of publications on the "instinctual" basis of human aggression, Lorenz (1966), Ardrey (1961, 1966, 1970), Morris (1967, 1969), Golding (1954), and Storr (1968) have pursued different but related lines of inquiry during the past decade. All of these men—including Freud (e.g. 1930), mentioned earlier—see a good deal of man's behavior, especially his aggression, as being innate or genetically determined, but they draw out the remainder of their arguments on somewhat different grounds. In his first book, *African Genesis* (1961), for example, the playwright Robert Ardrey developed the hypothesis that man evolved from a tool-using "carnivorous, predatory killer ape," and that through the process of evolution man has perpetuated his killer instincts. This fanciful but widely appealing thesis was later elaborated in his book, *The Territorial Imperative* (1966), wherein he argued that man's aggressiveness is based on his innate and unalterable, species-specific compulsion to gain and defend territory for his own exclusive use. Lorenz (1966), too, sees man's aggressiveness as being phylogenetically adaptive and programmed; the source of man's violence lies in his genes. Morris, however, takes a somewhat different point of view in *The Naked Ape* (1967). He agrees with Lorenz and Ardrey that we cannot understand man's current aggressive impulses until we recognize his infrahuman origin (i.e. recognize that *Homo sapiens* is still a "naked ape"), but doubts the existence of an innate, *spontaneously aggressive* drive in man. Rather, he sees much of our aggressive behavior as genetically governed by certain environmental conditions and by signals sent to us by other people. In effect, Morris is reacting against the Lorenzian "hydraulic" model—or "toilet flush" model, as it is sometimes whimsically called—where aggression is seen as building up in the organism much like urine in the bladder until it has to be relieved (i.e. "flushed out"). If it is not relieved in controlled ways, it will spontaneously "pop off." It is for this reason, Lorenz tells us, that aggression in humans is so dangerous. Thus we are informed that human nature is innately depraved, a familiar theme going back at least to the nineteenth century.

Most of these arguments share several flaws. First, they tend to generalize facilely by way of analogy from animal behavior to human behavior. The presumption is made that the behavior of living species of animals reflects man's own infrahuman ancestry, and that the trait of aggression, for example, has been carried forward phylogenetically from earlier times. More cautious scholars recognize the very real difficulties that exist in comparing even the behavior of one strain of laboratory mice with that of another strain, or in comparing localized subspecies of monkeys with monkeys of the same subspecies living in a different ecological niche —let alone those that exist in leaping generic bounds from animal behavior to human behavior. This interest in the parallels between man's behavior and the behavior of animals, however, goes back at least a hundred years to Darwin's *The Expression of the Emotions in Man and Animals* (1872). Darwin believed that the behavior as well as the anatomy of animals evolved through the process of natural selection, and that, since man is in many respects like other animals, his social and emotional behavior also results from evolutionary processes.

A second flaw in this line of argument is that in the absence of organic, measurable data, the principal standard of credibility used by expositors of the evolutionary-ethological view seems to be the same as the one used in functionalist theory, namely: "Is the interpretation internally consistent and satisfying?"[5] But these theories are not falsifiable by the conventional standards of science; their scientific status therefore remains dubious. Moreover, the theories contain many undefined concepts (What is meant by aggression? for example), and undisciplined generalizations. Conclusions are often founded on what we may term conjectural evidence.

Finally, the evolutionary-ethological arguments tend to be mechanistic, in that human behavior is portrayed as being phylogenetically programmed. This view leaves little room for the effects of experience. In fact, the proponents of this position usually ignore the massive experimental evidence demonstrating the importance of learning for displays (or inhibition) of aggression and other behavior.[6] (We review in Chapter Three some of the evidence regarding the consequences of experience for the development of aggression in humans.) As conjectural as they often are, however, we must acknowledge that the evolutionary-biological-ethological views expressed by Lorenz, Ardrey, and others have helped to rekindle a popularized—and to a certain extent a scientific—interest in the question of the "nature of human nature."[7]

This interest has been pursued by Steven Goldberg, a sociologist who is interested in the purported biological basis for sex-role differences between males and females. In his book, *The Inevitability of Patriarchy* (1973)—a book which he boldly subtitles "Why the Biological Difference Between Men and Women Always Produces Male Domination"—he argues that in all societies males do and should dominate females, not only in the principal political, leadership, and other high status roles but in virtually all task-oriented activities except childbearing. His argument is founded on the presumption of a genetically determined hormonal difference between males and females, whereby males are not only more aggressive but superior in their capacity for logic and abstract thought. It is principally the difference in aggression between the sexes, however, that leads males in all parts of the world to assert their "natural" dominance over females, thus producing males' "inevitable patriarchy." Goldberg's thesis, which is superbly critiqued by Eleanor Maccoby (1973), draws almost solely on the biological component of the evolutionary-biological-ethological chain; evolution appears only by implication, and ethology figures hardly at all.

Goldberg is not the first person to draw attention to behavioral differences between males and females. The psychologist Daniel Freedman earlier interpreted widespread sex differences in such behaviors as passivity and aggressiveness as being rooted in man's infrahuman ancestry, rather than being a result of social learning in infancy or childhood. To quote: "Thus when we find little boys less passive, more negativistic, more aggressive, more rivalrous, and more investigative than little girls, we probably have our mammalian-primate ancestry to thank and not some make-shift social force. This is not to deny, of course, that cultural institutions do indeed support and differentially shape such biological trends" (Freedman 1968: 268).

Lionel Tiger, a political sociologist, amplifies on the universal sex differences theme in *Men in Groups* (1969). He asks the question: Why do men the world over form all-male groups excluding women? His answer is that men have a biologically transmitted propensity toward male bonding—a phylogenetically determined need to form cohesive defensive, foraging, and other cultural units. This predilection, Tiger argues, has the same adaptive or survival value as the male-female bond leading to reproduction. Tiger frankly admits that his evolutionary-biological argument is speculative, but he justifies it on the grounds that it will help to encourage a multidisciplinary orientation to social science (by introducing the subject matter of biology).

The work of Tiger, Goldberg, Bowlby, and others described above is relevant to the question of the evolutionary-biological basis of culture, a problem in which anthropologists have shown increasing interest in recent years. The idea here is that man has a phylogenetically evolved predisposition to create certain *general* forms of culture—analogous to the universal structure of human language, which we discuss later—with room in man's behavioral repertoire for a wide but definitely limited range of specific cultural variability. Thus as Thomas Sebeok puts it, all cultural systems are regarded as but "superficially different representations of one abstract structure, namely of human culture" (Sebeok 1968: 4). Presumably, certain general organizing principles of culture underlie this universal cultural design (Keesing 1973: 319). Man's species-specific capacity for culture (and for the complex personality organization from which culture is derived) has emerged over the past millennia in interaction with the evolution of a large and highly differentiated brain. (This line of reasoning is developed further by Hallowell 1950, Henry 1959, LaBarre 1955, Spiro 1954, and Wallace 1970).

Some writers add an ethological dimension to the evolutionary-biological explanation of human culture. Lionel Tiger and Robin Fox (1966, 1971) and Fox (1970, 1973), for example, postulated that man's social behavior is programmed phylogenetically, i.e. it is genetically wired through evolution. As "Darwinians," Tiger and Fox (1971: 4) take it as an article of faith that all regularities characterizing a species must be the result of successful adaptation in the evolution of that species. Their thinking, and the thinking of many other writers on this subject, have been inspired by Lorenz, and by the accumulating ethological data on infrahuman animal populations. Along with Lorenz, they argue that it is reasonable to make inferences about man's nature and culture based on primate social behavior, because man and the other primates—indeed many other mammals—share a common biological ancestry. Thus Fox (1970: 22) writes, "much of our behavior and in particular our social arrangements can be seen as a variation on common primate and gregarious mammalian themes." He extends his argument further, saying that as a result of the evolutionary process of natural selection, man is now genetically "wired" much like a computer to produce certain universal forms of culture, such as the family, myths, religion, and kinship systems.

This interest in the universal structure of culture is partly an outgrowth of the quest for linguistic universals. Many linguists today are turning away from the traditionalist interest in linguistic diversity and relativity toward the search for language universals. Linguists (e.g. Chomsky 1965) have identified two types of universals, substantive and formal. Substantive universals refer to particular "things" within a language; e.g. all languages have proper names and parts of speech, such as nouns and verbs (although these may be hard to identify in some languages). The work of the anthropological linguist Joseph Greenberg (1963, 1966) is especially noteworthy in this context. Other linguists, such as Roman Jakobson (1968) and Morris Halle (Chomsky and Halle 1968), suggest other substantive universals from their theory regarding distinctive features in phonology.

Formal universals refer to formal, abstract conditions— general rules—manifested in varying forms within the grammar of all languages. Transformational rules and phonological rules, for example, are regarded as formal universals in transformational linguistic theory, just as phonemes and morphemes are formal universals in traditional descriptive linguistics. Noam Chomsky (1965, 1966), an eminent American linguist, emphasizes the general and universal structure or design that seems to underlie the idiosyncracies of each unique language. "The existence of deep-seated formal universals," he writes, "implies that all languages are cut to the same pattern, but does not imply that there is any point by point correspondence between particular languages" (1965: 30).

Chomsky (1973), along with others like the prominent psycholinguist Eric Lenneberg (1964, 1969), argue that these linguistic universals reveal a biological-evolutionary foundation to man's capacity for language. In support of this view, Lenneberg writes:

> . . . every language, without exception, is based on the same universal principles of semantics, syntax, and phonology. All languages have words for relations, objects, feelings, and qualities, and the semantic differences between the denotata are minimal from a biological point of view. . . . Phonologically, all languages are based on a common principle of phonemitization even though there are phonemic divergences.

> Language universals are the more remarkable as the speakers live in vastly different types of cultures ranging from an essen-

tially Neolithic type to the highly complex cultural systems of Western civilization. Further, language and its complexity is independent of racial variation. It is an axiom in linguistics that any human being can learn any language in the world. Thus, even though there are differences in physical structure, the basic skills for the acquisition of language are as universal as bipedal gait.

Owing to these considerations, it becomes plausible to hypothesize that language is a species-specific trait, based on a variety of biologically given mechanisms [Lenneberg 1964: 68-69].

Pursuing this theme, but from a different perspective, Chomsky (1968) argues that at birth a child knows *language*, but he does not yet know a particular language. According to Chomsky, the basic structure of human language is biologically channeled, and in the process of language acquisition a child simply has to learn the peculiarities of his own language (or even several languages), but not the basic structure of language. Thus, Chomsky assumes that language acquisition is based on the child's innate knowledge of a theoretical model—a generative grammar of his language. How else, linguists ask, can the fact be explained that tiny children everywhere—dull children as well as bright children—uniformly and reliably learn the complex structure of their language from the seeming jumble of speech sounds they hear? Surely some children would be more adept at this task than others if each child, in order to learn a language, had to construct from scratch his own "theory" of language; surely at least some children would devise more appropriate theories than others, while some otherwise normal children might never learn to talk at all. Also, if language were created anew by the members of different societies around the world, rather than being an evolved species characteristic, we would expect to find far greater variations in the structure of human language than actually exist. These and other evolutionary-biological and universalist arguments are made by increasing numbers of scholars in the linguistic sciences.

Charles Osgood, a distinguished psycholinguist, and his associates have studied the universal affective or connotative aspects of language for nearly two decades. They conclude that people the world over, regardless of their cultural experiences or language, appear to use the same semantic standards for making affective judgments. Using the semantic differential technique, Osgood and his colleagues find three principal but independent (i.e. orthogonal) factors reappearing again and again in both their intracultural and cross-cultural studies of semantics: an evaluative factor (Evaluation), represented by such dimensions as good-bad, pleasant-unpleasant, and positive-negative; a potency factor (Potency), represented by such dimensions as strong-weak, heavy-light, and hard-soft; and an activity factor (Activity), represented by such dimensions as fast-slow, active-passive, and excitable-calm. The evaluation factor is intimately associated with the rewarding, satisfying, or reinforcing property of a stimulus or with its nonreinforcing counterpart; the potency factor has to do with a person's perception of the effort required to resist a stimulus or with the force that could be exerted on him by a stimulus; and the activity factor is connected with the rapidity of movement expected of a stimulus-object. The latter, Activity, seems to be concerned with a time dimension, whereas Potency is more closely associated with space and includes size and weight (Carroll 1964: 105). In a frankly speculative mood, Osgood (1964: 199) attempts to explain this universal phenomenon: "I would suggest that this affective meaning system is intimately related to the nonspecific projection mechanisms from the hypothalamic, reticular, or limbic systems and their cortical connections in the frontal lobes. Both are gross, nondiscriminative, but highly generalized systems, and both are associated with the emotional, purposive and motivational dynamics of the organism." Osgood provides an illustration of a "biologically" oriented universalist perspective. Evolution appears by implication, but ethology seems not to figure into his scheme at all (see Osgood 1969, 1971; Adams and Osgood 1973).

Brent Berlin and his collaborators developed an explicitly universalist-evolutionary orientation in ethnosemantics; ethology and biology concern them little. A significant part of this work is also synchronic (i.e. nonevolutionary or non-historical) and structural. To be more specific, Berlin, a cognitive anthropologist, is interested in discovering synchronic (i.e. structural) and diachronic (i.e. evolutionary) semantic universals, or general, worldwide semantic processes in color lexicons and in ethnobiological lexicons—i.e. in the way people name the plants and animals in their universe (Berlin 1970, Berlin, Breedlove, and Raven 1973). Regarding color lexicons, for example, Berlin and Kay (1969) found that in all parts of the world men recognize precisely eleven *basic* color categories: black, white, red, green, yellow, blue, brown, pink, purple, orange, and gray.[8] These basic color terms represent timeless or structural universals. In addition, and more surprising, Berlin and Kay found that not all languages contain all eleven terms, and that when terms are missing, they are almost always restricted in a predictable sequence. All languages have color terms for black and white, for example, but if a language has three basic color terms, these terms will be black, white, and red; the language will contain no other basic color term. Those languages having four basic color terms have black, white, red, and either yellow or green, but not both. Finally, languages having eight or more terms contain words for black, white, red, yellow, green, blue, brown, and, in addition, gray, orange, pink and/or purple. Moreover, Berlin and Kay found that this distribution of color terms is linked—they postulate in an evolutionary sequence—to overall cultural complexity: technologically simpler societies have fewer basic color terms than technologically and economically complex, industrialized nations.

Much of this work drawing from the linguistic sciences, especially the work of Osgood and associates, approximates the requirements of the universalist approach. It is nomothetic, comparative, often interdisciplinary, and, unlike much of the work mentioned earlier, it strives to conform to at least the minimally acceptable standards of science.

Interest in scientifically derived generalizations about human behavior, especially in universal causal-functional relationships, has been stimulated more by the cross-cultural survey (or holocultural) method than by any other single influence. As we describe in the following section and again in Chapter Four, the cross-cultural survey method employs a worldwide sample of societies from the ethnographic record in anthropology. Relevant variables are coded in these ethnographies for the purpose of statistically testing hypotheses about the transcultural relationship between two or more psychological, social, cultural, or other variables. By its very nature, the logic of the holocultural method is oriented toward universalist principles. Over 300 studies have been made using this method. More appear each month. The cross-cultural survey method implies no particular conceptual orientation. Indeed, many theoretical points of view can be accommodated by the method, including at least part of the evolutionary-biological-ethological universalist viewpoint. For instance, several holocultural studies have been done on worldwide relationships between socialization practices in infancy and subsequent biologically related processes such as age of menarchy and adult stature (see, for example, Landauer and Whiting 1964; Whiting 1965). Holocultural studies have also been used to help develop evolutionary arguments (see, for example, Otterbein 1970). Moreover, many studies have been completed using social structural variables (e.g. type of marriage, postmarital residence patterns, divorce, kinship, household organization, descent systems, and the like); life cycle and socialization, including initiation ceremonies, parent-child relationships, menstrual and pregnancy taboos, and so forth; the effect of the physical environment on behavior; and the relationship between child-training practices and (a) personality development and functioning, including problems of dependence, aggression, achievement, anxiety, and responsibility; (b) expressive features of a social system, such as art, games, and religious beliefs; and (c) maintenance systems antecedent to parental behavior, such as subsistence economy and family and household organization. Some of these studies more closely approximate the requirements of the universalist approach than any other line of inquiry developed so far, but, as we point out in the following section, these studies are not sufficient in themselves to establish unequivocably the species-wide principles of human behavior for which we are searching. We turn now to a multimethod research strategy that *is* sufficient for establishing these universalist principles.

A UNIVERSALIST RESEARCH STRATEGY

As mentioned earlier, successful universalist efforts must not only be generalizing in intent but must also conform to the minimum standards of science, deal with transculturally equivalent variables, and at some point test their principal hypotheses in an adequate pancultural sample. These are but minimum standards for the universalist approach. In addition, researchers should recognize that each "methodology" and each specific research procedure (or, more simply, "method") has certain strengths and weaknesses; each will give certain kinds of information and not others; and each has the potential built into it for systematic error or bias. By the term "methodology" we refer to distinguishable classes, traditions, or paradigms of research, each with its own natural history, employing a somewhat different logic and basic assumptions—i.e. epistomology—and each comprising one or more discrete methods (i.e. research procedures), such as questionnaires, field schedules, interview schedules, or behavior observations. In this sense, then, the cross-cultural survey method described in the preceding section is a methodology. It is a class of research that has a different logic, requires different assumptions about the world, and commits the researcher to different concrete procedures from the experimental method often used in psychology or from anthropological fieldwork (Rohner 1975).

Since each method (and methodology) has certain forms of error potentially built into it, it is possible for research results to reflect this method bias, rather than to be a true measure of the behavior we wish to know about. Any such results are disastrous, no less for the universalist approach than for any other kind of research. To avoid the possibility of interpreting "method bias" as being a true measure of the behavior under question, serious universalist researchers *triangulate* their results whenever possible by employing a multimethod research strategy (see Figure 1 below). They employ two or preferably three discrete measures (i.e. methods) or, even better, two or three independent methodologies in order to determine the extent to which the same conclusions emerge when multiple and independent measurement processes are used—none of which shares the same weaknesses or potential for bias (see Webb et al. 1966: 3). Our confidence is increased insofar as we get converging results from the use of different tests, especially when these tests are performed within the framework of separate methodologies.

In addition to calling for a multimethod research format, the universalist approach also generally assumes a probability model of social, psychological, and cultural behavior, rather than a mechanical model, where a single exception to one's hypotheses or theory is sufficient evidence to discredit that theory. Practitioners of the universalist paradigm—including the author of this volume—generally assume as a matter of course that exceptions to their theories will occur. Generally the best that scientists of human behavior can hope for is that their theories will lead them to make predictions with tolerably few exceptions. The probability model is largely a matter of statistics and of the *probability* of certain events happening in a population under specified conditions. The mechanical model, on the other hand, assumes that behavior is strictly "ruleful"; if we can discover the rules, we can make predictions with perfect fidelity. Much of the research in linguistics and in allied fields using the linguistic model come close in contemporary universalist research to this orientation. Most other behavioral scientists search for statistically significant regularities in behavior, rather than for exceptionless uniformities.

All these methodological and conceptual guidelines are incorporated into the research design directing the work of this volume—the question of the worldwide causes and consequences of parental acceptance and rejection. (The concepts of acceptance and rejection are defined at length in Chapter Two. Briefly, however, they refer respectively to parental warmth and affection, and to the absence or with-drawal of warmth and affection.) In this book we ask the question: "Do human beings throughout the world respond the same way to parental acceptance (or rejection) regardless of cultural context, physical type, environmental conditions, or other limiting conditions?" We also ask: "Do parents everywhere who live under specified conditions tend to interact with their children in the same way with respect to warmth, hostility, and neglect?" These are universalist or specieswide questions, questions which, when appropriately answered, may be elevated to the level of universal "principles" of human behavior.

FIGURE 1.   Triangulation of Methodologies

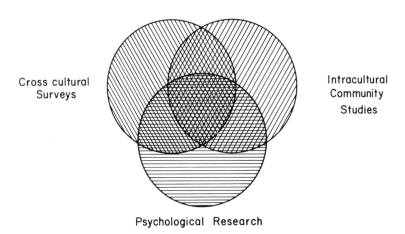

Cross cultural
Surveys

Intracultural
Community
Studies

Psychological   Research

In order to deal with an issue as complex as this one, we employ a research strategy that incorporates three distinct traditions of research or methodological components (diagrammed in Figure 1), namely: the cross-cultural survey component, the psychological research component, and the intracultural community study component. Figure 1 shows that the methodologies used in this research produce overlapping results. It is in the hatched area, where all three methodologies converge, that the results have successfully survived the onslaught of the multimethod research strategy, and it is in this area that the universalist or specieswide principles are to be found.

The most highly developed component of this work is the one using the cross-cultural survey method, where we employ a worldwide sample of 101 communities (i.e. "societies"), representing a stratified sample of the world's known and adequately described cultural systems. (Sampling rules and other methodological procedures in the cross-cultural survey component are described in the Appendix.) The objective here is to test statistically various hypotheses about the worldwide relationship between parental acceptance-rejection and: (a) specific personality characteristics of children and adults; (b) expressive features of society, such as religious beliefs, art, folklore, and music—generally non-utilitarian features of a social system that are expressive of personality; and (c) societal maintenance systems, including family and household organization, subsistence economy, social stratification, and political organization. (These points are amplified at length in Chapters Two and Four). Our goal in this component, as it is in the project as a whole, is to develop a theory that will allow us to predict reliably the worldwide consequences of parental acceptance-rejection for personality development and functioning—as well as for selected institutionalized expressive features of society—and to predict specific psychological, environmental, and maintenance system conditions under which parents everywhere accept or reject their children (see Figure 2 in Chapter Two).

The ethnographies on which the cross-cultural survey method is based describe the "typical" behavior of a population of people. The cross-cultural survey method thus measures regularities in standardized or customary behavior within total communities the world over. For this reason, the method is outstanding for distinguishing culturally conditioned from universal causal/functional relationships, but it provides no information about individual variability in behavior. (Results of the cross-cultural surveys on rejection-acceptance are described in Chapter Four.)

The second component, the psychological research component, involves research in the United States on various aspects of the rejection-acceptance problem, including child abuse. This component also incorporates cross-species research on aspects of developmental psychobiology, ethological studies, and other disciplines relating to the maternal behavior of mammals (see, for example, Denenberg 1969, DeVore 1963, Harlow 1971), and it includes an intensive and systematic survey of a vast literature in the psychological sciences on the causes and consequences of acceptance-rejection. (See Chapter Three for an extended discussion of the results of psychological testing within the United States.) Psychological research complements cross-cultural survey research in that the former deals with interindividual variability; whereas hologeistic or cross-cultural survey research deals with intercultural variability. It is often possible to experimentally manipulate and control psychological variables within the United States in ways that cannot be done in cross-cultural research; the cross-cultural survey method is nonetheless indispensable, because, among other things, it lets investigators measure the extent to which psychological research done in the United States can be generalized to the entire world. Psychological research within America cannot by itself distinguish culturally dependent from specieswide developmental tendencies. In fact, the vast portion of all psychological research is in one sense culture-bound, in that it has been done within the United States. More particularly, it has been conducted on a minuscule and unrepresentative sample of the American population (i.e. college students, especially introductory psychology students; see Carlson 1971: 204). As a result, many psychologists and anthropologists have raised serious questions about the pancultural generalizability of a good portion of psychological research. For example, DeVos and Hippler (1969: 324) concluded that the "universality of conclusions based on psychological research conducted within Western culture has received severe challenge from comparative anthropological data." Making an even stronger point, the psychologist Jahoda (1970: 2) wrote: "I strongly suspect that a high proportion of the generalizations contained in textbooks on the topic [of experimental social psychology] would not stand up to cross-cultural replication" (see also Dawson 1971: 291; Jahoda 1975).

Intracultural community studies form the third part of our work. This component includes long-term anthropological and psychological field investigations of communities within the United States, but especially in culture areas outside North America. The general cultural setting as well as parent-child relationships are studied within each community, and a personality assessment is made of the sample children and their parents.[9] Community studies provide invaluable information about the influence of natural (e.g. cultural, climatic, etc.) settings on behavior and personality development. The community study methodology also provides the opportunity to vary systematically cultural and other social, psychological, and environmental conditions, while simultaneously allowing for the measurement of individual variability as well as behavioral uniformities within each community. This component, like the psychological research component, employs an interdisciplinary and multimethod research strategy.[10] Unlike the other two methodologies, however, the community study component concentrates on within-community consistencies *and* variability in behavior. In every community, some parents are warmer and more accepting than others, even though the general cultural norm may tend toward rejection. We find similar variation in other relevant forms of behavior within all communities as well. The universalist theory in our research postulates that rejection (or acceptance) by itself is sufficient but not necessary to produce certain specified consequences, regardless of the "culture" of a people, their physical type, or any other conditions that might alter their behavior. Thus to take an extreme example, the theory predicts that an accepted child within any given family will develop certain characteristics (detailed in Chapter Two) that are more like the characteristics of accepted children elsewhere—perhaps under widely different cultural and other conditions—than the characteristics of his own rejected sibling.

The community study component and certain aspects of the

psychological research component provide the opportunity to study in situ many of the relationships found in cross-cultural surveys.[11] This technique of subsystem replication (i.e. testing within a single cultural system the results reached in cross-cultural surveys) contributes to the assessment of the validity and panhuman generalizability of results coming from the other two methodologies.

The universalist, multimethod research strategy is likely to involve investigators in interdisciplinary research—as it has in the work of this volume—because, it seems, most behavioral sciences have only one or a very few methodologies (i.e. general classes or paradigms of research) which are regarded as being appropriate for answering the questions that are customarily asked within each discipline. The experimental method(ology), for example, is used universally and is regarded as sacrosanct within "scientific" psychology, but it is virtually unknown within anthropology. Even if they were expert with it, many anthropologists would be offended if the experimental method were employed on the conventional problems of social anthropology —as experimental psychologists are scientifically offended when it is not. In this way, keepers of the disciplinary faith unintentionally inhibit a unified science of man from developing simply because they insist that anthropology, psychology, sociology, or whatever is properly conducted only within the bounds of the profession's customary scientific paradigm (see Kuhn 1970). For this reason, many of the most productive advances in human knowledge are yet to come, and many will be made only insofar as behavioral scientists feel free to work at the boundaries between two or more established disciplines.

As an illustration, we expect an interaction between anthropology and psychology to produce significant universalist advances. Neither discipline by itself, however, can find the principles for which we are searching, because both are, in certain respects, critically handicapped. Theory in anthropology, for example, is poorly developed, some say virtually absent, and the profession is unconcerned and untutored in scientific methodology. Moreover, anthropology is limited by its idiographic bias. Psychology, on the other hand, has both powerful theory and sophisticated techniques of data collection and analysis, but on the whole the discipline is ethnocentric and culture-bound. Probably the majority of American psychologists—given psychology's nomothetic bent—assume at least implicitly that if an experimental result can be replicated on a second American sample the results would be universally valid. We have already pointed out how this conclusion has been challenged by both anthropologists and psychologists. Even scholars who work in cross-cultural psychology, however, tend to be culture-bound, especially in their overintellectualized view of the reality and force of "culture learning," but also in their assumption that experimental procedures that work in the United States necessarily produce valid and interpretable results cross-culturally (see Triandis, Malpass, and Davidson 1972: 2). Anthropology's deep phenomenological understanding of the influence of culture learning is yet to be achieved by the majority of cross-cultural psychologists.

The strengths and weaknesses of psychology and anthropology are thus complementary. Together they make possible what neither alone can do: they provide a means for pursuing universalist questions such as the ones raised in this book. Murdock (1971: 22) emphasized this point when he wrote that: "only if the two disciplines collaborate to the full, with anthropology trusting psychology to reveal the basic mechanisms of behavior and with psychology trusting anthropology to ascertain the relevant configurations of conditions, will a genuine and full-fledged science of man emerge."

The same productive union is also possible for research on the interface between other fields, but in all universalist research, an adequate *anthropological perspective* is probably required. The anthropological perspective comprises several elements. It includes a profound familiarity with "culture," not as an abstract or as an explanatory concept (see Murdock 1971), but more as a pervasive, existential-phenomenological experience. True understanding of the effects of culture learning on behavior and on behavior potential comes from a deep immersion in ethnographic materials and, for most people, from an extended period of participant-observation fieldwork or from something equivalent to participant-observation research, such as the investigator's having grown up in a cultural system different from the one in which he is now working. In addition, the anthropological perspective implies a worldwide comparative orientation and a personal introjection of the concept of cultural relativity (but not radical relativism). Moreover, respect for the fact of cultural (and personal) holism or functionalism (but not extreme functionalism) is a part of the perspective. Even for those scholars who have internalized the anthropological perspective, however, anthropology per se, as a behavioral science discipline, is likely to play a focal role in a great part of the universalist paradigm. By its very nature—its idiographic bias notwithstanding—both social and cultural anthropology are committed to exploring human (especially social and cultural) behavior on a worldwide basis. A massive body of ethnographic data is ready for use in this effort.[12]

*We are moulded and remoulded
by those who have loved us; and
though the love may pass, we
are nevertheless their work, for
good or ill.*

FRANÇOIS MAURIAC

CHAPTER TWO

The Universalist Study
of Acceptance-Rejection

Five-year-old Azu trails after his mother as she walks along
the village path, whimpering and tugging at her skirt. He wants
to be carried, and he tells her so, loudly and demandingly,
"Stop! Stop! Hold me!" His mother shows no sign of attention.
She continues her steady barefooted stride, her arms swing-
ing freely at her sides, her heavy hips rolling to smooth the
jog of her walk and steady the basket of wet clothes she carries on her head. She has been to the washing pool, and her
burden keeps her neck stiff, but this is not why she looks im-
passively ahead and pretends not to notice her son. Often before she has carried him on her back and an even heavier load
on her head. But today she has resolved not to submit to his
plea, for it is time for him to begin to grow up.

Azu is not aware that the decision has been made. Under-
standably, he supposes that his mother is just cross, as she often
has been in the past, and that his cries will soon take effect. He
persists in his demand, but falls behind as his mother firmly
marches on. He runs to catch up and angrily yanks at her hand.
She shakes him off without speaking to him or looking at him.
Enraged, he drops solidly on the ground and begins to scream.
He gives a startled look when this produces no response, then
rolls over on his stomach and begins to writhe, sob, and yell.
He beats the earth with his fists and kicks it with his toes. This
hurts and makes him furious, the more so since it has not caused
his mother to notice him. He scrambles to his feet and scampers
after her, his nose running, tears coursing through the dirt on

39

his cheeks. When almost on her heel he yells and, getting no response, drops to the ground.

By this time his frustration is complete. In a rage he grovels in the red dirt, digging his toes into it, throwing it around him on himself. He smears it on his face, grinding it in with his clenched fists. He squirms on his side, his feet turning his body through an arc on the pivot of one shoulder.

Azu is left alone, but it takes several minutes for him to realize that this is the way it is to be. Gradually his fit subsides and he lies sprawled and whimpering on the path.

This has been Azu's first painful lesson in growing up. There will be many more unless he soon understands and accepts the Palauan [an island group in the Pacific] attitude that emotional attachments are cruel and treacherous entanglements, and that it is better not to cultivate them in the first place than to have them disrupted and disclaimed. . . . There will be refusals of pleas to be held, to be carried, to be fed, to be cuddled, and to be amused; and for a time at least there will follow the same violent struggle to maintain control that failed to help Azu. . . . Children must grow away from their parents, not cleave to them. Soon or late the child must learn not to expect the solicitude, the indulgence, and the warm attachment of earlier years and must accept the fact that he is to live in an emotional vacuum, trading friendship for concrete rewards, neither giving nor accepting lasting affection [Barnett 1960: 4-6].

This illustration of a rejected Palauan boy shows two universal processes working, or rather two facets of a single socialization process: socialization as an idiosyncratic, enculturative process and socialization in its phylogenetic or species perspective (see Mead 1963; Wrong 1961). The specific content of Azu's mother's behavior toward the boy is very much a matter of enculturation or culture learning.[1] She behaved toward him in roughly the same way that other Palauan mothers behave toward their children—and in the way that they themselves were treated as children. Here we see some fragments of the gradual transmission of culture from one generation to the next. But we also see in Azu's behavior what are probably universal or specieswide response-tendencies to the loss of love (i.e. parental rejection). When he responds predictably with aggression, dependency, and frustration, we are witnessing socialization in its phylogenetic (i.e. evolutionary and biological) perspective. Animals in other species respond to the withdrawal of nurturance in very different ways.

In part, here, we are dealing with the ontogenetic manifestation of potentialities characteristic of our species. This view of the socialization process is part of a growing belief that man has certain phylogenetically acquired potentialities for behavior, potentialities that are encoded in our DNA. Experience—including culture learning—interacts with these genetically encoded "blueprints" or "programs" for behavior to produce a seemingly inexhaustible diversity of individual behaviors as well as human cultures, languages, and other superficial variations on man's generalized but specieswide behavior patterns.

To illustrate this argument, let us consider man's species-specific capacity for conscience development, at least conscience in the sense of guilt from anticipating a wrongdoing in advance of committing an act. Even though this is a phylogenetic characteristic, we know from an ontogenetic viewpoint that some individuals do not have the experiences necessary for conscience development and, as a result, do not actualize this species capability. Moreover, the contexts that produce "bad conscience" (i.e. guilt) are partly a function of culture learning or of the variability of norms from one cultural system to another. The actual development of conscience within any single person is therefore simultaneously a matter of socialization as idiosyncratic and cultural experience and as a species-predisposition.

Moving closer to the specific interests of this book, we recognize that man has the capacity to form strong, enduring attachments loosely called "love"; this capacity to form attachments is also shared by some other species of animals, notably the other primates. Our interest at the moment, however, is with humans, who may be predisposed genetically toward becoming attached to someone during the first year of their lives. The specific person(s) to whom an infant becomes attached is a matter of the child's experiences (see Ainsworth 1972: 102).

The proclivity in man to form attachments in infancy no doubt has had significant adaptive or survival advantage for the perpetuation of our species during the several million years of man's hominid (i.e. protohuman) evolution. It is clear, however, that as with conscience development, not every human actualizes this potentiality. An individual must have certain experiences in order to develop the species capacity for attachment and for love-giving. Specifically, an infant must be loved in order to develop the general capacity to give love. It is also likely that the love given an infant must occur at a certain time developmentally if the child is not to be forever crippled in his ability to form warm, . emotionally responsive relations to others (see Bowlby 1969; Ainsworth 1973). (This point is explored further in Chapter Three.) Thus there may be a "sensitive period," or a period of heightened vulnerability in human development, when it is especially critical that a child receive affection if he is to develop normally.

Part of the rationale for this phylogenetic or "evolutionary-biological-universalist" perspective lies in the common observation that normal infants everywhere do form attachments to certain individuals sometime during the first year of life. Not all species share this proclivity, suggesting that there is something in man's biological constitution which explains this normally invariant human fact. If the development of human attachments and the ability to give love were purely matters of experience or learning—if genetics or other biological factors were not in some way implicated —then surely some societies in human history would have failed to provide the proper learning experiences for the successful development of these predispositions. Of course it is possible that some such societies have existed, but that we have no record of them, because, without the capacity for affection and for attachment, such social systems probably disintegrated within a generation or two, thereby failing to reproduce themselves. Perhaps this is what is now happening to the Ik, an isolated people in the mountains separating Uganda, the Sudan, and Kenya. These people probably anchor the lowest level in recorded history of man's indifference for his offspring:

> We should not be surprised when the mother throws her child out at three years old. She has breast-fed it, with some

ill humor, and cared for it in some manner for three whole years, and now it is ready to make its own way. I imagine the child must be rather relieved to be thrown out, for in the process of being cared for he or she is carried about in a hide sling wherever the mother goes, and since the mother is not strong herself this is done grudgingly. Whenever the mother finds a spot in which to gather, or if she is at a water hole or in her fields, she loosens the sling and lets the baby to the ground none too slowly, and of course laughs if it is hurt. I have seen Bila and Matsui do this many a time. Then she goes about her business, leaving the child there, almost hoping that some predator will come along and carry it off. This happened once while I was there—once that I know of, anyway—and the mother was delighted. She was rid of the child and no longer had to carry it about and feed it. . . . [A leopard in the vicinity found the sleeping child an easy kill.] The men set off and found the leopard, which had consumed all of the child except part of the skull; they killed the leopard and cooked it and ate it, child and all. That is Icien economy, and it makes sense in its own way. It does not, however, endear children to their parents or parents to their children [Turnbull 1972: 135-36].

The evolutionary-biological perspective described in this book rests on the assumption of an inextricable interaction between experience (e.g. learning, including culture learning) and genetics—or, more broadly, an individual's "biological state," including his genetic endowment and "biological states of readiness" and also his history of disease, nutritional status, and so forth. A major point is that experience affects both the *time* of appearance and the *forms* of evolved behavioral potentialities. This view does not impute immutability of any kind to these evolved, genetically encoded behavior predispositions. To the contrary, the universalist perspective recognizes that within limits, man's genetic predispositions are plastic, or variable within the species. Ginsburg and Maxson (1974) attach the felicitous label "genomic repertoire" to this fact. The concept of genomic repertoire recognizes that the way genetically encoded behavior predispositions are revealed within any individual (or breeding population) is a function of experience in interaction with his biological state.

We should also note that a phylogenetic argument in no

way lessens the fact that each human is unique. The apparent paradox coming from the recognition of species uniformities while simultaneously acknowledging individual uniqueness is resolved by the following facts: all humans share in common a great many species traits and states-of-biological-readiness. These predispositions have been transmitted phylogenetically from our infrahuman ancestors. Yet at the same time, within the limits of our species genomic repertoire, each individual has his own unique genetic endowment. In fact, genetic variation within individual members of a species is the very basis of evolution, especially of natural selection. Not only is each individual's genotype unique but his experiences are also unique. The interaction between a unique genotype and unique experience must produce a singular human being, who, at the same time, can be compared with every other human being any of us has ever known (see Freedman 1968: 274).

We are concerned here more with socialization as a universal or species predisposition than with the peculiarities of individual or cultural experience. Nonetheless, part of our procedure is to study the enculturation process on a worldwide basis to see if the species proclivities of interest to us are universally manifested, as predicted in the theory described later in this chapter.

The remainder of this chapter deals with love, the kind of love that parents can give or withhold from their children. The consequences of parental love, warmth, and affection (i.e. acceptance) are profound and generally productive of positive social and emotional health. Here, however, we place a somewhat greater emphasis on the absence or significant withdrawal of parental love (i.e. rejection), because its effects are more immediately and conspicuously apparent than the effects of parental acceptance. The withdrawal or absence of love by itself seems to be sufficient to produce stark and often profoundly damaging consequences for growing children as well as for adults who were rejected as children. Rejected children, by the mere fact that they are rejected, seem to have a clearly identifiable constellation of personality characteristics, even though many of the effects of rejection can be changed. It is also true, of course, that experiences having little or nothing to do with parental behavior can sometimes intrude into a young person's life, producing in a child from a warm and loving family some of the same personality characteristics we find in the rejected child.

Parental warmth forms a single, unitary dimension or continuum. In oth *r* words, rejection stands in opposition to acceptance o*r* ~tinuous scale, with warmth and affection at one ~ absence of warmth and affection at the oth*r* ~ be placed on this continuum, because ᐟ experienced more or less warmth, a ʻility), or neglect (indifference) from t. ᐢst important to us, usually our parents. ᐤarental behavior that is characterized b ᐧal of warmth and affection. Rejecting ᵢ ᐢrove of, or resent their child. In ma. a burden and they sometimes c ᐧly with other children.[3]

The absence of warmth and af. ᐧled around the world in two principal ways, by ᐧuised hostility or aggression toward the child, or ᐧerence, which is often expressed as neglect. Parental ho. ᐧty is an internal emotional reaction of anger, enmity, or ᐧesentment toward the child and may reveal itself in forms of overt physical or verbal aggression. Hostile parents, for example, may be irritable toward their child, critically impatient, or antagonistic; they may curse him or speak to him in other harsh, deprecating tones of voice. Hostile, aggressive parents may also be very rough or abrupt in their handling of their child and they may punish their children often and severely. Punishment per se, however, is a form of parental rejection only insofar as it is a clear expression of hostility or aggression toward the child. Punishment among the Aymara of Peru, for example, seems to express rejection as described by Tschopik (1951: 165), who writes: "Physical punishment, although infrequently employed, tends to be severe and it is meted out in the heat of anger. Adults of sixty years can recall vividly isolated instances in which they were beaten by their fathers. The basic idea in punishment is . . . that the family has suffered as a consequence of the child's shameful, willful, or careless act. Thus the threat of rejection, often explicit, is ever present."

Indifferent, neglecting parents, on the other hand, are not necessarily hostile toward their children. They may be simply unsympathetic, cold, and distant; they are often physically and emotionally unavailable or inaccessible to their children, and they tend to be unresponsive to their children's needs and wishes. Such parents show a restricted concern for their child's welfare. They pay as little attention to him as they can, and they spend a minimum amount of time with him. Not infrequently they forget promises they have made to him, and they fail to attend to other details or needs important to his happiness or well-being. Colombian mestizo in the South American village of Aritama illustrate both neglect and hostility. In this regard, the Reichel-Dolmatoffs (1961: 89) write: "Carelessness, ignorance, and at times, open hostility toward the child . . . may lead a woman to neglect an infant's health to such a point that serious disease and death are the natural consequence." Mestizo children in this community are not valued as human beings in their own rights, but as tools and assets to their parents. These children are rarely shown affection, never played with, and as infants they are often left in the care of child nurses who are hostile and resentful of them. "Men as fathers demonstrate not only indifference toward their newborn children, but quite often show a marked loathing for them" (Reichel-Dolmatoff and Riechel-Dolmatoff 1961: 87). Mothers, too, are unconcerned about their children's well-being: "Frequently the baby is handled rather roughly, with rapid and clumsy movements and with little regard to his comfort. No efforts are made to avoid letting the bright sunlight fall on his face or to protect his body from exposure to a draft of cool air. He is handled like a dead weight, devoid of all feeling, and hardly any thought is given to his being comfortable and safe" (Reichel-Dolmatoff and Reichel-Dolmatoff 1961: 79). Accentuating this point, the authors later write:

"A baby's crying is always interpreted as a desire for food and few women believe that during the first three or four months of life an infant could have other reasons for crying. Cold or pain are hardly ever taken into account, and the need for affection and company are never thought of" (1961: 84).

Violent temper tantrums are a characteristic outcome of the callous, indifferent handling of these mestizo infants and young children: "The temper tantrums of the first year continue in more and more violent form, up to the seventh year at least. Children will roll on the floor, beat their heads against the wall, and may even break their teeth while doing so. Very often they beat their fists against their chest and head, tear out their hair, or twist their ears. As soon as children have learned to speak, they scream threats against their mother, which become increasingly verbose and insulting as the child acquires a wider vocabulary" (Reichel-Dolmatoff and Reichel-Dolmatoff 1961: 97-98).

Firth's (1963: 150-51) description of a Tikopian mother, portraying an episode of spontaneous affection, contrasts profoundly with this description of rejection: "Coming round the corner of a house near mine one day, I was able to watch unnoticed the wife of one of my neighbours as she sat playing with her babe. She held it on her knees and looked at it with fond smiling eyes, then caught it up to her with a sudden movement, and began to press her nose in a greeting of affection to its nose, its cheeks, its ears, its breast and the hollow of its neck and limbs, with swift but soft caresses in an abandon of obvious pleasure." The warmth characteristic of Tikopian parents is the opposite end of the emotional and behavioral continuum we have been describing. Parental acceptance is marked by overt displays of warmth and affection on the part of parents toward their children. Acceptance is revealed by parents doing things to please their children, such as playing with them, comforting them, holding them, cuddling them, praising them, singing lullabies to them, caressing, fondling, and hugging them. Accepting parents generally like their child, approve of his personality, and take an interest in his activities and well-being. They are not necessarily effusive or demonstrative in their love, but they give love without qualification. We should note, however, that parents are not necessarily "warm" when they routinely care for or amuse their child as part of a schedule or simply as a matter of duty or responsibility.

Drawing on this conceptualization of acceptance, can there be any doubt about how the Hutterites of North America feel about their children?

> Everyone in a Hutterite colony loves a baby. Children of both sexes will crowd around a baby to play with him and gently vie for the privilege of holding or caring for a tiny baby. A child as young as two will be rewarded by being allowed to hold a baby. When the adults are not working, the babies are always held. After supper, in a group of men sitting around informally discussing colony affairs, one or two will be seen holding babies on their laps; a grandfather may hold two or three children on his. Adult Hutterites, colony members, visitors, and everyone who passes a very young child gives him cheerful attention. The baby is spoken to, picked up, tickled, played with. . . . Although he is disciplined quickly and frequently, the child is considered entertaining and is petted, played with, and desired. . . . [By the end of the first three years of life, the Hutterite] child has passed from complete dependency on his family to a moderate degree of independence. . . . He has learned to respond positively to every person [Hutterite] who comes within sight or earshot. . . . He is happy to be with people [Hostetler and Huntington 1967: 60-61].

Earlier we wrote that acceptance-rejection is a single dimension or continuum of parental behavior. This conceptualization of warmth notwithstanding, we have already shown that different manifestations of the rejection-acceptance process can be distinguished in actual measurement. Rejection may be differentiated as either hostile or aggressive rejection, or as rejection shown in the form of indifference or neglect. Hostile rejection, in turn, is revealed in either verbal or physical form, or both. Each of these is further revealed in concrete, observable behavior. Physical aggression (as a form of rejection), for example, may be manifested behaviorally by hitting, slapping, pinching, kicking, biting, scratching, throwing things at the child—or throwing the child himself—and so forth. Verbal aggression, on the other hand, is expressed in such forms as ridicule, cursing, sarcasm, or saying thoughtless, cruel, or unkind things to or about the child, or by nagging, scolding, and humiliating him. The point here is that investigators may analyze the rejection-acceptance process at various levels of abstraction. For some purposes, it may be more productive theoretically to ask about the relation between parental praise and some subsequent child behavior than to ask about the effects of the global construct "acceptance," which includes various forms of physical warmth as well as verbal warmth, of which praise is only one expression.

In our work, we consider it important to assess the overall quality of the social and emotional environment (in terms of warmth, aggression, and neglect) in which children are raised. Children respond to their total environment, an environment of interacting elements. Some elements are, to be sure, more salient than others. Some discrete forms of parental behavior have more impact on a given child than others, but nonetheless the effect of any specific behavior is modified (i.e. exacerbated or mollified) by other experiences in the child's day-to-day life within his family. Thus a sarcastic mother who says hostile, thoughtless, unkind things to her child (i.e. who is verbally aggressive) but who also hugs and kisses her child (i.e. is physically responsive) will probably produce a less disturbed child than a mother who is both verbally and physically aggressive. So, for the questions we ask in this book, we regard it as more productive theoretically to make assessments of the overall social and emotional environment wherein children are raised than to study the effect of single, concrete forms of parental behavior in isolation from other behaviors.

We now ask the question: "Do rejected children everywhere tend to become hostile and aggressive?" Is rejection universally implicated, as the psychological literature within the United States suggests, in such personality and behavior problems as autism, schizophrenia, neurosis, and delinquency and in psychosomatic reactions (including allergies), poor concept formation, disturbed body image, and academic problems, and in personality disturbances such as anxiety, insecurity, negative self-evaluation, and hostility? In effect, we are asking here a fundamental universalist question: "Do the personality and behavioral characteristics attributed by Western psychologists to parental acceptance-rejection appear in all human populations under comparable conditions, regardless of cultural context, physical type, geographic region, or other limiting conditions?" As we noted in Chapter One, a critical problem in the universalist approach is to distinguish culturally dependent responses (or other such restricted responses) from universal causal-functional relationships and from universally valid descriptive statements. This is what we have attempted to do in this study of the worldwide causes and consequences of parental acceptance-rejection. Thus the following pages should be viewed as an inquiry into the nature of human nature.

In this inquiry we try to discover why and under what conditions parents around the world are most likely to accept or reject their children.[4] How, for example, does the natural and social environment influence the way parents treat their children? Do the environmental conditions, or economic, political, and other institutions of a society predispose parents to be affectionate, indifferent, or hostile to their children, and, if so, can we predict how parents will behave in these different contexts? In many cases we can.

Regarding personality, we predict that parental rejection is universally associated with a specific cluster of traits, including hostility and aggression, dependency, low self-esteem and feelings of low self-adequacy, emotional instability, emotional unresponsiveness, and negative world view. Personality characteristics of rejected children may be modified over time, however, by a variety of intervening experiences between childhood and adulthood. The negative effects of parental rejection can be muted, for example, if the child is able to establish warm, responsive relations with his siblings, peers, or other adults. Effective psychotherapy can also render startling transformations in an individual.

Adult personality is not simply shaped from a biography of developmental experiences in preadult life. Adults are, of course, also affected by current experiences, including the stress of economic depression, armed combat, the threat of losing someone they love, or by less dramatic daily experiences; the shift from robust adulthood to old age, too, is often accompanied by personality alterations. In the absence of counteracting experiences, however, adults who were rejected as children are likely to express the same constellation of characteristics as they did in childhood: hostility, dependency, negative self-evaluation, emotional instability, emotional unresponsiveness, and negative world view, among others.

Not only do we expect to find a link between parental rejection and the development of this set of personality characteristics but, as suggested earlier, we predict that parental acceptance-rejection is transculturally linked with certain expressive, environmental, and maintenance systems of society. Institutionalized expressive systems of society, such as religious beliefs, magic, art, music, dance, games, medical beliefs, folklore, and mythology—i.e. ubiquitous but usually nonutilitarian features of society—reflect the personality structure of society's members. The games people choose to play express their personalities, including often unrecognized needs, unresolved conflicts, desires, or wishes.[5] Institutionalized expressive features of a society are not simply imperfect reflections of personality but are in turn modified by the natural and social environment. These systems change not only in response to changes in personality but also in response to other features of the environment. In addition, because these expressive systems preexist even before the birth of any single individual, they also affect his behavior as he grows up. It would be surprising, for example, if a child's actions were unaltered by his belief that powerful men in his community could punish his misconduct through sorcery.

The natural environment, including climate, plants, animals, and the other natural resources around us, imposes certain limits on the variety of forms taken by maintenance systems, i.e. the technological, economic, social, and political organizations of a society—the "basic customs surrounding the nourishment, sheltering, and protection of [a society's] members" (Whiting and Child 1953: 310). People also alter or reshape their natural environments through their maintenance systems.

The conceptual model shown in Figure 2 graphically portrays the universal connections we envisage between parental behavior and personality development in children and adults. It also maps the association between parental acceptance-rejection and expressive, environmental, and maintenance systems features of society. The model in Figure 2 is constructed to show how the natural environment and maintenance systems are two prominent forces shaping

FIGURE 2.   Conceptual Model

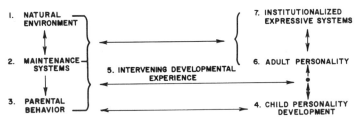

the customary behavior of parents toward their children. As the single-headed arrow indicates, however, we have difficulty imagining how parental behavior per se influences maintenance systems; e.g. how parental behavior can change a community's settlement pattern, system of social stratification, subsistence activities, technology, household structure, kinship system, or political organization. It would be a mistake, though, to overlook the fact that a substantial part of parental behavior is shaped by the personality of parents themselves. And as the double arrow suggests, it would also be a mistake not to recognize that a good deal of parental behavior (in both humans and animals) is a response to the actions and the personal, including constitutional, characteristics of their offspring (see Bell 1968; Harper 1971; Lewis and Rosenblum 1974; Yarrow, Waxler, and Scott 1971).[6] In addition, the model expresses our view that personality is the outgrowth of a variety of developmental experiences, including notably a child's experiences with his parents, and that expressive systems are shaped in large part by personality—but that once created, expressive systems can also have a measurable impact on personality as well as the other systems of behavior within the model.

Earlier we stated that adults who were rejected as children are likely to have a distinctive set of personality traits, and that rejected children too are prone to share a number of characteristics in common. We explain these commonalities in the following way: we as human beings—all human beings—have a profound, generalized need for positive response (love, approval, warmth, affection) from the people who are important to us. The bare minimal care that we must have for physical survival is not enough for normal psychosocial development. This need for positive response is probably rooted in man's biological and evolutionary development, and it is reinforced in the experience of infantile instrumental dependency. The absence or significant withdrawal of warmth and affection is sufficient to produce massive and predictable consequences for personality functioning. For example, rejection inhibits or distorts aspects of normal personality functioning, such as feelings of positive self-esteem and self-adequacy (i.e. positive self-evaluation). All of us tend to view ourselves as we imagine significant others view us, and if our parents rejected us as children, we are likely to define ourselves as *unworthy* of love, and therefore as unworthy and inadequate human beings. In this way, we develop a sense of overall negative self-evaluation.

Moreover, a rejected child is likely to be more dependent —to be clingy, intensely possessive, and to seek parental approval, nurturance, attention, and physical contact—than the accepted child. As we noted earlier, all humans have a basic need for positive response, but if a child's "significant others" are rejecting, his needs for warmth and affection are unfulfilled and he will, *up to a point*, increase his efforts to get love and attention. In other words, he will become dependent.[7]

Beyond a certain point, the dependency response may be extinguished. The seriously rejected child has not learned how to give love, because he has never known a loving parent after whom he can model his own behavior, and, for reasons described below, even though he craves affection he has difficulty accepting it. In order to protect himself from more emotional hurt, the rejected child tends to wrap his emotions in cotton, to encyst his emotions. Ultimately he stops trying to get affection from the people who are important to him. Dependency responses disappear. Thus the rejected child becomes emotionally insulated, unable to freely and openly form warm, lasting, intimate relations with others. His attachments tend to be troubled by emotional constriction or defensiveness, and in extreme cases the rejected child may become apathetic or emotionally bland or flat. In addition, as a result of the grave psychological damage brought about by rejection, the rejected child is inclined to have less tolerance for stress, and he is therefore likely to be less emotionally stable than those who were accepted as children.

The rejected child is apt to become resentful or angry at his parents, as well as fearful of more rejection, thereby producing a "defensive" independence—or emotional withdrawal—from them. In so doing, the child initiates a process of counter-rejection. (Beaglehole and Ritchie [1961: 502] describe something of this process among the Rakau Maori of New Zealand.) Behind his defensive independence or emotional detachment is often an unrecognized longing to reestablish a warm, nurturant relationship with his parents.

The child is especially likely to be hostile, aggressive, or passive-aggressive if rejection takes the form of parental hostility. Under these conditions, he is provided with an aggressive model to emulate, and thus his own aggressive responses may intensify (see Bandura and Walters 1963). In societies where persons are not allowed to overtly express aggression, however, rejected children are likely to have problems managing their hostility. Suppressed, over-controlled aggression is often expressed in such disguised or symbolic forms as a worried preoccupation about aggression, aggressive fantasies or dreams, or an unusual concern about the real or imagined aggression of others. Lewis describes part of this process when he writes about the Tepoztecans, the people of the village of Tepoztlan, Mexico:

> A good deal of suppressed hostility finds indirect release in malicious gossip, stealing, secret destruction of others' property, envy, deprecation and sorcery. The [use of] indirect criticism is a common, accepted form of aggression. Assault in the form of surprise attack and murder occurs from time to time. Men in a position of wealth, power, or authority often carry a gun for protection and prefer not to venture out at night. The most feared, although perhaps the least common, form of indirect aggression is sorcery. . . .
>
> The sanctions against any overt expression of aggression sometimes give rise to an interesting type of illness known as muina or anger, in which the aggression is apparently turned inward against the self. . .
>
> Tepoztecans view people, too, as potentially hostile and dangerous. [Lewis 1960: 87, 90].

Finally, the rejected child—one who is anxious, hostile, insecure, emotionally unstable, and who devaluates his feelings of self-worth and self-adequacy—is likely to generalize these feelings onto the nature of the world as being an unfriendly, hostile, unpleasant place in which to live. The child who has experienced so much psychological hurt at the hands of the people who are most important to him comes to expect little more from life itself. The very nature of life for him is threatening, dangerous, and an unhappy experience. This child is likely to develop a negative world view. This process derives from the fact that the interpretations we make about the world are based on our own experiences with it, both experiences we have had as individuals and experiences we know or believe others to have had. An individual's world view extends this interpretation about the empirical world—including interpretation of the experiences we have had at the hands of the people who are

most important to us—into an interpretation of the very
nature of the world.

Even though they may want to reach out to others, rejected
children are often unable to form fully satisfying social relations with their peers, and so their already damaged senses
of self-esteem are reinforced, and they may withdraw even
further into themselves. Thus in the absence of positive,
counteracting experiences (such as rewarding peer group
relations), these rejected children are likely to grow into
adults who are hostile, insecure, and dependent—adults
who have feelings of low self-esteem and low self-adequacy
and who have a negative world view. Referring again to
Tepoztlan:

> To Tepoztecans the world and nature present a constant threat
> of calamity and danger. A strong fear of natural forces and a
> high anxiety about the imminence of misfortune, disaster,
> and death were revealed in Thematic Apperception Test
> stories. . . .
>
> The world in which Tepoztecans live is filled with hostile forces
> and punishing figures which must be propitiated if their good
> will and protection are to be secured. El Tepozteco withholds
> rain if he is neglected; *los aires*, the spirits who live in the
> water, send illness to those who offend them; and *nuguales*,
> humans in pact with the devil, can turn themselves into a pig
> or dog to do harm at night. Catholic figures, too, are seen as
> threatening. God is a punishing figure rather than one of
> love, and most misfortunes are ascribed to Him. He brings
> good fortune only rarely [Lewis 1960: 86].

Adults who were rejected as children tend to have strong
needs for affection, but are unable to return it because they
have become more-or-less emotionally insulated or unresponsive to potentially close interpersonal relations. Any of
these adults who become parents are therefore much more
likely to reject their own children than parents who were
accepted as children. In this way, the rejection cycle is
perpetuated—and along with it the personality syndrome
we have just described. Hostility, dependency, low self-
evaluation, emotional instability, emotional unresponsive-

ness, and negative world view in no sense represent a complete roster of the consequences of rejection, but they seem to form a constellation or syndrome in the rejected child and, to a somewhat lesser extent, in the adult who was rejected as a child. We therefore concentrate on these behavioral predispositions throughout the remainder of this book, but not to the exclusion of other consequences of the rejection-acceptance process. Not only are the effects of rejection profound for personality development and functioning but, as we noted earlier and will elaborate on in the remaining chapters, they permeate widely throughout the social system.

We began this chapter with a description of Azu, a young Palauan boy. It seems fitting that we should end with a description of Palauan adults. In this way, one may begin to see why Azu's mother treated him the way she did and to see in a specific social system many of the effects of rejection we have described. Obviously, however, not all of the Palauan personality described below can be attributed to parental rejection.

Palauan "emotions of love, delight, hope and yearning," writes Barnett (1960: 13), "are shallow and constricted, outbalanced in intensity by resentment, alarm, suspicion, embarrassment, anger, shock and surprise." Palauan adults tend to be hostile, dependent, chronically anxious, constrained, and emotionally unresponsive, and they have feelings of low self-esteem and low self-adequacy. They have a negative world view and tend to be emotionally unstable, but they are achievement oriented and ambitious. Barnett attributes this ambition to an overreaction to their real feelings of inadequacy. Achievement aspirations generally surpass the capabilities of the individual, and ambition, because Palauan goals are unrealistic, becomes primarily satisfied in daydreams and imaginary successes. Man is believed to be at the mercy of an impersonal universe, and life is a series of events which must either be manipulated to personal advantage or simply adjusted to. A Palauan does not believe that he controls his destiny, but adapts himself

to pressures or diverts the pressures to others. The superficial calm of these people, the display of indifference, is a
mask for chronic anxiety. Any sudden event, such as an
accident, typhoon, or a show of strong emotion, shakes their
masks. Palauans become fearful, distrustful. "Such anxiety
produces a psychological state that might be described as
fear of fear. It apparently stems from lack of self-acceptance,
a rejection of impulses as damaging; and it produces the
sensation of being torn by an inner struggle which cannot
be faced or expressed. It obstructs action and thought as
well as feeling" (Barnett 1960: 15).

Better is a dinner of herbs where love is than a stalled ox and hatred therewith.

PROVERBS XV.17

CHAPTER THREE

They Love Me Not: Psychological Effects Of Rejection

by Evelyn C. Rohner and Ronald P. Rohner

Drawing from the evidence provided by psychologists and psychiatrists regarding the effects of parental rejection in the United States, we now focus on five major topics: (1) developmental problems created by "maternal" deprivation in humans and in monkeys (2) child abuse (3) personality disturbances arising in children and in adults as a consequence of parental rejection (4) behavior disorders and conduct problems, and (5) psychopathology (mental illness), especially schizophrenia, early infantile autism, and neurosis. We concentrate principally on studies having relatively few problems of research design, and we deemphasize purely descriptive articles and individual case studies. Our greatest confidence is placed in studies that attempt to objectively quantify the relationship between parental behavior and the social and emotional development of children and adults.

"MATERNAL" DEPRIVATION

"Maternal" deprivation is an elastic concept used in the psychological literature to cover a variety of related issues

59

including the "institutionalized child," "hospitalism," "maternal separation," "emotional deprivation," and "inadequate mothering." Most of these terms have one condition in common, the child is physically separated from his mother or other warm, nurturant, and intimate caretaker. This elasticity of use makes it difficult to explore the processes of "maternal" deprivation, because of the variety of ways in which the concept has been used and because of the variety of ways researchers have tried to assess the social, emotional, and physical development of the deprived child. Yarrow (1964), for example, points out the need for distinguishing between the effects of maternal deprivation, maternal separation, multiple mothering, and distortions in maternal care. He argues that one of the problems with studies on maternal separation is that current data "do not differentiate clearly between the effects of separation per se and the reinforcing conditions following separation" (1964: 127). Another difficulty in the study of "maternal" deprivation is the one of locating homogeneous groups of subjects for comparison in different environmental settings, such as foundling homes, orphanages, foster homes, and hospitals. Moreover, the infant's age at the time of separation, his relationship with his mother or other caretaker prior to separation, and many other such factors need to be controlled in order to compare studies of "maternal" deprivation.

A great deal of research on "maternal" deprivation assumes that a single maternal figure is crucial for normal social, emotional, and cognitive development. As we pointed out in Chapter Two, this belief is culture-bound and is challenged by the facts of human life in numerous societies throughout the world where children are cared for by several people—fathers, older siblings, grandparents, or even nonkinsmen. Margaret Mead (1956) claims that a child's social adjustment is best facilitated if he experiences warmth and affection from a number of nurturant persons, rather than from a single maternal figure. Whether or not Mead's conclusion is correct is yet to be demonstrated, but it is probably true that an emphasis on *maternal* deprivation or separation fictionalizes the importance of mothers per se. "Mother" can be anybody.

What happens to the "maternally" deprived infant, the infant who is deprived of love, warmth, and affection? The short-term response to mother's absence is modified by the child's age (his distress seems to be most marked between the ages of six months and four years), by his temperament, his previous relationship with his mother, and whether he is in a strange or a familiar environment. Acute distress and temporary developmental retardation are two major short-term consequences of deprivation.

Ainsworth (1966) summarized the results of deprivation. Utilizing the concept of "sensitive periods," she explained the differential effects of deprivation as being dependent on the child's age when he was first separated from his mother and when he was reunited with her. Specifically, she noted that children usually make a good recovery from a single, brief separation and that they usually make at least a fairly good recovery from a prolonged but single separation. But if a child is separated from a warm and a nurturant caretaker (i.e., if he is "maternally" deprived) between the ages of six to twelve months, and if the separation lasts three years or more, the effects are likely to be severe, both for personality development and for intellectual development. Separation occurring when the child is two may also have severe adverse effects, but at least the negative effects on intellectual functioning seem to be reversible. Skeels (1966) and Wolins (1970), too, say that for many babies the effects of parental deprivation in early infancy are reversible. When the infant receives emotional solicitude as well as physical care, he has a chance to show spectacular gains in IQ, and he can grow up to be a self-sustaining adult. As Rutter (1972: 122) points out in his extensive review of the literature, "acute distress is probably due in part to a disruption of the bonding process (not necessarily with the mother)."

Long-term "maternal" separation and institutional care have been associated with language retardation, mental retardation, growth problems, psychopathology, and at a later age with delinquency. It appears that babies between the ages of three and twelve months who are not fondled, held, loved—infants who, in effect, are given only the minimum care required for their survival—fail to develop normally. According to Goldfarb (1943), they become detached, insulated from others, and incapable of forming deep and lasting ties. Nevertheless, for many babies the effects of maternal deprivation in early infancy are reversible when the infant receives emotional solicitude as well as physical care. Bowlby (1966, 1969), however, claims that "good mothering" is futile if it is postponed until after the child is two or two-and-a-half years old.

In extreme cases, institutionalized children may develop a syndrome called marasmus, a high mortality illness. The symptoms of marasmus include extreme lethargy and loss of interest in environmental stimuli, deteriorated body reflexes, increased pallor, and muscular flabbiness. The following case history of a young child illustrates the physical and psychological effects of marasmus:

> The child weighed six pounds three ounces at birth. Both mother and child were thriving when they left the hospital two weeks later. On returning home, the mother found that her husband had suddenly deserted her—the climax of an unhappy relationship. The deep emotional reaction affected her milk secretion; the infant refused the breast and began to vomit. Later he was taken to the hospital, and the mother did not call to see him.
>
> In spite of careful medical attention this baby remained for two months at practically the same weight. He was in a crowded ward and received very little personal attention. The habit of finger-sucking developed, and gradually the child became a ruminator, his food coming up and going down with equal ease. At the age of two months he weighed five pounds. The baby at this time was transferred to a small children's hospital, with the idea that this institution might be able to give him more individual care.
>
> This baby actually looked like a seven months' fetus, yet he had also a strange appearance of oldness. He took large quantities of milk but did not gain weight. With concentrated nursing care the child began to improve slowly. It was possible to introduce the services of a volunteer "mother" who came to the hospital twice daily in order to give him some of the attention he so greatly needed.

As soon as the child's life was no longer in danger, he was transferred to a good foster home in order that he might have still more individual attention. Under this regime his development proceeded well, and gradually he mastered such functions as sitting, creeping, standing. His speech was slow in developing, however, and he did not walk until after the second year. The general health of this child was excellent at the end of his third year; also his IQ was high on standard tests, but his emotional life remained deeply damaged. With any change in his routine, or in a prolonged absence of the foster mother, he went into a state which was quite similar to a depression. He became inactive, ate very little, became constipated and extremely pale. His emotional relationship to his foster mother was receptive, like that of a young infant, but he made little response to her mothering activities except to function better when she was there. He had little capacity to express affection, displayed no initiative in seeking it, yet failed to thrive without it [Maslow and Mittlemann 1951: 317-18].

An infant who is not given a parental substitute often becomes depressed after losing his mother or other caretaker if he has developed a strong prior attachment to her. Spitz and Wolf (1946) studied a large group of infants who had been separated from their mothers and who were not provided with a mother surrogate. After six months of separation these previously happy, smiley, outgoing infants became weepy, and eventually this weepiness was replaced by withdrawal. "The children . . . would lie in their cots with averted faces, refusing to take part in the life of their surroundings. When we approached them we were ignored. Some of these children would watch us with a searching expression. If we were insistent enough, weeping would ensue and in some cases, screaming" (Spitz and Wolf 1946: 313). This weepiness was often accompanied by insomnia, loss of weight, greater susceptibility to colds or eczema, and a gradual decline in physical motor development. After three months, 19 of the 123 infants examined by Spitz needed strong provocation to induce even so much as weepiness. Typically, these 19 infants lay or sat with wide-open, expressionless eyes and with frozen, immobile expressions on their faces which made them look as if they were dazed, oblivious to what was going on in their environment. At this stage, the children became increasingly difficult to contact, and finally contact was impossible. Spitz describes the major symptoms of this anaclitic depression as apprehension, sadness, weepiness, rejection of the environment, withdrawal, retardation of physical development, slow reaction to environmental stimuli, slowness of movement, dejection, stupor, loss of appetite, refusal to eat, loss of weight, insomnia, and depression. The children who showed these characteristics had been removed from their mothers, with whom they formerly had warm ties, but not all of the children who were separated from their mothers developed anaclitic depression. "Maternal" separation appears to be a necessary but not a sufficient condition to cause anaclitic depression.

Spitz (1949) reports that if children are able to reestablish positive emotional bonds with parental figures within five months after institutionalization, those who were suffering from anaclitic depression rapidly attain the level of physical development characteristic of normal children. There is disagreement on this point, however, and some investigators believe that if a child is not given the opportunity to establish such ties, his physical development will become retarded and remain so. Overall recent evidence seems to suggest that the physical health of "maternally" deprived children is likely to improve, but that long-term bone development and body weight do not necessarily catch up to age norms. In addition, the intelligence level of these children seems to be affected, and their ability to form lasting relations with others is impaired.

The long-term developmental effects of severe and prolonged deprivation are not yet fully known. It is not entirely clear, for example, what cognitive, emotional, physical, or social handicaps deprived infants will experience when they reach adolescence. Goldfarb (1945) examined adolescent adjustment in relation to the age at which the youths had been admitted to an institution. He compared children fostered at birth with those fostered at age three, and reported that institutionalized children who were not placed in foster homes until they were three were, when tested in adolescence, restless, hyperactive, unable to concentrate, impudent, and destructive, and that they expressed their hostility by displays of temper. Many children were also mentally retarded, and most of them were emotionally apathetic, passive, and restricted in their capacity for adapting to change. They were also more withdrawn and less capable of entering into responsive human relations than the children who had been placed in foster homes at birth.

An example of the consequences of such deprivation is provided by the case study of an eight-year-old girl who was adopted by a family after six-and-a-half years without a consistent parental figure.

After an illegitimate birth, the child was shifted about from one relative to another, finally brought to a child placing agency, and then placed in a foster home for two months before she came to the referring foster parents. The complaints were lying and stealing. The parents described the child's reaction to the adoption as very casual. When they brought her home and showed her the room she was to have all for herself, and took her on a tour of the house and grounds, she showed apparently no emotional response. Yet she appeared very vivacious and "affectionate on the surface." After a few weeks of experience with her, the mother complained to the husband that the child did not seem able to show any affection. The child, to use the mother's words, "would kiss you but it would mean nothing." The husband told his wife that she was expecting too much. . . . In a few months, however, he made the same complaint. By this time, also, it was noted that the child was deceitful and evasive. . . . After a contact of a year and a half with the patient her father said, "you just can't get to her," and the mother remarked, "I have no more idea today what's going on in that child's mind than I knew the day she came. You can't get under her skin. She never tells what she's thinking or what she feels. She chatters but it's all surface" [Bowlby 1966: 30-31].

Pringle and Bossio (1960) compared two groups of children who were placed in institutions at an early age. None of the eleven children in the first group entered an institution before he was a year old, and these children subsequently maintained no dependable ties with their parents or other adults. They showed more signs of maladjustment than did the second group, who had been institutionalized at a later age and who had retained ties with at least one parent, even though they were not living with the parent. Children in the first group showed signs of regressive social behavior and were retarded in language development as well as in reading; they were anxious, aggressive, unable to relate to others, and overly concerned with adult approval. Earle and Earle (1961) compared 100 adults who had been deprived in early childhood with 100 adults who had not. The authors discovered in their sample that early "maternal" deprivation was related to the later development of "sociopathic personality," childhood behavior problems, broken marriages, a history of prison sentences, and poor work records.

More recently Rutter (1972) examined the evidence for a connection between long-term maternal deprivation on the one hand and delinquency, psychopathology, language retardation, mental retardation, and growth problems on the other. Reviewing the literature, Rutter (1972: 58) found that early life experiences can have long-term effects for animals, but that the evidence among humans does not point to either protracted or irreversible consequences. He further suggested that a complete and permanent change of environment in infancy can reverse the ill effects of deprivation, but that the upper age limit for potential reversibility is as yet undetermined. Factors other than mother-infant separation per se may also have produced the disturbing long-term effects seen in "maternal" deprivation. Nutritional deficiency, for example, is probably a principal contributer to "deprivation dwarfism." Intellectual retardation is due more to a deficiency in both "stimulation" and necessary life experiences than to the loss of a maternal figure; later antisocial behavior and delinquency are produced mainly by distorted intrafamilial relations, including hostility, discord, and lack of affection; "affectionless psychopathy" is due primarily to the failure of the young child to develop bonds of attachment. "The evidence strongly suggests," Rutter (1972: 119) concludes, "that most of the long-term consequences [of 'maternal' deprivation] are due to privation or lack of some kind rather than to any type of loss. Accordingly the 'deprivation' half of the concept is somewhat misleading. The 'maternal' half of the concept is also inaccurate in that, with but few exceptions, the deleterious influences concern the care of the child or relationships with people rather than with any specific defect of the mother."

Deprivation in Monkeys

Human beings are not alone in being adversely affected by "maternal" deprivation. Long-term maternal separation has severe developmental repercussions for some species of monkey as well. Investigators have separated infant rhesus monkeys from their mothers, placed them in isolated cages, and fed them by propping their bottles on either wire or cloth-covered forms. Those male and female monkeys who were raised from birth to adulthood in social isolation became socially abnormal, as shown subsequently by their infantile sexual behavior, their failure to groom other monkeys, their excessive aggressiveness, and their lack of cooperation with other monkeys (Harlow 1962: 7-8). With guidance and with what Harlow refers to as a training program, a few of these motherless females did manage to become pregnant and have babies. The motherless mothers, however, were deficient in maternal behavior toward their offspring when compared with mothers raised by their own mothers (Arling and Harlow 1967; Seay, Alexander, and Harlow 1964). Harlow (1962: 9) poignantly describes mothers who never had real mothers of their own and who had no social experiences with other monkeys until adulthood as "helpless, hopeless, heartless mothers devoid or almost devoid, of almost any maternal feelings."

When motherless rhesus monkeys were given frequent opportunities to play with other monkeys, the behavior defects seen in motherless monkeys who were raised in social isolation were not as severe. When a motherless monkey was allowed to play with only one other monkey, rather than several monkeys, her social behavior as an adult fell somewhere between the monkeys raised in isolation and those allowed daily contact with other groups of monkeys. Some of the monkeys raised with mothers but allowed no peer interaction also showed severe social difficulties with agemates during adolescence (Arling and Harlow 1967). Whereas the motherless mothers observed by Seay, Alexander, and Harlow (1964) were either indifferent or abusive to their young, Arling and Harlow (1967) found that when they provided peer interaction, three of the four females approached a modicum of adequate maternal behavior. Generally, Arling and Harlow (1967) concluded that punitive and rejecting mothers produce hyperaggression in their infants, thereby disrupting normal mother-infant interaction. This indicates that early social deprivation disrupts the expression of adequate maternal behavior.

Mother-infant body contact appears to be an important factor in rhesus monkey socialization—as it may be in humans—but, as we just saw, monkeys raised in isolation but allowed peer contact do not show the severe effects of maternal deprivation. Thus the Harlows (1969) conclude that peer affection may serve as a substitute for normal mothering. By the same token, maternal affection may partially substitute for peer affection.[1]

In a longitudinal study on the effects of short-term, mother-infant monkey separation, Hinde and Spencer-Booth (1970) found that infants who were most upset by the separation had had "tense" relationships with their mothers. They defined tension as the frequency of maternal rejection and the infant's efforts to maintain proximity to its mother. Kaufman and Rosenblum (1967) examined the results of maternal deprivation among bonnet macaque monkeys. They found that a short-term (i.e. four-week) separation created an effect on the mother-infant relation, but they also found that many of the potential separation problems were mitigated by bonnet social organization. Unlike Harlow's rhesus, the female bonnet macaques take over the care of an orphaned young—rather than simply ignoring it. The possibility of alternate caretakers, then, mitigates the effects of "maternal" separation.

It is difficult to generalize from the behavior of monkeys

to the behavior of humans when making comparisons. Social isolation results in sexually and socially inadequate behavior among adult rhesus monkeys. Maternally deprived monkeys, for example, make very poor or even inadequate mothers. What kind of mothers do humans make who have experienced "maternal" deprivation? Part of the answer to this question is suggested in the following section on child abuse.

CHILD ABUSE

The term "child abuse" refers most commonly to the willful infliction of serious physical injury on a child, but the term is being increasingly expanded to include other forms of parental rejection, such as neglect, abandonment, malnutrition, and sexual molestation (see Helfer and Kempe 1968, Gil 1970). The incidence of abuse is widespread throughout the U.S. In fact over 60,000 cases of abuse are reported every year, and some authorities estimate that twenty-five times as many cases go unreported. Moreover, according to Apthorp (1970), "fantastic as it sounds, more children under five years old are killed by their parents each year than die of disease." Some authorities suggest that if we had more complete information about the incidence of abuse we might even discover that it is the most common single cause of death in young children. Abuse is not localized in any particular social class, ethnic group, or other segment of American society, but occurs at all levels. Early in 1972, five thousand cases of child abuse were reported in New York City alone; fifty-two of these resulted in death from beatings and other physical trauma, including burns and scaldings, falls down stairs or out windows, strangulation or suffocation, fatally ingesting dangerous drugs, abandonment, starvation and malnutrition. Half of these youngsters were less than one year old; all but one were under six.

Several years ago an organization called "Mothers Anonymous," modeled after Alcoholics Anonymous, was initiated to help both abusing and potentially abusing parents cope with their problems. Apparently the first chapter of the

organization was started in southern California by a woman
who was placed in therapy after four years of struggle to control her urge to severely punish her daughter. Early in 1970,
she put a series of ads in a local newspaper which read,
"Mothers Anonymous, for moms who blow their cool with
their kids, call . . . ." More than 200 mothers phoned and
joined M.A. During stressful situations, members call on
each other for support. They have found that exchanging
children is another effective method of helping tense situations. Most of these mothers stop beating their children
after three months in the organization. Mothers Anonymous
and several other comparable groups continue to develop all
over the country, signaling the fact that parents everywhere
are confronted with the same turmoil and many of the same
difficulties in managing their own behavior toward their
children.

What kind of parent is a child abuser? Melnick and
Hurley (1969) matched a group of ten abusive and ten control mothers in terms of age, social class, and education.
They found that abusers have lower self-esteem, less satisfaction in their families, less need to give nurturance, and
greater frustration of dependency needs than the control
mothers. Furthermore, abusing mothers do not empathize
with or administer to their child's needs, they are frustrated
in their own emotional needs, and they do not perceive their
families as sufficient to meet their personal needs. Abusing
mothers are more dependent and feel unable to cope with
life's responsibilities; these feelings are accompanied by a
perceived lack of emotional support from those around them.

Surveying the opinions of scholars who have studied the
psychological characteristics of abusing parents, Spinetta
and Rigler (1972: 296) found most professionals agreeing
that "(a) the abusing parent was himself raised with some
degree of deprivation; (b) the abusing parent brings to his
role as parent mistaken notions of child rearing; (c) there is
present in the parent a general defect in character structure
allowing aggressive impulses to be expressed too freely;
and (d) while socioeconomic factors might sometimes place
added stresses on basic personality weakness, these stresses

are not of themselves sufficient or necessary causes of abuse." Amplifying on some of these points, the authors note that abusing parents look to their children for the satisfaction of their own emotional needs, and that many of these parents believe that it is their natural right to use strong physical force with their children. Coupled with this belief is often a lack of impulse control, so that the abusing parents are prone to strike out violently against their children, especially when they are under stress or tension.

What about the children themselves? What happens to them? In a retrospective study, Elmer and Gregg (1967) examined children who had been admitted to the hospital between 1950 and 1962 for what was diagnosed as possible child abuse. They also interviewed each child's caretaker, as well as school officials. In all, their study included twenty children who had been treated in the hospital for bone injuries and were later judged to have been abused. Eleven had had normal births, and nine significant past medical histories. Only two of the twenty were normal in all areas of emotional health, intellectual functioning, speech, and physical development. Abuse caused physical defects in one-third of the children; 50 percent were mentally retarded. The investigators predicted that at least five would become public charges, several others would need sheltered environments in order to remain in the community, and that on the whole, only a few of the children would become self-sufficient adults.

PERSONALITY CHARACTERISTICS

Aggression and Hostility

Human aggression is usually defined as the *intent* to do harm to oneself or to others. The motivation to injure may not be deliberate or under conscious control, however. Behavioral scientists have become interested in this issue, because questions relating to the nature of human aggression are vitally important in modern society. Is there an inherited basis for aggression in man, as the Lorenzians claim? Can the expression of aggression be reduced or eliminated by certain kinds of parent-child interaction? Theoretical models vary in their approaches to the causes and the "cures" of aggression. As we indicated in Chapter One, Lorenz and other ethologists often relate human aggression to man's biological past. Drawing analogies from animal behavior to human behavior, they claim that man has an inherited and spontaneous tendency for aggressive behavior much like our biogenic drives to eat and to drink. Another viewpoint asserts that human aggression is not inevitable, but that it depends on experience as well as on endogenous states, i.e. that aggressive behavior results from an interaction between learning, genetic predisposition, and other biological states. This is the position we adopt here. Still another view essentially ignores biology and looks to experience, mainly learning, to account for the etiology of aggression.

The now classic learning-theory explanation of aggression is the "frustration-aggression hypothesis." This hypothesis rejects the idea of an "instinctive drive," but retains other aspects of psychoanalytic theory from which it was partly derived. Briefly, the frustration-aggression hypothesis postulates that frustration in an ongoing activity produces a goal response to cause injury to some person or object. Dollard et al. (1939), as the main proponents of this theory, argue that the strength of aggressive behavior is correlated with the intensity and frequency of the frustrating experiences. Feshback (1970) points out that the development of aggression may depend on the fact that ego injuries are potent elicitors of hostility. This fact suggests to him that a global phenomenon like parental rejection should produce more aggressive children than more molecular forms of child rearing, such as severity of toilet training or weaning. Mothers who are emotionally uninvolved with their children frustrate the children's dependency needs, and this frustration often leads, among other responses, to hostility and to aggression. Affectionate parents, on the other hand, tend to have children who are affectionate (i.e. nonhostile) (Feshback 1970: 210). From animal studies such as those of

Seay and Harlow (1965) comes evidence for the unlearned basis of the relation between frustration and aggression. Analogies between human and nonhuman animals, however, must be viewed most carefully, and it is important to keep in mind that among different organisms, similar responses to similar stimuli (1) may not serve a single function (2) may have different mediating factors, and (3) are probably mechanistically different. Concrete illustration of frustration producing aggression in children is shown in an early study by Sears and Sears (in Dollard et al. 1939: 28-29). The authors systematically removed the bottle while feeding a five-month-old baby and measured the latency of crying (crying here was viewed as a measure of anger). Results from this study supported the hypothesis that as frustration increases, the intensity of aggression (i.e. latency to cry) also increases. More recent experimental evidence shows that the behavioral changes that occur as a result of frustration really reflect a choice between aggression and nonaggression (see, for example, Mallick and McCandless 1966, Miller and Bugelski 1948). The type of behavior chosen, i.e. aggression or nonaggression, depends on the individual's prior experiences, such as having been exposed to an aggressive adult model.

Bandura and Walters (1963) have shown that imitation plays an important role in the acquisition of behavior, in that children identify with their parents and imitate their actions. Imitation of parental behavior is one of the ways of gaining parental approval that children often seek. In an attempt to understand the role of imitation or modeling in aggressive behavior, McCord, McCord, and Howard (1961) observed for five years a sample of lower-class, relatively nondelinquent boys between the ages of nine and fourteen. The investigators found that assertive but nonaggressive boys were raised by affectionate parents; 95 percent of the aggressive boys, however, were raised by parents either one or both of whom were hostile and aggressive (i.e. rejecting). Additional support for the importance of modeling was provided by Bandura and Huston (1961), who instructed a group of nursery school children to observe an aggressive person performing a discrimination task. A second group of children observed a nonaggressive person in the same situation. When the children themselves were given the task to perform, a great deal of imitation or modeling occurred: 90 percent of the children who had observed the aggressive model were in turn aggressive; whereas only 13 percent of the children who had observed the nonaggressive model were aggressive.

Studies such as these show that aggressive behavior has multiple etiologies. As noted in Chapter Two, through modeling and as a result of frustration, rejection-acceptance theory predicts that rejection is one significant instigator to overt aggression, passive aggression, or to problems with the management of hostility and aggression. The link between parental rejection and child aggression has been recognized for several decades. Symonds (1939), for instance, examined sixty-two children, half of whom were rejected by their parents and half of whom were accepted by their parents. He found that the rejected children were significantly more rebellious than those who were accepted. Subsequently, in thirty-three severely emotionally disturbed children, Wolberg (1944) found the same two types of rejection we have identified cross-culturally, i.e. rejection expressed primarily in the form of parental hostility and rejection expressed as parental neglect. Twenty-eight of the thirty-three children in Wolberg's sample had problems with aggression, including temper tantrums, fighting, and destructiveness. Stagner (1948) found aggression and destructiveness to be common consequences of parental neglect. Crum (1972) interviewed twenty junior high school boys exhibiting aggressive, antisocial school behavior, as well as their mothers, to determine whether a significant relationship existed between the boy's behavior and maternal acceptance, overprotection, overindulgence, and rejection. She found that the mothers of the behavior problem boys exhibited significantly more overprotection and rejection. Her findings also included a positive correlation between maternal overprotection and rejection and between rejection and aggressiveness in boys.

Dependency

Dependency is sometimes defined as a behavioral state which occurs when an individual finds other people satisfying and rewarding *as people*. For example a child who wants to be near or seeks the attention or approval of another or who resists separation from another is behaving "dependently." Some scholars also include "seeking help" and "asking questions" in the definition of dependency, but it is often difficult to know whether these behaviors indicate dependence or low self-reliance as we conceptualize the two forms of behavior. When a young child asks his mother to help him tie his shoe, for example, is this request an expression of low self-reliance or of dependence (see Appendix One for the definition of self-reliance)? Some researchers, such as Bandura and Walters (1963), seem to avoid the problem of having to decide by defining dependence as any behavior that gains positive, ministering responses from others. Other researchers (for example Beller 1955, Heathers 1955) define dependence as we do (see Appendix One for a formal definition), but reserve the term independence for forms of behavior we call self-reliance.

Various theoretical perspectives have been formulated to explain the development of dependency. Psychoanalytic theory, for instance, postulates the existence of a biological predisposition in infants not only to satisfy basic needs but also to relate to objects in their environment (i.e. to be dependent). Bowlby's (1958, 1966, 1969, 1973) theory, describing the nature of attachment behavior and the functions served by it, is an outgrowth of psychoanalytic theory. Bowlby discusses the mother-infant dyad and the development of the attachment bond in terms of control theory and an ethological model adapted largely from Lorenz and Tinbergen. The concept "attachment" should not be equated with "dependency," however. Attachment refers to behavior that maintains proximity to another individual or that restores proximity when it has been disrupted. To this extent, attachment is similar to dependency, but in their theoretical elaboration of the construct, Bowlby and others put the concept in a realm of behavior that is only ambiguously related to dependency.

Social learning theory, as formulated by Sears and others (see, for example, Sears et al. 1953, Sears 1970, Dollard and Miller 1950, Bandura and Walters 1963, Gewirtz 1972, and Whiting 1941), provides another major theoretical perspective on the origin of dependency behavior. Here the child's attachment to the mother or other caretaker is based on her nurturance of him, and this need-satisfaction provides reinforcement for his dependency behavior. Differences among individual children and among cultural systems are said to be brought about by differences in parental behavior. Different forms of dependency responses, such as whining, clinging, showing off, and so forth, develop according to which form of dependency parents respond to. Social learning theorists also emphasize the importance of observational learning in the child's acquisition of social behavior. Whether dependency occurs as a result of observational learning, or modeling, is still an unsettled issue, however.

The frequency and intensity of dependent behavior vary considerably, both contextually and with age. Rosenthal (1965), Kiesler (1966), and Ainsworth and Wittig (1969), to name but a few, have demonstrated that dependency increases in contexts where fear, anxiety, and stress occur. Children who are rewarded frequently for seeking help are highly susceptible through social reinforcement to continue this behavior as an enduring personality disposition.

Beginning with Wolberg in 1944, investigators have found that parental hostility (i.e. rejection) is one significant factor producing dependency in children. Maccoby and Masters (1970) explain this fact by arguing that if mothers withdraw from their children, become unavailable to them, or reject them in other ways, the children are frustrated and seek to regain parental attention, help, praise, approval, or physical contact. Nonreward or punishment for this dependency behavior generates further conflict within a child, and his dependent behaviors increase.

Sears, Maccoby, and Levin (1957) demonstrated that the very dependency that was rewarded in early childhood may be punished or ignored in later childhood, thus producing conflict in the child, which incites him toward more dependent actions. In their classic Boston study, these authors (Sears, Maccoby, and Levin 1957: 146-51) rated dependency by the way parents responded to several interview questions including: "How much attention does [the child] seem to want from you?" "How about following you and hanging onto your skirt?" "How does [the child] react generally when you go out of the house and leave him with someone else?" The authors found that withdrawal of affection as a form of punishment was a strong reinforcer of dependency. Whether the child's dependency led to the mother's withdrawal of affection as a way of punishing the child, or whether the mother's rejection as a form of punishment led to the development of the child's dependency remains an unanswered question.

Using a sample of thirty-one boys from the ages of five to sixteen who were patients in a mental health clinic, Finney (1961) examined the effect of maternal warmth on dependency (which he defined as the child's attempts to solicit help rather than to rely on his own actions). He found that warm, responsive mothers do not have dependent children, but that dependency tends to be related to maternal overprotection, where the child is not allowed to mature socially or to engage in independent behavior. Finney also pointed out that overprotecting mothers often extend the culturally standardized times for terminating breast feeding, dressing, feeding, and bathing children. Finally, he found that dependent children from overprotecting homes tend to be anxious, pessimistic, and hostile.

Sears et al. (1953) also examined the relationship between child-rearing practices and the development of dependency, but in their work they used a sample of forty preschool children. The authors found that girls tended to be more dependent than boys, but that boys were slightly more aggressive than girls. It is instructive to note, however, that whereas teachers viewed attention-getting behavior from girls as a sign of aggression, they interpreted attention-getting behavior from boys as a sign of dependency. Mussen and Parker (1965) found that girls with nurturant mothers are less dependent, as rated by teachers, than other girls. Heilbrun and Norbert (1970) tested late adolescents who rated their mothers as more or less nurturant. They too found that high maternal nurturance facilitates independence in the child—and low nurturance promotes dependency. Further evidence for an association of rejection with dependency appears in the studies of Winder and Rau (1962), Marshall (1961), McCord, McCord, and Verden (1962), Wittenborn (1956) and Smith (1958), among others.[2]

Marshall and McCandless (1965) found that children who are dependent on adults have low social status with other children and tend not to participate in group activities. They also found that dependent children become more dependent on adults in group situations, while independent children remain nondependent on both adults and peers. Observing mother-child interaction of nursery school children in a free play situation, Brody (1969: 66) found that children of "high-rejecting mothers demanded more attention, praise and approval from their mothers [i.e. they were dependent] but paid less attention to what their mothers were doing, played more independently, and complied less with their mothers' requests."

Many gaps and inconsistencies appear in the literature on the relation between socialization and dependency behavior. It is clear, however, that infants are instrumentally dependent on the nurturant caretakers who fulfill their needs. How instrumental dependency later develops into "emotional dependence"—attention seeking, clingyness, asking for understanding, praise, approval, proximity—is not always clear, but it does seem apparent that parental behavior in the form of aggression, overprotection, or neglect plays a central role in the development of dependency behavior. The complementary assumption that warm, responsive parents will generally have independent children has been implied throughout the preceding pages.

Self-evaluation

Self-evaluation relates to the feelings we all have about ourselves, ranging on the one hand from liking and approving of ourselves to perceiving ourselves as being essentially worthless persons, worthy of condemnation. Self-evaluation includes two closely related dimensions, self-esteem and self-adequacy. Self-esteem is the global assessment we make of ourselves with respect to a feeling of personal *worth*. Positive self-esteem, for example, implies that a person likes himself, thinks well of himself, is comfortable with himself, and sees himself as being worthy of respect. Self-adequacy, on the other hand, refers to feelings about one's *competence* to manage satisfactorily his daily problems and to satisfy his needs. Positive self-adequacy implies that a person shows confidence and assurance in his day-to-day interaction with his peers, thinks of himself as a success, and feels competent to deal with his daily affairs. We will not always attempt to clearly distinguish self-esteem from self-adequacy, since they are closely related and are often merged in psychological studies.

Coopersmith (1967) claims that youths develop self-appraisal before middle childhood, and that even though self-evaluation may be affected by specific events, it reverts to its usual level when these events disappear. Once developed, overall self-evaluation resists permanent change, even though self-esteem with respect to specific tasks or roles—such as one's self-evaluation as a mother, teacher, or student—may vary. Individuals are not always consciously aware of their self-attitudes, but these self-evaluations are likely to be revealed in an individual's voice, gestures, mannerisms, and other behaviors. Sears (1970: 267) examined positive versus negative self-evaluation of eighty-four girls and seventy-five boys in the sixth grade. The mothers of these children had been interviewed seven years earlier, when the children were in kindergarten. Sears found high self-concept related in both boys and girls to "(1) high reading and arithmetic achievement (2) small family size (3) early ordinal position (4) high maternal and paternal warmth. For boys only, high self-concept was associated with (5) low father dominance in husband-wife relations. In both sexes, femininity was associated with poor self concepts." After testing Ellis's assertion that our feelings of self-worth reflect the feelings of how others perceive us, Brainerd (1969) concluded that women's perceptions about the way their parents evaluate them predicts women's feelings of personal worth. He found, however, that there was no predictable relationship between the way men think their mothers evaluated them and their own self-evaluations. Gecas (1972), after finding a strong relationship between parental support and adolescent self-esteem, further examined self-esteem in terms of context by asking about variability in adolescent self-esteem. He found that parental support is context bound. In other words, adolescents may have low self-esteem when they are among adults doing adult tasks, whereas among their peers, adolescent self-esteem may be high.

How does self-esteem develop? Why does one person regard himself with approval, whereas another person regards himself with disapproval? Wolberg's early research (1944) led to the isolation of one major factor in the development of positive and negative self-esteem, namely the child's reaction to parental behavior and beliefs. Specifically, he discovered that rejected, unloved, unwanted, and neglected children have feelings of insecurity and helplessness, leading to feelings of low self-esteem. Exaggerated positive self-evaluation, however, results from the attitudes of excessively permissive parents, who give in to the child's every whim and who fail to set limits. Jourard and Remy (1955) found that children have feelings of high self-esteem if they believe themselves capable and competent to handle life's problems and if they believe themselves liked: self-esteem is positively related to self-adequacy. Insecure children in his sample viewed themselves negatively and believed that their parents also viewed them negatively.

In a massive, comprehensive, and thorough piece of research on *The Antecedents of Self-Esteem*, Coopersmith (1967) found that parents who are emotionally stable—i.e. who have few mood fluctuations and who have high self-esteem—tend to have children who regard themselves with approval. Coopersmith explains this relationship in part as being due to the fact that these parents permit greater independence and give their children greater freedom. Children with high self-esteem have more frequent, more rewarding, and more satisfying social relationships with both family and nonfamily members than do children with low self-esteem. In addition, Coopersmith found that children with low self-esteem come from homes where parents fail to guide their children, where there is relatively harsh and disrespectful treatment of the child, and where parents withdraw their love as a form of punishment. It also appears that parents of children with low self-esteem themselves have low self-esteem. They lack the confidence necessary to establish a family framework, and they rely on harsh treatment to control their children and to resolve differences (Coopersmith 1967: 215). It seems, then, that parents who have feelings of low self-worth—who view themselves negatively—are also likely to have children who view themselves negatively. Sears (1970), too, found that early parental warmth (measured when the sample children were five) is associated with high self-concept (measured when the same children were twelve). Thus he concluded that there is a tendency for warm and accepting parents to have children with high self-esteem.

What are some of the antecedents and personal characteristics of individuals who evaluate themselves negatively? In a test of self-esteem, Heilbrun and Orr (1966) found that Yale College students who rated their mothers as rejecting were less consistent when betting on gambling tasks than those students who rated their mothers as accepting. The authors also discovered that members of the rejected group were more influenced by failure when setting goals for themselves than those of the accepted group. The authors attribute this relationship to the students' feelings of low self-esteem resulting from childhood rejection. Rosenberg (1962) associated feelings of negative self-worth and depression with self-reinforcing appraisals of inferiority, unworthiness, and incompetence. People with low self-esteem are often sad, depressed, and lethargic. "The corrosive drizzle of negative appraisal presumably removes the joy of today and the anticipation of tomorrow" (Coopersmith 1967: 130). Coopersmith also found that, in comparison with people with high self-esteem, people with low self-esteem are more destructive, more anxious, and more prone to psychosomatic illnesses, i.e. to organic illnesses resulting from emotional upset. On the other hand, persons with high self-esteem are more expressive, happy, and relatively free of anxiety than persons with low self-esteem.

Children with high self-esteem view their parents as placing a high value on school achievement and as deemphasizing excessive attention and concern for the opinions of others. Children with low self-esteem, on the other hand, perceive their parents as deemphasizing school achievement and as emphasizing attention and concern for the reactions of others. Coopersmith (1967: 101) concludes that both children with low self-esteem and their parents rely on pleasing others rather than relying on their own self-competence for their feelings of success. Sears's (1970) data suggest that a child's self-concept by age twelve is related not only to his academic achievement but also to certain family constellations which existed when he was five. Coopersmith (1967) found that even though low ability and low academic performance tend to be associated with feelings of low personal worth, ability and academic performance are not major influences in the development of high or low self-esteem. Finally, Rosenberg (1962) found that people with low self-esteem want success as much as people with high self-esteem, but that this desire creates a problem for those with low self-esteem, because they do not believe that they are capable of success in achievement-oriented ventures and in social matters, hence they begin with pessimism and the prophecy of failure.

World View, Emotional Stability, and
Emotional Responsiveness

Psychologists have given only modest attention to the relationship between rejection-acceptance and emotional responsiveness, and the association between parental rejection and emotional instability seems to be essentially unexplored. Moreover, so far as we know, no psychological study has yet looked directly at the relationship between rejection and world view.

World view. World view refers to the overall subjective feeling we all have about the nature of life and the universe itself as being basically a good, pleasant, secure, happy place in which to live (positive world view) or as being a threatening, dangerous, hostile, unpleasant, unfriendly, uncertain place in which to live (negative world view). Evidence in clinical psychology suggests that rejected children tend to have a negative world view (Coleman 1956: 117), but, as we pointed out above, no psychological study has yet looked squarely at this relationship.

Emotional stability. An emotionally stable person remains calm and does not lose his composure easily in stress situations. Moreover, he is not subject to the wide, frequent, and uncontrolled or unpredictable mood swings of the emotionally unstable person. Many emotionally unstable people, for example, are prone to sudden shifts in mood from happiness to unhappiness, contentedness to discontent, friendliness to hostility. They are often excitable, and they tend to become angry quickly and easily. Again, as with world view, the case histories from psychiatry and clinical psychology support the view that rejected children are more emotionally unstable than accepted children. Little solid experimental evidence exists to document this argument, but the cross-cultural survey data described in Chapter Four demonstrate unequivocally the connection between parental rejection and emotional instability.

Emotional responsiveness. Compared to world view and emotional stability, the relationship between parental behavior and emotional responsiveness is much clearer in the experimental research of psychology. By emotional responsiveness we refer to the ability of an individual to form close, warm, intimate relations with others. As with the other personality characteristics reviewed in this chaper, however, a person is not either emotionally responsive or emotionally unresponsive—rather we are all more or less responsive. Thus "emotional unresponsiveness" is a measure of the *extent* to which one is cut off from close interpersonal relationships, the degree to which one is unresponsive to or unable to become involved in lasting and affectionate relations with others. People who are emotionally insulated (i.e. unresponsive) are generally characterized by restricted emotional involvement with others. They usually have strong needs for affection but are unable to return it, thus their relations with others are likely to be distant and impersonal. Siegelman (1966) found that accepted children are motivated to continue with others the pleasurable experiences they found with their parents; he also found that boys in grades four, five, and six who had loving parents were perceived by their classmates as not being withdrawn. Boys who received insufficient affection from their fathers tended to be distant from their fathers and not to confide in them. In general, these boys felt more unjustly treated and less loved —in short, more rejected—than other boys. In turn, these boys were less supportive of and less affectionate toward their families—and by generalization, they were less warm toward others outside the family (Mussen, Conger, and Kagan 1963: 12). Boys who received sufficient affection were "calmer and happier, more achievement-oriented, and [manifested] fewer needs to manipulate and control others" (Mussen, Conger, and Kagan 1963: 12).

Several investigators have linked parental rejection with emotional withdrawal. Bandura and Walters (1958) hypothesized that aggressive boys who are punished for dependent behavior have more dependency anxiety and also feel more rejected by their parents. "Through such experience they would develop expectations of being disappointed and hurt which would lead them to resist and avoid dependency relationships. The insecurity surrounding dependency behavior would thus generalize to persons other than the parents and make these boys suspicious and resistant to entering into any close emotional attachments."

As we saw earlier, institutionalized children, as well as other children suffering from severe emotional deprivation during early childhood, are typically reluctant or unable to become involved with other people. In fact, according to the early research of Hattwick (1936), the most outstanding and consistently found trait among rejected children is their inability to form warm attachments to others. Fitz-Simmons (1935) reported parallel results when he wrote that children who are rejected by their fathers and overprotected by their mothers tend to be withdrawn. Wolberg (1944) noted that fourteen out of the thirty-three rejected children examined by him were detached and isolated from contact with others. Siegelman (1966), equating emotional withdrawal with introversion, found that withdrawn and/or introverted children have rejecting and punitive parents. Finally, Slater (1962) reported that the children in his study who received little parental support and warmth were also introverted and had less ego strength than children who were treated more warmly.

BEHAVIOR DISORDERS AND CONDUCT PROBLEMS

Behavior disorders and conduct problems include a variety of socially disapproved behaviors, such as theft, truancy, delinquency, criminality, cruelty, destructiveness, rebelliousness, lying, and sexual offenses. All of these disorders and problems have been related to parental rejection, but in this section we concentrate primarily on studies of delinquency.

Early theories of delinquency—behavior that brings youth into conflict with established authority (Zucker 1943)—were sociologically oriented and often dealt with such structural conditions of the local community as poverty, slums, poor housing, and so on. Inadequate employment opportunities, for example, were considered by many authorities to be a "cause" of delinquency, and slum life was considered to be a related "cause." True, delinquency is high in many slum and ghetto neighborhoods, but few experts would argue any more that these neighborhoods are sufficient by themselves to produce delinquency; not all slum or ghetto youths are delinquents, and delinquency is not confined solely to these communities. An important constellation of factors, aside from the structural features of the community that contribute to delinquency, revolves around the home, including parental models and parental behavior, especially parental rejection. In this regard, Feshbach (1970: 215) concludes that a comparison of delinquent boys with their nondelinquent siblings and with their nondelinquent peers matched for socioeconomic background reveals that delinquent youths have grown up in an environment of rejection and affectional deprivation.

Jackson (1950), who defined delinquents as youths who pilfer, willfully damage property, and who are truant from school, administered projective tests to three groups—delinquent, neurotic, and normal youths—to determine how these youngsters view the world. She concluded that delinquents approach life unrealistically and are more detached from their parents than neurotics and normals. Furthermore, she says that delinquents are more likely than the others in her study to see children as being bad, and parents as being ready to mete out severe punishment. These youngsters are aware that their parents reject them, but they do not admit that they in turn are hostile toward and therefore reject their parents. Moreover, these youths do not openly recognize their own hostility toward and rejection of their rival siblings. Finally, Jackson believes that the delinquent children in her study are more detached and less deeply involved in family loves and hatreds than the children in the two other groups. Zucker (1943), too, found that delinquent children have less affectionate relationships with their parents, identify less with their parents, and tend to reject parental values and standards. These youths retaliate against their parents for rejecting them by engaging in behavior they know their parents disapprove of, and by willfully taking the things they want. As a result, these delinquents are in constant conflict with their parents. Similarly, Zucker (1943) found that parents of delinquent boys do not have good relations with their sons and that, consciously or unconsciously, many of these parents themselves have antisocial tendencies.

Becker et al. (1959) examined two groups of families, one in which the children needed psychotherapy and the other where the children did not need psychotherapy. The investigators further classified the children who needed psychotherapy into two other groups, one involving conduct problems and a second involving personality problems. We report here only on the children who were listed as conduct problems. These children were aggressive and uncontrollable, and had parents who were maladjusted, gave vent to unbridled emotions, and tended to be arbitrary with their children. In addition, the mothers tended to be active, dictatorial, and directive, and to block expressions of individuality in their children; the fathers tended to be permissive. Winder and Rau (1962) measured social deviance in preadolescent boys. They, too, found that the parents of deviant boys had feelings of low self-esteem, that they were punitive and restrictive, and that either they were rejecting or that they vacillated between rejection and demonstrative affection. McCord and McCord (1958) examined 253 delinquent boys and concluded that maternal affection decreased criminality, whereas maternal rejection or maternal passivity increased criminality. In addition, these authors (1958: 72-74) wrote:

> In families where neither parent was loving, the crime rate reached a high level regardless of the paternal model. . . . If the father is criminal and the mother is also a deviant model, criminality generally results regardless of parental affection. If the father is criminal but the mother is non-deviant, and only one parent is loving, consistent discipline apparently deters the son from becoming criminal. If the father is criminal but the mother is non-deviant . . . parental affection seems to be crucial [in deterring criminality]. . . . The son is extremely likely to become criminal unless either (a) both parents are loving and the mother is non-deviant, or (b) parental discipline is consistent and one parent is loving. Twenty-four out of twenty-five boys whose fathers were criminal had criminal records as adults.

After examining the literature on deviancy, Rutter (1972) suggested, however, that lack of parental warmth is not sufficient by itself to produce antisocial behavior. Instead, active discord in the home, as well as lack of warmth, are associated with antisocial disorders in the child.

PSYCHOPATHOLOGY (MENTAL ILLNESS)

Schizophrenia

Schizophrenia is the most common of the various forms of psychosis, accounting for about 50 per cent of all patients in public mental hospitals. Schizophrenics suffer from cognitive, perceptual, emotional, and social disturbances of such magnitude that many of them must be hospitalized for their own well-being, and sometimes for the protection of others. Many schizophrenics have lost contact with "reality," they sometimes suffer from hallucinations and delusions, and some are totally disoriented in space and time. Moreover, the behavior of schizophrenics is often withdrawn, regressive, and bizarre, with chaotic speech and confused thought processes. Of course, as with the other forms of mental illness, not all patients show the same degree of pathology, malfunction, or disturbance. Some schizophrenics manage to function, at least marginally, in their social environments and occupations.

The causes of schizophrenia are incompletely understood, but it seems clear that genetic predispositions are involved in the development of the illness; so too are physiological and organic determinants, and psychological and social factors are also important. Kohn (1973: 74-75) argues for the interaction of three factors in the etiology of schizophrenia: genetics, stress, and social class position. The relevance of any one factor depends on the salience of the other two. In his view, no one factor produces schizophrenia except in combination with the other factors.

Regarding the significance of heredity, Kallman (1959) postulated that the more closely an individual is genetically related to a schizophrenic, the more likely he is to develop schizophrenia himself. In support of his argument, he showed that when one identical twin is schizophrenic, the other twin is six times more likely to be schizophrenic than would be the case with fraternal twins. He also showed that when one parent is schizophrenic, a child is sixteen times more likely to become schizophrenic than if neither parent is schizophrenic. Moreover, the odds of becoming schizophrenic are eighty times greater if both parents are schizophrenic than if neither one is. In further support of a genetic theory of schizophrenia, Heston (in Lerner 1968) studied psychiatric disorders in foster children who had been separated from their schizophrenic mothers by the time the infants were two weeks old. He found that about 17 percent of the children born to schizophrenic mothers became schizophrenic themselves, thus indicating either a high heritability of the illness or the possibility that the mothers supplied the fetuses with a schizophrenia-inducing intrauterine environment. In addition, Heston found that the incidence of mental deficiency, neurotic personality disorders, and criminal behavior was also well above average among these children. Bender and Grugett (1956) examined case histories of thirty hospitalized schizophrenics and compared them with a group of nonschizophrenic but emotionally disturbed children and with a group of thirty "normal" children. These researchers found that twelve of the schizophrenic children had schizophrenic fathers, fourteen had schizophrenic mothers, eleven had relatives who were emotionally disturbed, and twenty-one had either one parent or one sibling who had emotional disorders. Out of the control group of normal children, on the other hand, only four had parents with any kind of psychological disturbance. Because of these and other sources of evidence, investigators now generally agree that some individuals are genetically predisposed toward schizophrenia, making them especially vulnerable to certain kinds of environmental stress. But of course schizophrenia-sensitive persons are not necessarily exposed to these precipitating stresses. In short, genetic predispositions are a necessary but hardly a sufficient cause for schizophrenia.

Genetic theories of schizophrenia, especially those based

primarily on twin studies, have been seriously challenged. A major criticism focuses on sampling methods—samples often consist largely of already hospitalized schizophrenics. A second criticism relates to the question of how one arrives at the diagnosis of "schizophrenic," and a third criticism revolves around potential experimenter bias when testing twins. Other arguments against a strictly genetic transmission of schizophrenia have been aptly summarized by Zax and Cowen (1972: 164-65).

> These include: the hypothesized tendency of schizophrenics or those from schizophrenic families to mate selectively with others from similar backgrounds; higher mortality rates among schizophrenics than in the general population; and the fact that schizophrenics are less likely than normals to marry and have children. The overall effects of these factors would be to reduce the number of offspring of schizophrenic parents and, ultimately, the total percentage of schizophrenics from generation to generation if genetic factors are all-important. That such a reduction in the number of schizophrenics has not occurred argues against a strictly genetic theory. . . .

It seems clear that psychological, developmental, and environmental stresses are also associated with the onset of schizophrenia. But what are some of these stresses? Lidz, Fleck, and Cornelison (1965: 38) reviewed the literature on schizophrenia and compiled five conditions adversely affecting persons who later become schizophrenic. These include (1) deprivation of a parent (2) chronic emotional instability of a parent (3) chronic hostility or serious friction between parents (4) serious deviations from cultural norms in child rearing, such as extreme forms of oversolicitude or rejection, and (5) mental illness in the family tree.

Rejection has been clearly related to the development of several forms of psychopathology, two of which are described below. The extent to which parental rejection is importantly associated with schizophrenia per se, however, is a point of controversy; the bulk of the evidence connecting rejection with schizophrenia is equivocal, although several studies have concluded strongly that parental rejection is a significant factor in the etiology of the illness.

Friedlander (1945), for example, studied the early family life of sixteen adolescent schizophrenics and found that these youths came from homes characterized by either rejection, overprotection, or extreme disciplinary inconsistency, where one parent was stern and the other overindulgent. She also found intense family friction in 75 percent of these homes. Reichard and Tillman (1950) found a similar constellation of factors in a sample of seventy-nine schizophrenics. Ten of these patients (13 percent) had overtly rejecting mothers, and fifty patients (63 percent) had covertly rejecting and apparently overprotecting mothers. Moreover, twelve (15 percent) of these patients had domineering, sadistic, and rejecting fathers. More recently, in a study of 568 schizophrenics in the United States Navy, Wahl (1956-57) discovered that slightly more than half of these men had been severely rejected as youths, especially by their fathers. Overprotection, too, appeared as a visible factor in Wahl's study, but much less importantly so than in the studies of Friedlander or Reichard and Tillman.

Other research reports comparable to Wahl's have also revealed the father's importance in the context of schizophrenic children. In fact Lidz, Fleck, and Cornelison (1965: 50) conclude from their data that paternal influences are noxious as frequently as are the maternal influences. Actually, they found that schizophrenic sons and daughters tended to come from different types of families. Schizophrenic sons tended to grow up in families where the mother drew the son to herself and rejected the father; schizophrenic daughters tended to come from families in which the father dominated and humiliated the mother. Other investigators (for example Ellison and Hamilton 1949, Frazee 1953) have found fathers of many schizophrenics to be rejecting, sadistic, domineering, and cruel—often in the context of an overly solicitous and over-protective mother. Rousell and Edwards (1971), in a follow-up in 1968 of children used by Sears, Maccoby, and Levin (1957) in 1951, were able to relate warmth, overall permissiveness, and overall punitiveness to adult psychopathology. They found a correlation between a cold, punitive, home atmosphere in childhood and the development of psychotic disturbances in young adults. Heilbrun (1973) has proposed a theory of schizophrenic development postulating aversive maternal control as the principle stressor responsible for schizophrenia. By aversive maternal control, Heilbrun refers to maternal rejection, which he defines as low nurturance and high control over the child's behavior (Heilbrun 1973: 50-51).

Even though these studies testify to the importance of parental rejection in the development of schizophrenia, other studies fail to expose rejection as a significant factor. In fact Wolman (1965: 986) concludes that: "This intrafamilial relationship (productive of schizophrenia) does not fall into the usual descriptive categories of rejection, overprotection, overindulgence, etc." Thus we are left with uncertainty about the role of the more obvious forms of rejection in the development of schizophrenia, although it is clear that rejection may be involved in the onset of some schizophrenic episodes.

Autism

In 1943, Kanner described a rare behavior pathology which he named early infantile autism. Autistic children stand aloof, withdrawn from the world; they appear to be living by choice in a private inaccessible dream world, isolated from contact with others. They act as if other people do not exist, sitting for hours, motionlessly staring into space in a dreamlike trance. They are so lost within themselves that outsiders are often unable to attract their attention by calling their names or talking to them, and many of them do not even display a startle reaction to loud noises. For this reason, parents sometimes incorrectly assume their austistic child to be totally deaf.

The typical autistic child has exceptional motor and manual abilities, a photographic memory with an extraordinary interest and memory for music (one seventeen-month-old boy spontaneously recited a complete aria from Don Giovanni); he spends a great deal of time in utter preoccupation with mechanical objects, such as door knobs, light switches, stoves, and the like; and he has an acute intolerance for any environmental changes. Even the slightest displacement of a chair from its usual position is enough to evoke a temper tantrum. Language development is generally accelerated in autistic children, who often have unusually large vocabularies, but their speech is characterized by several anomalies, including extreme literalness (if an autistic child originally learned that "down" means "on the floor" then down for him will always mean "on the floor"), and delayed echolalia (for no apparent reason, autistic children may hour after hour repeat phrases, songs, television commercials, and the like). The single most striking symptom of these children, however, is the "autistic aloneness" described above, where the child is profoundly withdrawn into his own private world. Early infantile autism is often misdiagnosed as childhood schizophrenia, because distinctions between the major forms of childhood psychosis are blurred, and clinicians not infrequently disagree in their clinical diagnoses. Childhood schizophrenia, however, usually includes hallucinations and delusions in its symptomatology, whereas these pathologies are characteristically absent in autism. In any event, clinicians seem to agree that autistic children have serious difficulties with receptor behavior—i.e. in perception, language, social attachments—and with a sense of self-identity (Mosher, Gunderson, and Buchsbaum 1973: 29).

Some authorities favor a biogenic (biological causation) interpretation of autism, and some prefer a psychogenic (psychological causation) interpretation. Rimland (1964), a major adherent of the biogenic view, argues that early infantile autism is a distinct behavioral pathology caused by the inheritance of certain constitutional inadequacies of the brain, thereby causing cognitive dysfunction. More particularly, Rimland (1964) concludes that children with early infantile autism are grossly impaired in cognition, that is, in the ability to relate new stimuli to remembered experiences. The child is able to perceive external stimuli, such as the arrangements of blocks, but he is unable to comprehend, interpret, or integrate the stimulation, hence causing a "closed loop" between stimuli and response. Material is absorbed, stored, and recalled without ever being changed, supplemented, or integrated into the child's total memory bank.

Autistic children come from social and psychological backgrounds with many features in common. They are, for example, usually first-born, they are characteristically male (by a ratio of four to one), and they come more frequently from Jewish homes than from elsewhere. Moreover, studies by Eisenberg (1957), Kanner (1949), and Singer and Wynne (1963), show that autistic children typically come from families where fathers are successful scientists, professors, clergymen, business executives, or other professionals; mothers have usually attended college. The parents of autistic children are characteristically cold, detached, and emotionless, i.e. rejecting. In fact, for this reason some investigators have explained autism by asserting that the autistic child has withdrawn, become detached, and sought comfort in his own total solitude as a way of coping with this stressful environment. Whatever the proper explanation of autism, the evidence seems clear that the parents of autistic children do lack warmth. They are impersonal and mechanical in their care of their child, and they tend to be cold and distant. Kanner (1949: 417-25), for example, described the parents of autistic children as colder, more intellectual people, who stimulated their children less than parents of normal children. Eisenberg (1957) characterized the typical fathers of autistic children as being obsessive, detached, humorless, perfectionistic, bitter, and critical, and as being men who intellectualize life around them. Only fifteen out of fifty autistic children examined by Eisenberg had fathers who were warm, generous, and devoted; but eleven of these fifteen men were married to emotionally disturbed women. Singer and Wynne (1963), too, found fathers of autistic children to be lacking in empathy and sensitivity toward their children. These fathers were dissatisfied with their children and expected conformity and perfection from them. Moreover they were cynical, they attributed negative motives to others, and they were scornfully contemptuous of warm, tender feelings, expressing doubt about the worth of intimate relationships and interactions with others. Many investigators, however, suspect that some of these parental characteristics develop *after* the autistic child is born, as a response to the stress of rearing such a child.

Neurosis

Clinicians do not fully agree whether neuroses and psychoses are two different illnesses (differing as two distinct physical diseases would do), or whether neurosis is a milder form of mental illness, sliding into psychosis in its more extreme form. It is certain, however, that neuroses are generally less severe than psychoses. A neurotic rarely requires hospitalization, because he does not suffer from the same cognitive, emotional, perceptual, and social disturbances as the psychotic. Neurotics continue to evaluate "reality" more or less adequately; they usually have some insight into the nature of their problems; and they are unlikely to be dangerous to themselves or others. Consciously or unconsciously felt anxiety, plus the "inappropriate" use of defense mechanisms (ways of coping with stress, such as repression, dissociation, projection, and displacement) which normally protect an individual from directly experiencing anxiety are considered by most psychiatrists and clinical psychologists to be the major signs of neurosis.

The history of clinical evidence affirms the importance of a child's home life in producing either a neurotic or a "normal," happy child. Parental rejection figures conspicuously among the antecedents of neurosis (see, for example, Brown 1937, Ferenczi 1929, Horney 1937). According to Bender and Grugget (1956), distorted parental relationships and severe emotional deprivation produce neurotic and asocial behavior in normal children. Other researchers have found that hostile, emotionally withdrawn, unhappy, infantile, or neurotic parents are likely to produce neurotic children. Jacobs et al. (1972), in a study of 179 male college students seeking treatment for physical ailments, found that the neurotic group recalled the highest amount of unhappiness while growing up; they reported high paternal rejection and a high incidence of mothers who were domineering, cold, and harsh.

The authors find this consistent with other research, supporting the notion that "parents of children with psychological symptoms appear more pathological than parents of children with physical illness" (1972: 55). Ingham (1949) also found neurosis to be a common problem in unhappy families, in families where the parents are no longer living together, in families where the parents are overly strict, and in families where the child encounters serious conflict with his parents. Lewis (1954), too, related neurotic behavior to a stressful family background, where parents lack warmth, are inflexible or overprotecting, and where at least one parent is dominating or hypercritical of the child. These and literally hundreds of other sources of evidence support the view that parental rejection is a notable predictor of many forms of mental illness.

Finally, parental rejection has also been implicated in a variety of behaviors not discussed in this chapter. Hurley and Hohn (1971), for example, showed that large family size is conducive to parental rejection, and Jacobs et al. (1972) found a relation between paternal rejection and allergic reactions in children. Testing four-year-old children and their mothers, Radin (1971) found a correlation between maternal warmth and IQ, with achievement being an intervening variable between IQ and maternal warmth. Cox (1970) related parental rejection to various types of maladjustment, including anxiety, aggressive behavior, inadequate self-concept, autism, and poor performance on intelligence tests. He (1970: 437) modestly concluded that the "empirical data support the theoretical position that loving-rejecting parental behaviors have a pervasive influence on the child."

From a more positive point of view, Hartup and Yonas (1971) found that parental nurturance or *acceptance* is associated with a definite cluster of traits: "(a) willingness to disclose things about oneself to others, (b) expectations that the words, promises and statements of other people are creditable, (c) susceptibility to influence by both adults and peers, (d) and attention to, seeking information from, and compliance with maternal requests."

A child forsaken, waking suddenly,
Whose gaze afeard on all things round doth rove,
And seeth only that it cannot see
The meeting eyes of love.

GEORGE ELIOT

CHAPTER FOUR

Parental Acceptance-Rejection: Cross-Cultural Evidence

Chapter Two discusses a constellation of personality traits that seem to characterize rejected children the world over. These traits include hostility, aggression, passive aggression, or problems with the management of hostility and aggression; negative self-evaluation; dependence; emotional unresponsiveness; negative world view; and emotional instability. Chapter Three documents the presence of most of these personality characteristics among rejected children in the Western world. Now we broaden our perspective, in order to explore the causes and consequences of parental rejection and acceptance cross-culturally, where we find additional support for our hypotheses regarding the panhuman effects of parental acceptance-rejection.

The cross-cultural survey (or holocultural) method employed in this chapter has several distinct advantages not shared by other methodologies.[1] One of its strengths lies in its ability to help discover whether a worldwide relationship exists between two variables, or whether discovered relationships are unique to a given cultural system or to several historically related societies, such as those nations comprising the Western world. By drawing on a large number of societies from around the world, investigators can tell, for example, whether rejected children everywhere tend to devaluate their feelings of self-worth

97

or whether this psychological reaction is produced by features unique to American or Western life.

A second advantage of the cross-cultural survey method is its ability to test for the effects of more extreme behavior than normally can be found in any single society. In any society, only a limited range of behavioral alternatives are open to people. Persons who exceed these limits are considered deviant, and negative sanctions are usually placed against them. Excessive or deviant behavior in one society, however, may fall within the range of acceptable or even preferred behavior in another. In a study of child rearing in Kansas City, for example, Sears and Wise (1950) found that only five out of eighty children had not been weaned from the breast by seven months of age; no child was still being breast fed by the time he was three years old. Such late weaning shocks most Americans, but in a worldwide sample of thirty-seven societies, Whiting and Child (1953) discovered that the age of weaning cross-culturally ranges from twelve months to six years. And in only two cases in their cross-cultural sample were children weaned as early as most American babies, i.e. before six months. Thus from a pancultural perspective, the weaning habits of Americans as revealed in Kansas City are extreme.

Sears and Wise (1950) examined the relationship between age of weaning and amount of emotional disturbance shown by infants in their Kansas City sample. They concluded that the older a baby is when he is weaned, the more emotional disturbance he shows. Can this conclusion be incorporated into a general theory of human behavior? Is it universally true that the older a child is when he is weaned, the more likely he is to find it disturbing? Whiting and Child (1953) showed that scholars who generalize from the Sears and Wise study will be misled. As we saw above, the vast majority of children in Kansas City were weaned by seven months; thus the authors had a restricted time perspective on which to draw their conclusions. Basing their data on the great variability of behavior occurring cross-culturally, Whiting and Child discovered that *up to thirteen to eighteen months*, children really are more likely to become disturbed the older they are when they are weaned. Beyond that age, however, children show steadily fewer signs of emotional stress the older they are at weaning. Thus a curvilinear relationship apparently exists between age of weaning and emotional stress. We could not have known about this curvilinear relationship without access to the greater variability or extremes in behavior found cross-culturally than within any single society. We must point out, however, that our knowledge about the relationship between age of weaning and emotional disturbance would be incomplete without the data provided by Sears and Wise, because only two societies in the transcultural sample fell in the same time range (weaning from birth to seven months) as reported in the Kansas study. Without intracultural information such as this, we would have no way of knowing what the effects of weaning are at the lower age limits. Thus we see the complementary nature of intracultural and cross-cultural studies.

A third advantage of the cross-cultural survey method, one that is related to the point we have just discussed, is that it allows behavioral scientists to ask questions that cannot be explored within a single cultural system, either because the appropriate forms of behavior do not occur there or because, if they do occur, they are so deviant that careful investigators would be hesitant to use them. For example in America we could not test an hypothesis about the relationship between hunting and gathering economies on the one hand, and parental behavior on the other, because there are no hunters and gatherers in America (except for several North American Indian tribes, which take us "across cultures"). If, on the other hand, we want to look at the relationship between mother-child (father-absent) households and parental behavior—as indeed we do later in this chapter—we could, if we wished, do the research in the United States with relative ease. But we would want to recognize that certain risks are involved. Mother-child households in North America are often the product of divorce, desertion, or some other stressful circumstance. Thus investigators will have difficulty interpreting their results if they observe that women in father-absent households are not as warm toward their children as women in nuclear family households, where fathers live together with their wives and children. At least two conclusions are possible. First, women who live by themselves with their children—by this fact alone—may develop a different style of interaction with their children from women who live with their children and husbands. If this were true, one could conclude that the simple fact that a woman lives alone with her children is a sufficient condition, all other things being equal, to induce her toward the withdrawing of warmth. As we noted earlier, however, mother-child households in North America are often "broken homes." It is entirely possible that women in such homes experience external stress which has little to do with child rearing per se, but which almost certainly affects their relationship with their children. Therefore one cannot be sure whether it is mother-child households as such or whether it is these other extraneous stressful forces—or whether there is an interplay between these two factors—that contribute to the differences between father-absent and intact nuclear family households. Researchers do not have this problem of interpretation, however, when they use the cross-cultural survey method, because mother-child households are institutionalized (i.e. conventionally preferred) in many societies, and the stress that is so often present in father-absent American homes does not exist in these other social systems.

PARENTAL BEHAVIOR AND PERSONALITY

Several times we have spoken about the importance of parental warmth and affection for "normal" personality development. We now review the cross-cultural evidence for additional information about the profound effects of parental acceptance-rejection on the personality of children and adults. Table 1 shows that where relevant holocultural data are available, the predictions made in Chapter Two about the consequences of rejection are supported, i.e. that compared with accepted children, rejected children throughout the world are significantly more hostile, aggressive,

or passive aggressive.[2] These children also tend to devaluate themselves, to dislike themselves, to be uncomfortable
with themselves, and to perceive themselves as being worthless or worthy of condemnation.[3] Moreover, rejected children are often more dependent than accepted children;
they are more "clingy" and attention seeking than children
who are accepted. Dependency may also be related to a
rejected child's "conflict over nurturance" (see Table 1),
i.e. his conflict over positive desire to give succorance or
love, on the one hand—especially to people in need—and,
on the other hand, his fear or anxiety about committing
himself emotionally and thus exposing himself to the threat
of further rejection.

As shown in Table 1, after controlling for the effects of
"ethnographer bias" (see Appendix Three), the relation-

TABLE 1. Relationship Between Parental Acceptance-Rejection and Personality Development

Personality Characteristic	Children			Adults		
	r	p	N	r	p	N
Hostility	−.49	.001	60	−.32	.005	75
Self-evaluation	(.72)	(.01)	11	.40	.025	33
Dependence	−.31	.05	42	−.41	.01	40
Emotional responsiveness				.50	.001	75
World view				.29	.025	68
Emotional stability				.62	.001	38
Generosity				.41	.005	42
Nurturance				.39	.025	35
Conflict over nurturance	−.36	.025	37			
Achievement	(−.04)	(NS)	36	(.21)	(.05)	77
Self-reliance	(.16)	(.10)	77	.08	NS	77
Responsibility				.27	.06	34

Note: Correlations are computed by Pearson's r. The first six traits plus
"achievement" and "self-reliance" were coded in the Rejection-Acceptance
Project (see Appendix Three). Codes for "generosity" were taken from
Bacon, Child, and Barry (1963); codes and definitions for "nurturance,"
"conflict over nurturance," and "responsibility" are published in Barry,
Bacon, and Child (1967).

The two statistically significant correlation coefficients in parentheses become nonsignificant when the effects of "ethnographer bias" are controlled
(see Appendix Three); the two non-significant coefficients in parentheses
become statistically significant when the effects of "ethnographer bias" are
controlled (see Rohner, Dewalt, and Ness 1973).

ship between parental behavior and children's achievement-oriented behavior becomes statistically significant ($r = -.29$; $p = .05$): rejected children are more achievement oriented than accepted children. The data in the table also show that when the effects of ethnographer bias are controlled, the relationship between children's self-reliance and acceptance-rejection becomes statistically significant ($r = .19$; $p = .05$). Accepted children tend to be more self-reliant than rejected children.[4] In other words, accepted children tend slightly more than rejected children to draw on their own skills and resources to meet their instrumental, physical, or practical needs, as distinguished from their emotional needs.

It was not possible to make reliable worldwide measures of children's emotional responsiveness, world view, or emotional stability—three personality traits discussed in Chapters Two and Three—because anthropologists rarely report on these characteristics in young children within the age range of greatest interest to us. Our principal concern in the holocultural phase of this research is with children from the ages of two to six, or for as long before two or after six as the parent-child relationship remains fairly stable.[5] These ages are chosen because by the time a child is two, he has begun to learn complex symbolic skills, most notably language, and the effects of rejection-acceptance become most clearly measurable in the ethnographic literature. In addition, parents or other socializing agents typically remain of fundamental importance to the child until he reaches about six years of age. At this time, his interests and capabilities begin to expand, and other people, such as peers, become increasingly important to him. It becomes difficult to sort out the effects of parental behavior from other social experiences when this happens.

We do have adequate measures of adult emotional responsiveness, world view, and emotional stability. As predicted earlier, adults who were rejected as children tend panculturally to be emotionally unresponsive.[6] They encyst their emotions in a cocoon, as it were, and as a result they are unable to become deeply involved in affectionate, re-

sponsive relationships with others. Moreover, they are less emotionally stable than accepted adults. They tend to lose their composure under minor emotional stress, and many adults who were rejected as children are subject to wide, frequent, and often unpredictable shifts in mood. In addition, adults who were rejected as children are hostile, aggressive, or passive aggressive, and they are more emotionally dependent than adults who were accepted as children. They also tend to devaluate their feelings of self-adequacy and self-esteem (negative self-evaluation). Several of these features, especially hostility and low self-evaluation, combine to produce a negative world view in adults who were rejected as children. Such adults are inclined to view the world, life, the very universe itself, as being an unfriendly, uncertain, insecure, and often hostile place in which to live. Not surprisingly, many of these adults are nonnurturant in their relations with others, not simply with children but with other adults as well. They are less likely than adults who were accepted as children to spontaneously give sympathy, comfort, or support to people who are in need or those who are sick, confused, lonely, disabled, or defeated. Adults rejected as children are also less generous and less liberal in their giving than others. Although his data are not included in Table 1, Martin G. Allen (1967) found that both childhood indulgence and anxiety are related to ego strength in adults. Ego strength refers to an individual's ability to cope effectively with his environment without undue emotional upset, "to deal adequately, directly, and realistically with problems that arise" (Allen 1967: 53). Childhood indulgence includes a measure of overt affection given the child and is significantly related to both rejection-acceptance ($r = .49$) and to adult ego strength ($r = -.40$). Thus the more consistently and attentively the child's needs are gratified by his parents, the more ego strength he will have as an adult. Childhood anxiety is even more strongly correlated with ego strength in adults ($r = .54$), but this relationship is negative; i.e. the more anxiety a child experiences, the less ego strength he will have as an adult.[7]
Even though achievement orientation *in children* is re-

lated to parental behavior, adults who were accepted as children are no more achievement oriented than those who were rejected (r=.12; p =NS).[8] The trend regarding self-reliance in childhood also breaks down in adulthood—adult self-reliance is unrelated to parental acceptance-rejection. Moreover Table 1 shows a weak relationship between parental acceptance and responsible behavior among adults. Adults who were accepted as children are more likely than adults who were rejected as children to willingly perform laborious tasks, routines, or duties, such as those related to economic responsibilities or religious obligations. These traits are also sex linked: parents throughout the world tend to put greater pressure on boys than on girls to be self-reliant and achievement oriented. On the other hand, parents cross-culturally emphasize nurturant, obedient, and responsible or dutiful behavior in girls (Barry, Bacon, and Child 1957). It is not yet fully clear theoretically why these traits —achievement orientation, self-reliance, and responsibility —should be related as they are to parental rejection-acceptance.

As shown in Table 1, the *intensity* of the relationship between parental rejection-acceptance and specific personality traits often decreases over time, i.e. the magnitude of the relationship dwindles. Adults who were rejected in childhood tend to be somewhat less hostile than they were as children, and they probably evaluate themselves more positively than they did earlier. In addition, the weak connection between parental behavior and self-reliance evaporates as the years go by. The propensity for personality traits to alter as time passes is not invariable, however. Rejected children are dependent, and they are no less dependent when they grow up.

It is not always clear why some personality characteristics of rejected children should become muted in adulthood, while others remain essentially unchanged or perhaps even intensify. Life experiences, of course, have different effects on one's personality at different periods of development. Children usually form warmer ($p<.10$) and less hostile ($p<.05$) peer group relations in societies where they are accepted than where they are rejected.[9] This fact notwithstanding, it is true that some rejected children are able to form relatively warm, nonhostile relations with their peers, and that where this happens, the rejected child is bound to benefit, especially if his friends are supportive and nonhostile. Under these circumstances, the rejected child may have enough rewarding experiences in interaction with his peers and others to help him soften his feelings of, for example, self-dislike generated by the (sometimes mistaken) belief that his parents do not love or want him—and that he is therefore unworthy of love.

The cross-cultural evidence so far marshaled supports fully (with the possible exception of the relationship between parental warmth and children's self-evaluation) the findings reached by psychologists regarding the consequences of parental rejection on personality development. We can conclude, therefore, that the conclusions reached by psychologists are cross-culturally generalizable and probably panculturally valid. Even now, it appears that behavioral scientists may make certain statements about the "nature of human nature," but we cannot be fully confident of these universalist assertions until the data needed from intracultural community studies have been collected.

PARENTAL BEHAVIOR AND INSTITUTIONALIZED EXPRESSIVE SYSTEMS

What effect do socialization techniques—notably acceptance-rejection—have on the expressive systems of society? How, for example, are the religious beliefs of a people affected by their child-training practices? What impact does acceptance or rejection have on the artistic traditions of a people? How are the games a people play or the songs they sing related to their socialization experiences? These represent but a few of the many questions that could be framed about the relationship between parental behavior and the expressive features of society.[10]

In Chapter Two we describe institutionalized expressive systems as being ubiquitous but usually nonutilitarian features of society, such as folklore, art, religious beliefs, music, certain medical beliefs, and the like. Even though these systems are found in all human societies, they are generally not directly related to man's immediate survival. They are symbolic systems, including belief systems, that seem to be closely related to the operation of psychological processes within individuals. Thus in order for expressive systems to maintain stability in form and content over time, they must be compatible with the personality characteristics of a significant portion of the people within the society. This linkage between personality processes and expressive institutions is most clearly observable, and often most strongly bonded in small, stable, and relatively undifferentiated social systems. Any major incompatibility between psychological processes and institutionalized behavior— i.e. conventional, customary, or expected forms of behavior in different social contexts—leads to personal stress. If enough people are uncomfortable with certain features of society for long enough, the system inevitably changes. Also, we should point out that child-training practices per se probably do not directly influence expressive behavior of adults. The connection between parental behavior and institutionalized expressive systems is mediated over time through the personality of children, and ultimately through the personality functioning of adults, as shown in the conceptual model (Figure 2) in Chapter Two.

The theory in this volume predicts that the supernatural world (God, the gods, spirits, or whatever form the supernatural takes) will be viewed as hostile and malevolent in societies where parents reject their children; we expect supernatural beings to be benevolently disposed toward man in societies where children are accepted. In general, parental rejection is sufficient in most cases to create a conception of the supernatural as being malevolent. Parental acceptance, however, is not sufficient by itself to produce a positive view of the supernatural world, because, as is frequently the case with parental acceptance and as we argued in Chapter Two, other stresses can occur in a person's life to produce effects similar to those of parental rejection.

The specific predictions made about the relationship between the supernatural world and parental behavior are graphically displayed in Figure 3. As shown in Figure 3 by the minus sign in the malevolent row and the plus sign in the benevolent row of the acceptance column, we expect most accepting societies around the world to believe in a benevolent supernatural, and yet at least a few such societies will undoubtedly have essentially hostile or punitive deities. The plus mark in the malevolent row is juxtaposed to a zero in the benevolent row of the rejection column, indicating that we do not expect to find any cases of benevolent deities when parents reject their children. This model

FIGURE 3. Model of Expected Relationships Between Rejection-Acceptance and Other Features of Society

Dependent Variable (e.g. *Characteristic of the Supernatural*)	*Independent Variable* (e.g. *Parental Rejection-Acceptance*)	
	(Rejection)	*(Acceptance)*
(Benevolence)	0	+
(Malevolence)	+	−

Note: The "−" and the "+" in the right-hand column symbolize the expectation that accepting societies will have fewer malevolent deities than benevolent deities. The "+" in relation to the "−" here indicates relative proportion, "more than" (+), or "less than" (−). The "+" and "0" in the left-hand column, however, indicate the general expectation that rejecting societies will tend to have no benevolent gods (as marked by the "0"), but that accepting societies should have only benevolent gods (hence the "+"). The "+" and "0" here symbolize a "present–absent" dichotomy.

should also be accurate for many other predictions about the relationship between parental behavior and institutionalized expressive systems—as well as for some of the personality traits and other correlates of parental acceptance-rejection discussed elsewhere in this volume.

Two independent tests regarding the hypothesized relation between parental behavior and the supernatural world show that people the world over conceive of a benevolent supernatural in societies where children are accepted, but that they see their deities as being malevolent in communities where children are rejected ($p < .005$).[11] Thus the model of *expected* relationships in Figure 3 is essentially accurate, but, as shown in Table 2, one society appears as an exception to the prediction that rejecting societies do not believe in benevolent gods. The exception is a community in Egypt that is part of the great religious tradition of Islam. By their very magnitude and because of the fact that they have a written dogma, religious traditions such as Christianity, Hinduism, Islam, or Judaism are slow to change, and they rarely reflect accurately the internal psychological state of their believers. This is why we wrote earlier that institutionalized expressive systems are most revealing of psychological processes in small, stable, and undifferentiated social systems. It is neither disturbing nor surprising when these great religious traditions emerge as apparent exceptions to our predictions.[12]

TABLE 2.   Relationship Between Parental Acceptance-Rejection and Malevolence-Benevolence of the Gods

Malevolence-Benevolence of the Gods	*Parental Acceptance-Rejection*	
	Rejection	*Acceptance*
Benevolence	1	13
Malevolence	15	5

$X^2 = 15.3$
$p = .0005$

Several other cross-cultural surveys (see Lambert, Triandis, and Wolf 1959; Spiro and D'Andrade 1958; Whiting 1959) reinforce the general hypothesis that harsh parental treatment during infancy and childhood is associated with the view that the supernatural is harsh and aggressive. Most of these studies explain this relationship in about the same way we do: parental rejection is anxiety arousing, and, as a result, the rejected child is insecure and often hostile; from these psychologically painful early experiences the rejected child begins to develop a generalized negative world view. The child who has suffered emotional hurt from his parents—the people who are most important to him and from whom he takes his earliest cues about the nature of the world—is not likely to develop a sense of trust and confidence in himself and the world around him, and, after a time, he is likely to generalize these feelings onto the supernatural world, conceiving of it as hostile, harsh, or punitive. This attitude of distrust toward the supernatural is consistent with the psychological processes within the individual. Adults who view their gods as being malevolent also tend to be hostile themselves (p =.023); on the other hand, adults who conceive of a benevolent supernatural tend to be cheerful (p=.03) and nonhostile.[13]

Parental behavior affects not only a people's religious beliefs, but other institutionalized expressive features of society as well, such as complexity of graphic art. In societies where children are rejected, artistic design tends to be complex, that is elaborately organized with little repetition of many figures.[14] In societies where children are accepted, however, design is typically simple in its organization with constant repetition of relatively few figures (p=.03).

Games, too, are related to parental behavior, as well as to other features of society. Games appear in nearly every society, and they are clearly expressive in character—much like music, folklore, or graphic art—in that they do not directly satisfy biological needs associated with survival but are a reflection of the needs, wishes, conflicts, or other psychological conditions within the members of a community.

The anthropologist John M. Roberts and his associates have identified three principal classes of games around the world: games of chance, strategy, and physical skill. The outcome in games of physical skill, such as marathon races, hockey, and prize fighting or bowling, is determined primarily by the physical ability of the players; the outcome in games of strategy, such as chess or "Go," is determined by a series of moves, each of which represents a player's choice among alternatives; and, finally, the outcome in games of chance, such as "High Card Wins," is determined by nonrational guesses or by reliance on some mechanical device, such as the roll of a die (Roberts, Arth, and Bush 1959).[15] Roberts, who has done more than any other anthropologist to develop and provide empirical support for the relationship between games and personality, views games and other expressive systems of society as models of the social sys-

tem and of cultural activities. He argues that by learning
to play a game, children also learn to simulate present (or
sometimes former) cultural activities. Many games of physical skill, for example, simulate hunting or combat, as in
competitive trap shooting and boxing; games of strategy,
such as chess or backgammon, may be models of warfare.
Roberts and his colleagues have found that games of strategy,
which they say are models of social interaction, do not often
occur in stateless and unstratified societies. Roberts views
games of chance as models of interaction with the supernatural, and he has found that such games are related cross-
culturally to the presence of benevolent, unaggressive, but
easily coerced gods and spirits. The evidence is less clear
for the argument that games of physical skill are models of
mastery over oneself and the environment.

The research of Roberts and his associates is especially
notable, because these scholars attempt to validate their
cross-cultural findings by replicating them within the United
States. In this way, they fulfill a significant part of the research strategy required in the universalist approach. For
example Roberts and Sutton-Smith (1962) found that games
of strategy are correlated cross-culturally with rewards for
obedience in childhood, games of chance with responsibility, and games of physical skill with achievement. Using
a sample of 1,900 American schoolchildren, these authors
tested and confirmed the hypothesis that achievement is
stressed more often for American boys, who prefer games
of physical skill, than girls; girls, on the other hand, are more
often trained to be obedient and responsible, and accordingly they prefer games of strategy and chance. Moreover,
Roberts and Sutton-Smith conclude that "persons with
semi-skilled occupations (emphasizing responsibility) have
been found to exhibit a greater preference for games of
chance when compared with people in the professions (emphasizing achievement and obedience), who show a greater
preference for games of physical skill and games of strategy"
(1962: 177).[16]

The musical traditions and song styles of a people are also
related to numerous aspects of the social system, including

modes of economic production, cultural complexity, and socialization practices (see Lomax, et al. 1968). Ayres (1973), for example, found that musical rhythm is regular (i.e. accents occur continuously at equal intervals throughout the composition) in societies where infants are carried a great deal, either in a sling shawl, net bag, pouch, or on the mother's hip or shoulder (gamma = .72; p < .001); whereas rhythm is irregular (i.e. time signatures appear to change from measure to measure) in societies where infants are kept relatively immobile in cradles, cradleboards, or hammocks. Ayres explains this relationship by saying that regular rhythm in music is modeled on the sensation of regular up-and-down and side-to-side motion experienced by the infant while being carried. This sensation assumes greater reward value the more the sensation is associated with physical contact, feeding, and other such rewards.

Ayres (1968) also found that in the preferred songs of a society, the range (i.e. notes ranging from monotone to two or more octaves) and accent (i.e. forcefulness with which notes or syllables are attacked by the singer) are related to the experience of physical stress in infancy: songs in societies where infants are stressed before the age of two are characterized by a wider range (p<.005) and by a more forceful accent (p =.025) than songs in societies where infants are not stressed. Stress here refers to piercing an infant's ear, nose, or lips for ornaments, innoculation, scarification, or skeletal molding.

Ayres' work draws stimulus from research on humans and on animals, which shows that, for example, handled or stressed rat pups are more exploratory, mature more rapidly, and are longer and heavier at maturity than nonstressed rats (see Levine 1960; Landauer and Whiting 1964; Whiting 1965; Gunders and Whiting 1968; Whiting, Landauer, and Jones 1968; Landauer 1973). Apropos of this tradition of research, we have found that adult males the world over are taller in societies where young children are accepted than in societies where they are rejected (r=.38; p =.021). Perhaps this is because parental acceptance often manifests itself in the form of body contact and physical handling or stimulation such as fondling, cuddling, caressing, and hugging.

ENVIRONMENTAL AND MAINTENANCE SYSTEMS ANTECEDENTS OF PARENTAL ACCEPTANCE-REJECTION

What are some of the significant forces within maintenance systems and the natural environment (elements one through three in the conceptual model shown in Chapter Two) that shape the attitudes and practices of parents toward their children? In the first place, it is clear that parents usually treat their offspring in roughly the same way as they themselves were treated. They may not intend to do this, but many parents find it difficult, even when they try, to behave differently over an extended period of time. This is especially true of parents who were rejected as children. As we have already seen, these people tend to develop a constellation of personality characteristics—including hostility, emotional insulation, and emotional instability—that make it particularly difficult for them to provide their children with a fundamentally different emotional environment from the one in which they themselves grew up.

Moreover, most parents in stable communities around the world raise their children in pretty much the same way as the other parents within their community. Child-training practices are fairly well standardized within broad limits in every society. Even recognizing the great ethnic, regional, and class differences within complex nations such as ours, it is true that persons living within a single neighborhood often vary less in their child-rearing practices than parents living in unrelated neighborhoods. Neither of these facts, however, explains how a set of child-training practices evolved in the first place. It is neither an accident nor a matter of random chance that parents in one social system or subsystem reject their children, whereas parents in another system accept their children.

One of our principal general hypotheses explaining the worldwide variability of parental rejection-acceptance relates to the intensity of interaction between parents and their children. Specifically, we assume that mothers (or whoever the major caretakers are) everywhere are more likely to reject their children whenever they are unable to break the intensity of continuous interaction with their children. Socializing agents are likely to become increasingly frustrated if they are unable to get away from their charges from time to time. Consequently, they are more likely to withdraw the warmth and affection they might otherwise feel, and for this reason, they are more likely to reject their children. With this hypothesis in mind, we tested and found a significant worldwide relationship between parental behavior and household composition, where mothers who are home alone all day with their children are more likely to reject them than mothers who have someone else in the household—especially another adult who does not have child-rearing responsibilities of her own—to help assume the burden of child care.

The father is one possible alternate caretaker. Indeed, a significant worldwide relationship exists between parental rejection-acceptance and households where fathers are present to varying degrees during a child's first few years of life. Children tend to be accepted more often in homes where fathers are present on a day-to-day basis—as in the kind of nuclear family households preferred in America—than in households where fathers are present less often—as in the extreme case of mother-child households, where women live alone with their children. Women in the latter type of homes tend to reject their children ($r=.35$; $p=.05$).[17] In addition, a complementary piece of evidence shows a tendency for children around the world to receive more warmth the more important their fathers are as socializing agents ($r=.40$; $p=.005$).[18] Moreover, a modest transcultural relationship exists between parental rejection and the proportion of time that fathers in relation to other caretakers spend tending their children: the more time fathers spend with their offspring relative to other caretakers, the more likely children are to be accepted ($r=.28$; $p=.01$). All of these facts reveal that fathers the world over are important and effective nurturant agents.

Grandparents, too, can be successful alternate caretakers, helping to alleviate the strain of daily child care for the mother. Where grandparents (either grandmother, grandfather, or both) are present as significant child-rearing agents, children tend to be given a fair amount of warmth (p=.04).[19] It is appropriate to point out here that the proportion of time that mothers spend with their children is unrelated to rejection-acceptance. Knowing that children spend more time with their mothers than with other caretakers gives no basis by itself for predicting that mothers will accept or reject. It is also interesting to note that the presence of siblings as important caretakers is totally nonpredictive of whether young children will be accepted or rejected by their parents.

Minturn and Lambert (1964: 260) give valuable support for the hypothesis that the presence of more than one adult caretaker increases the likelihood that youngsters will be accepted. These authors find a fairly strong tendency in their statistical summary of the *Six Cultures* study (Whiting 1963) for children in three of the six societies examined to receive more warmth in stem family households, where a set of grandparents lives with the parents and children, than in nuclear family households, where parents live alone with their children.[20] Minturn and Lambert interpret this trend the same way we do: children receive more warmth in households where alternate caretakers are available. In this respect they write: "these results lead us to conclude that the presence of grandparents in a house, particularly a grandmother, reduces the isolation of mothers in nuclear families, provides an alternate caretaker, and therefore allows the mother to express more warmth to the children than when she is their sole custodian" (1964: 260). They continue: "But, as we suspected, the presence of sisters-in-law or co-wives, often unrelated to the mother and with children of their own to care for, provides a fertile field for bickering and leads to a muting of affect to avoid such strife. In such houses grandmothers must also be wary of showing favoritism which might incite jealousies among their daughters-in-law" (1964: 260).

Our cross-cultural survey data support Minturn and Lambert's conclusion, in that a moderately strong tendency exists in polygynous societies for co-wives who live in the same house to reject their children more often than co-wives who live with their children in separate dwellings ($r = .50$; $p = .07$).[21] Whiting (1961) provides collateral support for the hypothesis that household composition is related to parental behavior. He found that the amount that infants are indulged during their first three years is roughly proportional to the number of adults living in the household. In his words, "Extended and polygynous families where there are more than two adults living in the household tend to be predominantly indulgent with their infants. Nuclear households with two adults are unpredictable. Finally, in the mother-child household where one woman alone has to care for her children the probability of high indulgence is slight" (Whiting 1961: 358-59).

We now turn to a different aspect of the maintenance systems and ask about the relationship between parental behavior and the economy of a people. Do the subsistence practices in a social system predict in any way the child-training practices? Indeed they do. A fairly strong relationship exists between parental behavior and two forms of subsistence economy: hunters accept their children and pastoralists tend slightly to reject their children ($r = -.68$; $p = .07$).[22] As a matter of fact, none of the hunters in this sample reject their children. Indeed, we predict that parents in hunting societies cannot reject their children if that kind of social system is going to persist. The theoretical rationale for this hypothesis draws stimulus from Darwin and the concepts of "adaptation" and "selective advantage," or natural selection: certain personality characteristics are more adaptive than others for the successful maintenance of a hunting way of life. Young men who are self-confident (cf. "positive self-evaluation"), self-reliant, and independent and who can cope with stress without undue emotional upset (i.e. who are emotionally stable) are, in the face of a sometimes hazardous, demanding, or uncertain food quest, more likely to become successful hunters than youths who do not have these characteristics. Successful hunters thereby have a selective advantage in a Darwinian sense, in that they are more likely to reach reproductive age and over the generations to have more surviving offspring than hunters who do not have the attributes that help make them accomplished hunters. It is not implausible that over time, rejected hunters are likely to die out altogether, taking with them the maladaptive personality traits and the child-rearing practices that produced these traits. It is perhaps for these reasons that we have not found a single hunting group in the world today who customarily reject their children. If such a group ever existed, as no doubt some have, it must have either died out, changed its socialization practices, or adopted a new subsistence base.

The negative consequences of rejection are not as devastating in other economic systems as they are in hunting societies. Pastoralists, for example, typically have a reasonably secure food base as long as they can keep their animals alive. At least their survival is not threatened daily by food shortages, as is the survival of some hunters. Presumably, then, the positive traits that are so important for hunters do not have the same overwhelming adaptive value for pastoralists, who *may*, therefore, reject their children without facing the disastrous consequences experienced by hunters who reject their children.[23] In other words, economic systems such as pastoralism provide neither a necessary nor a sufficient basis for parents to either accept or reject their children; acceptance or rejection does not form significant natural selective pressures in these subsistence economies. A hunting economy does seem to be sufficient in itself, however, for parents to accept their children; here the selective advantage of parental acceptance is more clear-cut.[24]

This line of reasoning is reinforced by Barry, Child, and Bacon (1959), who find that children in hunting and fishing societies—societies where food resources are rarely accumulated—tend to have pressures put on them to be assertive, i.e. to be self-reliant and achievement oriented. On the other hand, children in pastoral societies (as well as those in agricultural societies where animal husbandry is important) are trained to be more compliant, i.e. obedient and responsible, than hunters or fishermen (p = .001). Barry, Child, and Bacon (1959: 62-63) conclude that:

"... our findings ... are consistent with the suggestion that child training tends to be a suitable adaptation to subsistence economy. Pressure toward obedience and responsibility should tend to make children into the obedient and responsible adults who can best ensure the continuing welfare of a society with a high-accumulation economy, whose food supply must be protected and developed gradually throughout the year. Pressure toward self-reliance and achievement should shape children into the venturesome, independent adults who can take initiative in wresting food daily from nature, and thus ensure survival in societies with a low-accumulation economy."

On the basis of a comparative analysis of three societies, Berry (1967), too, concluded that in subsistence level societies, where food resources are not accumulated, parents raise children to be independent and self-reliant, but in social systems where food surpluses are available, parents tend to raise more dependent and "group-reliant" children.

Although it is unclear why it should be so, we have found that levels of cultural development or cultural complexity are also related to parental rejection-acceptance. The more complex a social system is, the more likely children are to be rejected. Three indicators of cultural complexity used are levels of political integration, degree of social stratification, and settlement pattern. The more complicated the political structure of a society (ranging at one extreme from an absence of political integration—where, for example, family heads acknowledge no higher political authority than themselves—to the other extreme of complex states with at least 100,000 people), the more likely children are to be rejected ($r = .30$; $p = .025$); the greater the degree of social stratification (ranging from unstratified systems to societies with complex social classes), the greater the likelihood that children will be rejected ($r = -.25$; $p = .05$); and, finally, parents in sedentary neighborhoods and compact towns tend slightly to reject their children, whereas parents in migratory bands and in seminomadic communities generally accept their children ($r = .25$; $p = .05$).[25] Apropos of this information, we might also observe that hunting societies are typically less culturally complex than pastoral societies, where children tend to be rejected. Other indicators of cultural complexity could also be used, such as the relation between complexity of graphic art and parental rejection. Fischer (1961), for example, found that complex art forms tend to be found in highly stratified societies.

A cluster of social attitudes and practices are predictive of parents' behavior toward their children. It is no surprise, for example, that the more parents want or desire children, the more the children are loved and nurtured when they are born ($\phi = .63$; $p = .001$). Sears and his associates found a similar but less intense trend in their classic study of American child rearing. They (Sears, Maccoby, and Levin 1957: 56) report that: "there was a clear tendency for mothers who were delighted over pregnancy to be warmer to the infant after it was born [$r = -.23$; $p < .05$]. The carryover was somewhat diminished by the time the child was of kindergarten age, however [$r = -.13$; $p < .02$]; there was a noticeable relationship between feelings about pregnancy and warmth toward the kindergarten-age child, but it was not highly significant ($p < .02$)." Elsewhere these authors conclude: "a mother's attitude toward her pregnancy forecasts slightly—but only slightly—the warmth she will show toward her child after he is born. The forecast is even poorer for the warmth five years later" (Sears, Maccoby, and Levin 1957: 36).

The relationship between acceptance-rejection and other social attitudes and practices is less obvious. Severe punishment for abortion, for example, is strongly associated with the behavior of parents around the world. It is interesting to note that the *less* severe the punishment for real or suspected abortion in a society the *more* the resulting children are likely to be loved ($r = -.76$; $p < .01$). It would appear that when "wanted" children are born, they are given affection. Severe penalties deter women the world over from having abortions, but when women have unwanted children, the children may be rejected. The frequency of infanticide is unrelated to parental behavior. Knowing that newborn infants are destroyed in no way predicts how parents will later treat their young surviving children in terms of warmth and affection. Finally, a nonsignificant trend exists for children to be rejected in societies where women are ridiculed, divorced, or placed in other painful situations for not being able to bear children, but children tend to be more accepted in those communities where no such penalties or disapproval for barrenness exist ($r = -.28$; $p = .10$).[26]

Not only are current social attitudes and practices predictive of later parental behavior but certain cultural practices in infancy also reveal the way parents will treat their children in the future. One distinctive custom, for example—the practice of beautifying newborn infants through the use of adornments, nose molding, head shaping, and the like—has a fairly widespread distribution throughout the world. This custom reflects a basic concern, warmth, and solicitude for the infant, and wherever these practices are important, parents tend to continue showing affection for their children as the youngsters get older ($r = .40$; $p < .05$).[27] This fact assumes greater significance when we recognize that, overall, the display of affection toward *infants* is transculturally unrelated to the acceptance or rejection of *young children*. Parents around the world may be warm toward their infants and later reject them, or vice versa.[28] We should note, however, that most parents everywhere—even in societies where they reject their children—give their infants a fair amount of warmth and affection. There are a few notable exceptions to this rule, however.

Other features of the parent-infant relationship are predictive of later acceptance or rejection. Parents who are quick to protect infants during the first year from such environmental discomforts as excessive heat or cold, bright lights, or insects are also likely to be warm toward their two-year-olds and older children. On the other hand, parents who do not pay much attention to these sources of discomfort in their infants are also likely to reject their older children ($r = .30$; $p = .025$). Moreover, parents who are concerned about reducing such drives in their babies as hunger, thirst, and unidentified discomforts are also parents who are likely to give their older children more affection than parents who do not attend to these matters as solicitously ($r = .24$; $p = .05$). The *immediacy* with which parents attend to these discomforts in their infants is not related to later parental behavior, but the *consistency* with which they respond to the drives of their infants is predictive of later parental behavior ($r = .38$; $p = .005$). Thus it is no surprise to discover that the overall "indulgence" of infants, a measure which is based largely on the above characteristics, is related to the care given to slightly older children: "indulged" *infants* tend to be loved *children*, and "unindulged" infants tend to be later rejected ($r = .24$; $p = .05$).[29] Part of the reason for this is that the indulged infant is a happier infant, an infant that is easier to be with because it cries less, is less fretful, and less fussy. The warm mother produces a more lovable infant, so she can continue over time to be relaxed and pleasant with her child, but the nonnurturant mother is preparing her own less satisfying future. In this context, it is pertinent to observe that the earlier mothers reduce intensive contact with their young infants during the first year, the more likely these mothers are to become rejecting when their offspring reach early childhood ($r = .46$; $p = .025$).

Nowhere in this chapter have we commented directly on the effects of the natural environment upon parental behavior, even though a weak relationship between the two does exist. Parents in comfortably cool and fairly dry climates tend to accept their children, but parents in more tropical (hot and humid) regions are just as likely to reject as accept their children ($r = .18$; $p < .10$).[30] We shall not dwell on this correlation, however, because we suspect that the true relationship between climate and parental behavior is an indirect one. Careful exploration of the problem will probably show that certain types of economic systems, household types, or other maintenance systems tend to occur in certain climatic regions, and that it is these other ecological or cultural variables that account for a large part of the apparent relationship between climate and parental rejection-acceptance.

For some kinds of behavior climate may have a more direct effect, however. A fair amount of evidence links temperature to stress and emotional reactivity. In relation to "cool" societies (where the mean winter temperature is 49°F. or less), Robbins, Pelto, and DeWalt (1972) found that warm societies (where the average winter temperature is 50°F. or more) tend toward: greater indulgence of aggression ($\phi = .37$; p < .01); less anxiety induced by the socialization of aggression ($\phi = .40$; p = .01); relatively permissive premarital sex codes for females ($\phi = .23$; p < .02); greater emotional expressiveness ($\phi = .31$; p < .15); and, in 1965, a higher cross-national homicide rate (r = .50; p < .05) but a lower suicide rate (r = -.58; p < .05). Thus it appears that climate may be a significant stressor, producing nonrandom psychophysiological responses in the organism—both in man and in other animals. Related to these conclusions is the finding of McClelland (1961: 338), who reports that societies in temperate climatic zones are more achievement oriented than societies in either hot or cold climates.

Finally, Whiting (1964) argues a complicated sequence of relationships between climate and features of social systems. As summarized by Triandis, Malpass, and Davidson (1972: 3): "(a) climates with tropical, rainy forests, and (b) little production of meat in the form of cattle, result in (c) too limited a protein intake in children, which makes adaptive (d) a long postpartum sex taboo, and hence increases the probability of (e) polygyny, in which case (f) the father sleeps in a different place from where the baby and mother sleep, and so (g) the boys get very attached to their mothers and require (h) a severe initiation ceremony to introduce them to the male role. . . ."

When your heart is full of love
you are nine feet tall.

From a child's song,
"THUMBELINA"

CHAPTER FIVE

Love and Rejection
in Two Societies

THE PAPAGO

Papago Life Space

The term "Papago" is a White man's name for one of several Piman-speaking American Indian tribes who call themselves the "Desert People." Their reservation in southern Arizona (see Figure 4) lies within the Lower Sonoran Desert. Their climate is one of the hottest and driest in the United States and is characterized by extreme drought, torrential rainfalls, and large daily as well as seasonal temperature fluctuations. The reservation itself covers roughly sixty-five square miles and is divided into an acculturated eastern portion and a less acculturated western portion, where people are poorer and more conservative and tend to resist the instrusion of White "culture."[1]

Even though the Papago have intermarried with other Indian tribes, particularly with the Pima and the Yaqui Indians, the "Desert People" discourage marriage outside the tribe, especially with non-Indians. Thus few non-Papago are found on the reservation except for some White missionaries, traders, miners, and government officials. School teachers are either Whites or acculturated Indians from other tribes.

Papago Maintenance Systems

Except for increasing involvement in wage work on nearby ranches, in the mines, and for the government, the Papago

122

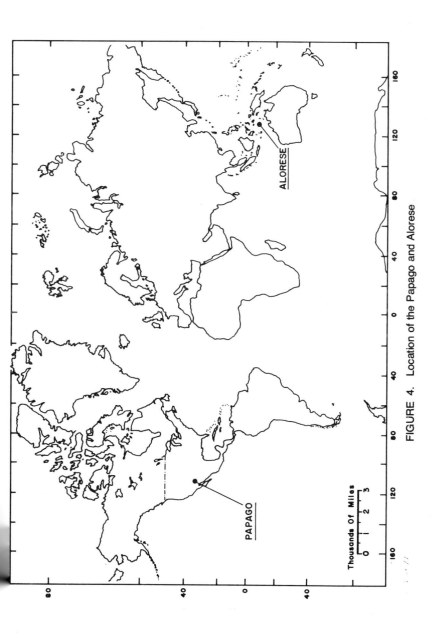

FIGURE 4. Location of the Papago and Alorese

live as they have lived for centuries, by farming small fields and raising cattle and horses. Farming and ranching are men's work. They till the fields and raise crops of corn, squash, legumes, and wheat. Men also tan leather and braid rope for barter or for sale. Women are responsible for domestic essentials, and they weave baskets and make pottery for barter and for sale. Depending on their ability, children help with household or farm chores. Even though the division of labor is clear-cut, all the Papago work together when it is time to bring in crops or to gather wild plants and berries. Cattle, though the largest single source of cash income, are not prestige animals. Horses, on the other hand, contribute to problems of overgrazing and are of little economic value, but they have great prestige.

In recent years, wage labor has become increasingly important. Accordingly, Papago men work in the mines, on ranches, or in government positions. They are considered by White employers to be good, steady, but slow workers. These greater chances to achieve and consume wealth draw the Papago off the reservation in increasing numbers, but at the same time the men send money home and usually plan to return to their old lands. Off-reservation living is regarded as but a temporary stage in their lives.

The extended family is the basic labor unit. These families are headed by an older adult male and include his wife, unmarried children, married sons, and their wives and children. The family head may occasionally be the maternal grandfather of the third generation; granduncles and grandaunts, too, may be household heads. The composition of any given extended family is flexible, because other relatives are always given a place in the house as long as they share the responsibility. Indeed, any kinsman who is willing to work hard is admitted into a family. The importance of kinship relations depends more on residential proximity and on the amount of work shared than on the actual closeness of kinship relationships. Besides providing labor and gifts, kinsmen are also expected to help each other in times of need. Moreover, two married couples often serve as godparents to each other's children, and kin terms are accordingly extended between the two families.

A man usually chooses his bride from a village other than his own, and as transportation improves brides even come from other dialect groups. Girls who speak a foreign dialect are often ridiculed for their mannerisms as well as their speech, but the teasing is generally good natured. Young people choose their own mates, but they usually seek prior parental approval. Marriage involves public recognition of the agreement between the spouses and their families. Church ceremonies are becoming increasingly common in the east, and the newly approved tribal code-of-laws now requires a marriage license and a ceremony by a religious or other authorized official, as well as a certificate of marriage. Men are usually eighteen to twenty when they marry, and women are sixteen to eighteen. After marriage, the couple either moves in with the groom's father or builds a house nearby. Sometimes the needs of the bride's family induce the newlyweds to stay with the bride's parents, but even though the young couple leaves the groom's home territory for various periods of time, "home" is always near the husband's father's house.

The new family possesses little prestige or influence in the extended family until the husband and wife demonstrate their adulthood by becoming parents. This change in status is particularly important for the woman, since she is now much less likely to leave her husband, and the husband's kinsmen begin to regard her as one of them. Now, too, she can show off her child to visitors instead of hiding in the background.

The Papago disapprove of premarital and extramarital sexual relationships, but children of such unions are given the same indulgent care as children born within marriage. Interpersonal incompatibility, not infidelity, is the principal reason for divorce among the Papago. Catholics, however, are forbidden to remarry after divorce, and to the devout this restriction constitutes a powerful deterrent. The grandfather is the head of the family, although he may delegate his authority to the ablest, though not necessarily the eldest, son. The household head has final authority, but he is obliged to consult the other household members before he reaches his decisions. The Papago allow each other great freedom of choice; even little children are allowed to decide matters that concern them directly. At the same time, discussions of morality, tales told by elders, criticism, ridicule, and denial of privileges are forceful mechanisms producing conformity. Junior and female members of a family are protected from subservience by the household head's responsibility to consult everyone before making decisions and by the freedom of choice allowed individuals in personal matters. Conformity to both family and legal authority comes in large part from respecting the legitimacy of such "authority."

All reservation land belongs to the tribe, and the village or district council assigns each family as much land as it needs. Usually the land remains in the family after the death of the head. The sons then inherit equally, sometimes without subdivision. Theoretically, all family members are entitled equally to use the land, but difficulties can arise. When the household head dies, the main herd generally goes to the new head unless prior arrangements were made. The new code-of-laws provides for wills and for the settlement of inheritance disagreements by the tribal court.

Villages, consisting mainly of groups of related households, play an important part in the political organization of the Papago. Along with a few houses, a typical village has a Sonora Catholic church, a dance ground, and perhaps a school to mark the center of town. The rest of the houses are scattered around the countryside, connected only by wagon trails. A village of fifty households may cover as much as two square miles. The land around each village is thought of as belonging to the community and technically may be apportioned to individuals by the village council. In practice, most people regard the land as belonging to whomever uses it; the village does little reapportionment.

Within each community, the Papago organize themselves cooperatively to care for their livestock, to keep washes (i.e. stream channels carrying water only after rain) clear of brush and sandbanks, to repair fences, and to maintain a blacksmith shop. The equipment in the shop is for everyone's use, and each family contributes money for gasoline to run the shop's well pump. Intervillage activity is greatest between parent and offshoot villages, where there is much visiting, cooperation in each other's roundups, and participation in each other's fiestas. Physical proximity and number of blood ties are the main determinants of closeness.

Beyond the village, each person feels that he belongs to a dialect group which shares certain peculiarities of speech and tradition. Today six main dialect groups are distinguished, as well as several mixed groups. Members of these groups share strong in-group feelings, and villages of the same dialects are likely to coalesce on social and political issues. People in the different dialect groups banter good-naturedly with each other about the superiority of their respective groups.

Each village elects a chief and two assistants. The chief serves in office until he retires or until the people become dissatisfied with him. The chief not only settles personal and family disputes and disagreements over water and land but is also the head of the village council, which formerly met every evening to discuss village affairs—it now meets less frequently. Unanimity was once required before any action could be taken, but now, under pressure from the Whites for prompt action, unanimity is sometimes impossible. As is true within the family, the most influential people within the villages are the elders, and those persons under twenty-five have little or no power. Also as with family structure, the village chief has the final word, but he must consult others before he makes his decisions. Power in leadership comes from interpersonal respect.

The new Papago constitution divides the reservation into districts, each with an elected council. It also stipulates two delegates to the tribal council, who serve two-year terms unless recalled. The tribal council has authority over tribal enterprises: arts and crafts, fairs and rodeos, loans and maintenance, and improvement of the herds. The council defines tribal membership, administers tribal law, levies taxes, and distributes monies. While the Superintendent of the Indian Agency has ultimate authority on many issues, he still discusses most matters with the council. Much of what the council discusses is suggested by the Agency. The eastern villages are the most active in the tribal council; other districts are without interested leaders. They often fail to send representatives to the council, and for this reason they lose influence. Tribal leadership is thus in the hands of a few. District councils have a lower achievement record than the tribal council. While district lines roughly follow the boundaries of the dialect groups, they were drawn primarily to facilitate range management, and they do not command the loyalty of the people. These councils are not organized, they meet irregularly, and they rarely accomplish anything.

The tribal court is subject to federal regulations on felonies such as arson, murder, and larceny. The court also enforces tribal law, which consists mainly of Indian customs mixed with some White laws, such as provisions for marriage licenses. Indian judges are appointed by the Agency superintendent and approved by the tribal council. The typical sentence imposed is a few days in jail, but this is a powerful sanction, because the Papago dislike the inevitable public gossip and ridicule. The Indian agency staff is generally seen as distant; indeed, the small staff seldom has time to consult with individuals. Among the White government employees, only teachers in the isolated districts get to be known by the Indians.

Growing Up Papago

Papago adults want children very much. The household looks forward joyfully to the coming of another baby, for children increase the status of parents, insure future solidarity and prosperity of the household, and protect the elders against the privations of helpless old age. Children are received with love, and even though males are socially dominant among the Papago, children of either sex are welcomed and treated with care. Nonetheless boys are regarded as more useful when they grow up, and the loss of a boy is felt more keenly. At the death of a son, people mourn, "and it was a boy, too" (Joseph, Spicer, and Chesky 1949: 117). Whereas overt displays of physical love are rare between adults, a small child's relatives fondle and make much of him. Parents dislike being separated from their children, and the "usually reserved Papago man will allow himself to express such joy and affection on being reunited with his children as he would never show for his wife in public" (Joseph, Spicer, and Chesky 1949: 51). All women are expected to long for children, and the occasional woman who expresses an unwillingness to rear them is severely criticized. Couples who cannot have children become upset and consult a medicine man for a cure. At the same time, even though the Papago strongly disapprove of abortion, they impose no strong penalties against it.

Growing up for Papago children is a long, gradual process, with no sudden breaks or changes; no ceremony suddenly admits them to a new status, although ceremonies exist for one-month-old babies and for girls at their first menstruation, as well as curing ceremonies for the sick and, for some, baptism. Except for baptism, all these ceremonies are private family and medicine-man affairs. They are intended to protect or to regain health, rather than to announce a new status. Even marriage is usually unmarked by ceremony or sudden change in status, since newlyweds have little more prestige than adolescents. Children gradually assume more responsibility and begin to live up to adult standards. No time comes when the standards for children are exchanged for adult standards, because childhood standards *are* adult standards. To gain approval, a child must be like an adult: industrious, honest, cooperative, and unquarrelsome. The only difference is that a child who fails to meet these standards does not receive strong public or family reaction. Youth excuses failure, but it does not redefine success.

Babies are swung gently in hammocks, watched, picked up and talked to whenever they cry or whenever the mother is not busy. A baby is usually within sight of his mother. When she is working he is either tied into a hammock, deep enough to be secure but open enough to see what is going on, or carried on his mother's hip. Mothers are constantly and warmly concerned with their babies, and babies are never neglected. Until the Papago infant learns to walk he spends his time in his hammock, on a bed, or in someone's arms. He learns to walk and to talk pretty much at his own pace.

Mothers do not keep track of the age at which their children begin to walk, and the "right" time for walking refers to the baby's size and strength at the time rather than to his age. Even though mothers do not systematically coach their children in walking and talking, they do, in their play, encourage them to take a few steps or imitate walking. Children are rewarded by obvious parental delight and caresses. Toilet training begins at about twenty months and is accomplished largely by imitating adults or older siblings who take the child to the bushes to urinate. At home mothers are lenient in toilet training, but their knowledge of White men's strictness makes them more concerned when they are among Whites. Mothers who are weaning their children try to avoid tears. Rather than enforcing strict, abrupt weaning, they either distract the child's attention whenever he attempts to nurse or leave him with one of his grandmothers for gradually increasing periods of time. Since the grandmother has already served as a mother surrogate, the mother's absence is not bothersome. After weaning, the child is usually assigned to a child caretaker—generally to a sister or female cousin, but occasionally to a boy if there are no available girls. Caretakers look after the child's physical needs and his safety. The baby may also be entrusted to a playgroup of three- to eight-year-old girls, who keep him from getting lost or hurt. The authority of older children is limited, however, because if the child cries, an adult usually appears to insist that the child get his way. Mothers as well as other family members believe that a little child should be happy and have what he wants. The effort with which they try to satisfy the youngster depends on the intimacy of their relationship with him and on their kin ties with him.

Everything that a child cries for he may play with. An adult may protect his belongings by hiding them, by trying to distract the child, or by providing a substitute, but if the child insists, the treasure will be delivered. The caretaker can only watch very carefully to see that the child does not break the thing. It is not unusual for Papago children visiting Whites to be treated somewhat more severely. For example a mother visiting one of the fieldworkers wanted to divert her child's attention from a Yaqui dance mask belonging to the White woman. When his interest would not be diverted, the mother said in a tone of fear: "You must not touch it. It's a ghost" (Joseph, Spicer, and Chesky 1949: 125). A widowed mother working in a trading post silenced her screaming three-year-old by dumping her into a bucket of cold water, saying: "I guess you are too hot, too hot in the head. Maybe this will cool you off" (Joseph, Spicer, and Chesky 1949: 125). Children at home seldom receive more than a scolding, however.

Grandmothers have even more time than mothers for children, although the ultimate responsibility for a small child lies with the mother. Grandmothers express their pleasure with their grandchildren with smiles, loving words, and caresses. Grandfathers, who also play with children, tell them old-time stories, sing old-time songs in the evening, and gravely lecture on the virtues of honesty and industry. Fathers fondle little children and are viewed by children as powerful protectors; children are delighted when their fathers come home in the evening.

The right of young children to be indulged supersedes the Papago obligation of deference to elders, but by the time a child is seven, he generally recognizes the Papago principles of seniority. As a result, older children achieve a certain power over younger siblings and cousins. Insofar as older children gain authority, elders are relieved from child care, thus preventing child rearing from becoming a burdensome chore for any single person.

Few demands are made on a child before he is four. The Papago believe that a little child should be humored as often as possible. His development should suit his own pace, and he should not be forced or even strongly urged to follow the wishes of older persons. When the child must be denied something, efforts are made to keep him from realizing he is being refused by distracting his interest to something else, or by mild deception. The Papago rarely use corporal punishment, but families who have had contact with Whites sometimes spank their babies. Ambulatory children must learn to stay away from wild animals and to fear ghosts, both of which cause sickness, but children are not expected to obey more rules than their well-being demands.

Subtle changes in child training occur when the child is five. Fathers become more reserved with the child, and grandmothers begin to direct the child's activities; it is she who is most likely to lecture him for misbehavior. Despite her disciplinarian role, her great affection for and pride in her grandchildren, and her freedom and willingness to spend time resolving their problems make her the one first turned to for help. She may also, particularly at cactus camp in the summer, show them legendary landmarks and tell and sing old-time Papago stories and songs. In the house, she oversees the girls at such household tasks as sweeping, rolling up bedding, washing dishes, and setting the table.

As they grow up, girls also take over child care duties and, along with the boys, they run errands and fetch water. Boys chop the firewood, but for the most part this is a freer time for them than for their sisters. Girls must play near their homes and be watched, but the boys are free to roam widely. Girls develop close relationships with their mothers while they do the housework together. In their leisure time, girls share gossip with each other, enjoy magazines and pictures together, and in the hot summer they often lie close together for naps.

As adults-in-training, children receive a great deal of instruction—not in *how* to do things but in *why* they should be done. Children are expected to cooperate and to learn work tasks by imitating their elders. In the evening, grandfathers and often fathers include among their stories lectures on the importance of industry, honesty, and peacefulness. During the day, children are reminded that only by willing obedience can these virtues be obtained. A child who is slow to work is not coerced, however, nor does he receive strong or lasting condemnation, even though industriousness is a prime Papago virtue. He is, after all, still a child.

Older children accept the virtue of peacefulness even more readily than they do that of industry. By now they have learned that quarreling, as well as animals and ghosts, can cause sickness. Not only is quarreling itself dangerous but so too is the type of thinking that causes quarrels.

Despite the often greater friendliness and familiarity of a partly retired grandfather, children respect and obey him even more than they do their respected and quickly obeyed father. After all, even father defers to and obeys grandfather. Older children claim indulgence from their elders and deference from their young siblings, and yet they are also responsible for indulging these same younger siblings. Any cry from the younger one because of demands from the older one will result in an adult insisting that the demands of the older child be dropped.

As noted earlier, both children and adults have freedom of choice in personal matters. Just as the head of a household or of a village must consult everyone on a course of action, so, too, parents consult their children on matters concerning the children. Whether a child goes to school, receives medical care, or eats a certain food is up to him. Parents do not feel that their greater experience or power gives them the right to determine decisions whose major effect is on the child. Only in regard to his responsibility to the group do they apply pressure, and even here a young child can get his way. His parents will be disappointed in him if he does not obey —they will lecture him, scold him, compare him unfavorably to others, threaten supernatural action, and slight him with their physical movements and poses—but they will not withdraw their love or apply the sharp derision nonconforming adults might have to face.

When they are about eleven, children generally give up their childish play. They begin to walk with deliberate, unhurried motion, and they identify with young adults of the same sex. Parents assign and entrust them with more labor and responsibility. Girls assume the full range of household chores; boys help with herding, farming, and repairs. Boys are still freer than girls to roam when their help is not needed, and they are not censured for disobeying women unless their fathers or grandfathers support the women. Girls must now be taken to town and to fiestas by male relatives. As children grow they are treated less and less like children;

gradually they become the youngest adults in the household seniority system.

Papago Personality

Few quarrels disturb children's play groups, and those that do occur cause the children to disperse until the trouble is forgotten. According to Papago norms, an individual should not express anger openly. Anger is most frequently provoked by aggressive or inconsiderate behavior of others. Aggression and overt hostility occur infrequently except among drunken men. Males, both boys and men, have greater problems with the management of aggression than women. But boys are only infrequently aggressive and they infrequently exhibit passive hostility. Some children, however, seem concerned with anger.

The Papago are fond of visiting, and kinsmen are always welcomed guests. Strong feelings of warmth and mutual responsibility unite members of the extended family, and few needy people have to rely on extrafamilial support. At least in public, adults usually disguise the emotions they feel for other adults, for "reserve" is proper behavior. Toward children the Papago are more openly affectionate. Relatives fondle and make much of the young child, and a Papago parent returning from a trip shows public delight on being reunited with his children. Children are equally as warm as their parents. Young girls rarely resent their little charges and they take friendly care of them. It is not unusual for a sister at a fiesta to take time to teach a toddler how to dance. Older siblings at school are eager to help the younger ones. Social and emotional ties are also strong among those who are in close residential proximity. This fact is indirectly revealed by competing school children, who ally themselves with other children in their own village.

Individual achievement motivation is not a major value among the Papago. Even though an elected village chief or roundup foreman is expected to work hard for the village, too much drive to achieve ostentatious success is accompanied by social disapproval. Those persons who have exceptional wealth or specialized skills or who hold office do not receive any special consideration. They are expected to play down their advantages. In traditional Papago culture, individual "superiority" and power were thought of as gifts from the supernatural world rather than as being the outcome of patient and planned labor, or as being connected with personal merit. Gifted or uncommonly successful persons are not admired as "self-made men," but are looked upon with friendly appreciation as long as they continue to work in cooperative harmony with others. In no way are Papago children encouraged to outdo their parents or their grandparents. Rather, children strive to become as much like their seniors as they can. Papago decorum asks the individual to avoid drawing attention to himself. Conspicuous behavior is ridiculed; being remiss in decorous behavior causes embarrassment. Major values for a smooth-running Papago social system include work, cooperation, and the avoidance of aggression. The mutual sharing of family work stresses the subordination of self-gratification to close cooperation within the group.

Even though personal achievement is deemphasized, self-reliance is important in making a living on the desert. Individuals have to be able to take care of themselves. The village elects men to organize those things that need organizing: some influential person becomes chief; another becomes foreman of the cattle roundups or member of the committee to host a fiesta. But the willingness of these individuals to assume responsibility does not mean that the other men rely on them for the fulfillment of their own instrumental needs. In fact, much of the appeal for adolescents of wage work away from home lies in the fact that it gives these youths greater independence and freedom to rely on their own resources, both physically and emotionally.

Younger Papago children accept responsibility with little pressure. In learning to work, they do not demand detailed instruction and supervision, but they learn by observing adults and then trying to take on the tasks as their own.

The Papago seldom demand affection or care from others, and any special intimacy between kinsmen arises from the personal choice of both parties. Preadolescent girls show signs of dependency when they seek the attention of female teachers and of young female adult relatives, but this seems to be more an attempt to identify with or model adult behavior than a need for reassurance, care, or affection. Papago adults typically preserve a calm, reserved demeanor, a composure that is difficult to disturb. Along with this quiet, steady, controlled behavior, the Desert People maintain a lively interest in their environment: they enjoy gossip, though they disapprove of vindictiveness; they are often pleasant but cool toward strangers, but among themselves they are quick to smile and to laugh. Papago children, too, seem generally at ease, with few episodes of emotional upset. The people laugh and enjoy life, but, as described below, they also see the desert as full of disease-causing and misfortune-causing agents, and they believe that evil medicine men can cause illness, natural disaster (such as droughts), epidemics, and even death. Benevolent medicine men can counteract these evil doings.

Papago Expressive Systems

Contemporary Papago religion combines indigenous beliefs with Christianity. Generally the larger, public ceremonies of the traditional religion are disappearing, along with the old men who knew how to conduct them; the public side of religion is being replaced by Christian ritual. Nonetheless almost everyone, except the strictest Presbyterians, uses a medicine man and a native singer to diagnose and to cure disease. The indigenous religion was mainly concerned with bringing rain and curing illness by manipulating the village fetishes.

Medical beliefs are closely tied to the traditional religion. Proper relationships must be maintained with the many supernatural forces causing disease. Care must be taken, for example, not to offend the dead, because they may return as owls or as other animals to bring sickness and misfortune. Almost any living animal is capable of producing disease or misfortune, but animals also have the supernatural power to help man. Nonetheless, because of their capability of bringing misfortune, animals, especially wild ones, should be avoided. When this is impossible, protective magic is used. Moreover certain kinds of thought can cause illness, especially thoughts that lead to quarreling, but also any undue concentration on sexual matters. Physical aggression and open displays of temper are generally controlled by the belief that mysterious illnesses and eventual death may come to those who strike, push, or touch others in anger. As noted earlier, malevolent medicine men can "shoot" individuals with poisonous substances that cause illness or death, or these men can interfere with sacred objects and natural phenomena to induce droughts and other disasters. Benevolent medicine men, however, can diagnose the cause of disease and prescribe a cure. They can remove the poisonous substances, prescribe cures for evils other than disease, and, in order to cause magically their death or disappearance, good shamen can locate the malevolent medicine men or witches who caused the injury. Medicine men can also determine the cause of droughts, foretell the weather, predict human behavior, and suggest ways of controlling both the human and the nonhuman world. The power of a medicine man is latent until it is revealed in a dream. Years may pass before he is certain he has such power, but once he is sure, he must practice his art or it will poison him.

A medicine man is usually consulted in the case of disease, but if he fails to cure the patient or if he diagnoses a "White man's" disease, a White doctor may be called in. Only in the case of broken bones is a White doctor sure to be called.

Through supernatural forces a person influences his own future by his good or bad behavior; both one's own future and the supernatural are at least partly under individual control. Thus for all the dangers that exist in the world, life can be managed safely through knowledge, through care, and through morality. Papago religion for most Papago includes the belief in many evil forces, which must be and can be controlled by good forces. The medicine man, whose power comes from the benevolent I'itoi, or God, knows how to cure the effects of these evil forces, while Christian saints and God (God alone for the Presbyterians) can help those who pray and care for them.

In addition to the traditional religion, many Papago are

adherents of Sonora Catholicism, a belief system developed from the teachings of early Spanish missionaries. Sonora Catholicism excludes mass, Latin, confession, and marriage ceremonies; godparents, not priests, baptize children; the people bury their own dead. Most villages have small churches where appointed adults lead prayers and where women sing hymns. Sonora Catholicism and the indigenous Papago religion work together to bring rain. Legend has it that a medicine man once diagnosed a drought as being due to insufficient care of the Christian saints. When this slight was remedied, the rains came.

Increasingly, Sonora Catholics (who compose the majority of the Papago on the reservation) are becoming Roman Catholics. The Roman Catholic priests are tolerant of both the traditional beliefs and Sonora Catholicism—even though they do not regard the latter as being Catholicism. Some of the nuns in religious schools raise doubts about the old beliefs. To a certain extent, the priests are regarded as foreigners and are accordingly mistrusted or are felt to be too distant from the people; nonetheless their help is recognized throughout the reservation except in the West, where they are not yet accepted.

Presbyterians use a different approach to gaining converts. They demand complete rejection both of traditional Papago religion and of Catholic beliefs, but they use the Papago language and Indian ministers. Papago elders govern the Presbyterian churches on the reservation. The use of tobacco, alcohol, and Papago medicine men is forbidden by the Presbyterians, and so is dancing. Presbyterianism appeals to the Papago for various reasons. It appeals to some because of its Papago involvement in the services, to others because of its strictness, and still to others because it appears more progressive than the other religious systems. Presbyterians are more likely than members of other religions to stress the importance of education. Partly because of the superior education offered in their schools, partly because of being located in one of the most acculturated areas, and partly because of White feelings in favor of Protestants, the Presbyterians, though few in number, are gaining substantial influence throughout the reservation. Much of the tribal leadership comes from their ranks.

THE ALORESE

His injured childhood bullied him.

ROBERT HAYDEN

Alorese Life Space

Alor is an island approximately fifty miles long and thirty miles wide, lying at the end of a long string of islands extending east of Java (see Figure 4). Monsoon winds on the island create a cycle of wet and dry seasons. The wet season starts slowly in October and builds up to steady downpours every afternoon in January, February, and March. After this time, the temperature cools slightly, and the dry season begins. The Alorese refer to the dry season as the "hungry period," because only cassava and sweet potatoes grow, rather than the preferred grains. "Good" years alternate annually with "rat" years in the cosmology of the Alorese. During the rat years, the supposed increase of rats makes planting rice and outlying plots futile—a belief which seems to have little basis in fact (DuBois 1956: 250).

Since the small island supports a population of 70,000 people, almost all possible land is cultivated. Steep, mountainous slopes make communication among villages within the interior difficult. This fact helps to explain the large number of dialects of at least eight mutually unintelligible languages. Except for the division between the coastal Muslims and the interior mountain people, the languages and their speakers fade imperceptibly into one another. The mountain district of Atimelang studied by Cora DuBois (1944) is described in this chapter.[2] The region of about 600 people within a radius of one square mile comprises four major villages, plus several offspring hamlets and individual dwellings, all under the authority of a single headman, the *tumukun*.

Prior to the arrival of the Dutch in Indonesia, social control in Alor was exercised only by kin and village groups. During the 1910s, however, political power was given by the Dutch to the coastal Muslims, certain of whom were designated radjahs of the four radjahships into which the island was divided. These divisions cut across both cultural and language boundaries. Each radjahship is further divided into districts administered by a kapitan with the aid of a few field police. The principal functions of both radjahs and kapitans are to collect taxes and to hear litigations. These, too, are the functions of the appointed chief of each village. Groups of friendly villages are unified under a *tumukun*. This Dutch-innovated political hierarchy—together with the system of litigation that replaces the now forbidden tradition of warfare and headhunting—have been accepted by the Atimelangers, but the enforced taxes are paid more reluctantly.

Villages in Alor are small, rarely housing more than 150 people. Most villages are located on mountain spurs and crests as protection against the once endemic warfare. Since springs tend to be located in ravines, water becomes a problem. The Dutch have been pressuring the islanders to move to more level ground, and after the villages of the Atimelang complex became involved in the murder of the last radjah and in the subsequent war of pacification, the Dutch government moved the people from the mountain ridges to the floor of an enclosed valley. Each of the villages has from one to seven dance places, roughly one to each patrilineage (i.e. the corporate descent group formed by a line of males and their children). Located on each dance place is at least one large lineage house, occupied by one branch of the lineage. Around the edge of the dance place are flat gravestones of the prominent dead. Narrow trails connect dance places and sometimes houses, which are raised, thatch pyramidal structures, with wide eaves. Smaller houses, a guesthouse, and spirit sheds are located around the lineage houses. Fields lie beside and between the houses, and some are located more than an hour's walk from the main village. Scattered temporary shelters dot the outlying fields. These have grown more attractive as possible dwellings since the cessation of headhunting.

Alorese Maintenance Systems

In the agricultural economy of the Alorese, women are responsible for the collection of vegetable foods and for cultivation; they own all plants produced, regardless of whose land was used or who helped grow them. Men are responsible for the financial system and the three currencies on which it is based—gongs, pigs, and *mokos*, or metal kettledrums; men are also responsible for flesh foods, such as chickens and goats, but not pigs. In addition, men engage in organized rat hunting for food and in wild pig hunts. Men who are accomplished horticulturalists and women who are skillful in the competitive financial system, however, are also admired by the Alorese.

Ideally, residence in Atimelang is patrilocal—i.e. the bride and groom set up residence in the hamlet of the groom's father—but brothers scatter widely rather than live together if they cannot get along. Within each house lives a nuclear family (i.e. parents with their children), occasionally supplemented by other kinsmen. Houses of a single patrilineage tend to cluster around their dance place. Another set of relationships, important in exchange relationships—particularly in death services—are the six "male houses" (a kind of kin grouping) of each individual. Less sharply defined in form and function is the "female house." One may call upon relatives in these "houses" or kin groups for supplementary assistance in ceremonies and for financial exchanges.

Children of either sex who are old enough to work productively receive garden plots from their parents, but neither rank nor prestige is inherited from parents; each man must accumulate his own wealth and his own influence. One's social position is determined largely by financial acumen, especially as manifested by wealth, i.e. available capital plus profit and interest. Business acumen, as we note later, includes an excellent memory, assertiveness, constant vigilance, ingenuity, and chicanery.

One of the principal functions of marriage in Alor is to initiate a series of financial exchanges between extended affinal kin (i.e. kinsmen related by marriage), which continue for as long as the marriage itself. The amount paid by the husband's kin—the bride-price—usually exceeds considerably the amount paid by the wife's kin—the dowry—so the wife's family is usually put in a debtor position. These financial affairs tend to stabilize marriage, since the liquidation of the bride-price and dowry agreements may take the better part of a lifetime. About once a week, a man and wife in the Atimelang area sit down to air their grievances publicly and to compare total bride-price paid to total dowry paid. The two amounts must be equal to permit divorce. On these occasions, the couple and their respective kinsmen quarrel energetically. But many more such confrontations than divorces occur. At the same time, a woman may find a new husband who is able to pay off the owed bride-price to the first husband, and in this polygynous society a man may take a second wife. The exchange function of marriage results in complicated transactions, because a man may enter into exchanges with the husbands of all his nieces and his female cousins, as well as his own sisters and daughters.

Marriages may be entered into for reasons of financial expediency on the part of adults. It is also possible for young couples who have met during all-night dances, tooth blackening ceremonies, or other such activities to ask their parents to make arrangements for the necessary marriage. If the parents agree to the marriage, the two sets of adults discuss how the bride-price and dowry exchanges will be initiated, and an engagement gift of an inexpensive *moko* is paid to the girl's father and mother, thus making the girl affianced. Before the marriage is consummated, the young man pays an expensive *moko*. Thereafter, barring divorce, the girl lives with him as a member of his village and lineage, but she is usually still loyal to her blood kin in the matter of bride-price payments. Women always marry early, sometimes before their breasts begin to swell at pubescence. Men, however, have to acquire financial backing, so few of them can marry until they reach their early twenties.

Marriage not only adds relatives and financial exchange partners but also serves to legitimize sexual relationships. The Alorese have brief affairs, but a man may also be forced to marry the girl with whom he has sexual relations. If she is already married, his life may be threatened or he may be forced to pay a fine to the offended husband. Forced marriages place the man's family in an awkward bargaining position, and pregnancies resulting from an illicit affair are usually aborted. Most marriages involve constant, jealous quarreling and bickering about property. Men, for example, complain that their wives spend too much time with their children and neglect their fields, and their jealousy of other men often results in beatings. As a result of this conflict, at least half of the Alorese who have ever been married have also been divorced at least once. Financial transactions that accompany marriage often make divorce difficult, but even where divorce would be too expensive for one of the families, estranged couples and their families undergo the public debt-reckonings and airing of grievances preparatory to divorce.

Through the creation of alliances with other men, certain rich men in Atimelang have captured substantial power. A rich man may intimidate his debtors into paying what is owed by menacingly appearing with a large group of allies before a debtor. Public shaming and ridicule are potent forces of social control in Atimelang life; fear of retaliation through murder, litigation, and battles, along with wealth, are pacifying forces among men who seldom physically strike or openly insult one another. In their economic systems, the Alorese recognize the concepts of profit, credit, reciprocity, interest, and, of course, debt. And since the three principal currencies are not wholly standardized in value, there is ample room in the system for vigorous bargaining. Profit is the ultimate economic motive, but wealth is measured more in terms of outstanding credits than in accumulated property.

Growing Up Alorese

Recognition of adulthood comes only with parenthood, but the benefits of adulthood are greater for men than for women. As a result, Alorese men want children, but many women resent bearing them. Hence the women often try to miscarry.

Most men do not approve of their wives' abortions, but the only penalty is likely to be a beating by an angry husband. The newborn infant is considered a delightful creature. He is held, fondled, joggled, and mouthed by all the people around him, especially the young men, who in this cultural system have the most leisure time.

The mother returns to her work in the fields within two weeks after her child's birth, thus ending the period of maternal solicitude. From this time forward, maternal care becomes inconsistent, undependable, and sporadic. The infant is left with his grandmother, or perhaps with his father, or with an older sibling who carries him about in a shawl tied over one shoulder and under the opposite arm. Fathers and grandmothers often have business of their own to attend to, however. Older men in particular may be involved heavily in financial affairs and so have little time for children, and older siblings frequently resent acting as nurses. Mothers fondle and nurse their infants when they return in the evening from the field, even though they find little pleasure in nursing. Sometimes adults sing dance-songs to soothe a fretting child. When the child learns to walk he is left to play under the casual supervision of an older sibling or aged adult. Food is given unreliably, and the child is no longer the object of constant and affectionate handling. Now he faces teasing, lying, deception, and other forms of mild aggression.

Young children are weaned when the mother again becomes pregnant. They are pushed away from the breast or slapped; recalcitrant children are sent away to live with some other kinsman. After their children are weaned, mothers may tease the youngsters by taking neighbors' babies to their breasts. Mothers do this in order to arouse jealousy in their own children. One day Padafon, a little boy who was nearly weaned, discovered his mother nursing a kinswoman's baby. At first he whimpered and tried to climb into his mother's lap, but when she failed to relinquish the strange baby he broke into a jealous rage and began hitting the infant. Mildly amused and smiling, the mother handed back the baby and nursed her son (DuBois 1944: 40).

Young children are ridiculed, teased, poked, and prodded,

all of which makes them irritable, but any show of temper is met by laughter, more ridicule, and such recommendations as "Hit him!" or "Kill him!" As a form of amusement, adults or older children sometimes frighten young children. One five-year-old, while watching a mechanical toy with calm interest, was frightened by a young man who shouted that it would bite. Other children standing nearby joined in the fake warning. Brandishing knives, adults also playfully terrify children by threatening to cut off an ear or a hand. Often, too, children are sent on fools' errands or falsely promised rewards. In one case, an adult passed by a girl after visiting her family. He told her to run home for some of the honey he had left there, but in fact the man had not left any honey at all. Children who cry are shamed or frightened with bogeys. A child who trips on the uneven ground is shouted at harshly for his awkwardness, because the Alorese greatly fear even accidental injury; adults are seldom sympathetic.

Adult support comes in large amounts, however, when children are ill. Parents give long death feasts to soothe an angry ghost, or, if another type of spirit is offended, they administer the appropriate, usually long-neglected, sacrifice. Much of the child's fear of the dead and of the supernatural begins during late childhood as a result of listening to his parents' speculations and gossip on occasions such as these.

Toddlers around two have long, violent temper tantrums. At this age, whenever the mother must go to the fields the child is likely to throw himself onto the ground and start kicking and raging in an effort to make his mother stay home. Children eventually give up temper tantrums, but tantrums continue longest and occur most frequently in contexts of desertion. The child finds it very hard to bear separation from his mother. DuBois (1944: 51) related her observations of a two-year-old over a period of nine months. Each morning the child attempted to follow his mother to the fields, but when she outstripped him he fell to the ground, rolled back and forth, and beat his head on the earth, screaming. These paroxysms lasted from five to twenty minutes. His mother's reaction was typical of Alorese mothers: sometimes she ignored him, sometimes she returned to slap him, and sometimes she returned, pretending to stay for the day, only to slip away when his attention was distracted. Neither mothers nor other caretakers are consistent in their care of toddlers. A group of toddlers trying to imitate adult behavior may at times get affectionate attention, but such moments are unpredictable. Children often get attention by playing one parent against the other; at other times they escape punishment from both parents by running off to a relative. Often a grandparent cares for them and takes their side against the parents. Overall, however, Alorese children have no stable or dependable source of care and affection. Young children live in an insecure world, where need-satisfaction is unpredictable and becomes available mainly through their own manipulations. Even with regard to food, young children are left without any assured provisions. Throughout the day they must rely on the handouts they can get by begging or screaming at older children and adults.

Toilet training is initiated after the child learns to walk and usually goes easily. The mother either takes the child to the privy or to the edge of the village in the morning and evening. The child watches his mother and learns by her example. Also the child is told to withdraw when he needs to eliminate. Children soon understand, and even though mothers hit or shout at a child who is not yet toilet trained, toilet training is seldom a problem. Bathing causes considerably more tension between parent and child. After a child can stand alone, the mother or some other older person begins to wash him by pouring cold water over him, scrubbing him roughly and then leaving him to dry. If the child has yaws, a common skin lesion in Alor, this experience is very painful. Children with yaws violently resist bathing, but their efforts are met with coercion and retaliation.

From the time children can walk, they are ordered about on errands in the same peremptory tone the Alorese use when they want anything. Children rebel against these officious commands, and their vocabularies soon become filled with curses and protests. Except during temper tantrums, however, small children are reluctant to talk much, because adults ridicule their verbal mistakes. Small children are generally not prohibited from doing what they want. The Alorese do not treat their ritual paraphernalia and other belongings with protectiveness or awe, and the few taboo restrictions they have are observed carelessly. The main prohibition is on physical fighting—a child seen to strike another is slapped immediately by an adult kinsman. As a result, small children resort to subterfuge; they become sly in their aggression. They will, for example, give a sly, sharp pinch and then run from the scene. Sexual behavior before five seems unrestricted, and little boys freely masturbate in public. Around six the child gets his first loincloth and begins to observe proper modest behavior. From this time on, sex play is frowned upon, although sanctions against heterosexual activity are slight.

Boys and girls begin to be treated differently when they are about five. Boys can expect to get food in the early morning and in the evening, but between these times they forage in play groups: they scavenge food by scraping the cooking pots, eating insects, or raiding nearby fields. Raiding is resented only if it is too persistent or if food is scarce. It may also be resented if the adult raided (usually a parent of one of the boys) feels that the boys should be engaged in productive activity. Rivalry and resentment between boys may develop if one boy's parents object, while the other parents do not. When boys are about twelve, they attach themselves to young men whom they serve as menials, thus permitting them a broader education than is offered to the girls—and at the same time giving them a chance to learn the procedures of financial dealings and to become thoroughly indoctrinated in cultural values. During the season of heavy garden work boys sometimes form work groups, helping to cut or pull weeds. For their work they are given a midday meal.

Girls are reared differently. They do not often steal, partly because they have more reliable access to food. They start working with their mothers in the fields soon after they are six, and by the time they are nine or ten they can do all ordinary household cooking. Girls are also taught to sew mats, weave baskets, and make barkcloth. They cannot, however, join visiting men for dinner, and they are seldom given presents at butcherings. At feasts, meat is distributed to each household in proportion to the number of males in it. Thus, whereas girls are given more purposeful instruction, have both substantial economic responsibilities and a more secure food supply, they also have less prestige, less access to scenes of financial exchanges, and less freedom, but also less pressure to steal than boys.

Older boys are admonished sternly to become circumspect in their language and behavior and to avoid fights, especially physical fights. In order to avoid a fine, even words must become guarded as one becomes older and wealthier. During the rare fights between boys, other children withdraw in fright, although older children safely ridicule and tease both younger children and helpless adults. A youngster can afford to be spiteful only toward those who have no redress.

Children and adolescents alike receive and lose property at the capricious whim of adults. Even when an adult admits that a piece of property belongs to the child, he may confiscate it without scruple.

A child between eight and fourteen is given a field by his parents. This only means that, if the family can afford it, a portion of the produce of that field will be used to buy clothes for the child. Since this benefit is rarely enough to make work attractive, children still have to be reminded forcibly of the virtues of industry.

In summary, parental behavior is characterized by continual neglect, only occasional warmth, and frequent aggression in the form of deceit, teasing, ridicule, and frightening children—often for the sole purpose of amusement. Adults are not considerate of their children for any length of time; they high-handedly confiscate children's property, leave them without food, and tease them without regard for their feelings or needs. Parental rejection in the forms of both neglect and aggression is conspicuous in Alor.

Alorese Personality

The Alorese are hostile and aggressive. Even though violent outbursts among men are strongly discouraged by the promise of retaliation, and insults are controlled by the prospect of fines, many outlets for hostility exist. Some of these are open to everyone, including women and children. Others are more restricted. Teasing, frightening, ridiculing, and deceiving both children and helpless adults are widespread activities: mothers tease children who are being weaned by nursing neighbors' babies; people ridicule little children's mistakes in speaking; for amusement, little boys are poked in the belly and crotch; children are sent on sham errands for rewards no one intends to give; lies are told to frighten those naive enough to believe them. As adults treat children, so older children treat younger children. Since they are slapped for openly hitting another child, very young children slyly pinch others and then run off. Toward adults they can only rage in futility. Temper tantrums are prolonged and violent before five, but later they begin to subside, coming to extinction by the time the child is eight or nine. Occasionally boys over five get into a fight. When they do, other children withdraw in fright, because they, like their parents, regard physical aggression as extremely dangerous. Physical violence against close kin is safer and does not result in severe retaliation, however; husbands beat their wives; adults and older children slap younger kin or strike them with weapons. In one case a man ordered his younger half-brother to fetch a sword promised him from another village. When the boy seemed reluctant to set out, the man in a rage chased his brother until the boy fell. The man then beat him with a thick length of rope. Witnesses disapproved of the brutal attack, but no one interfered until a distant kinswoman of the boy dragged him away. In another case, an uncle heard his eighteen-year-old nephew insult a third person. The uncle hit the youth so hard over one eye with a rattan club that the boy was stunned.

Women may engage in physical violence not permitted to men. It is assumed that co-wives will quarrel and fight, at least at first, and if feelings are truly bitter, almost all the women in the village may be drawn into several hours of brawling. A man who is afraid that the fight might go too far may try to restrain the women with a rattan switch, but not infrequently the women join to beat him off.

The Alorese are very sensitive to slights and public

humiliations; they lay great stress on saving face. What matters in Alorese life is what people say about you. Ridicule and derogation are the chief forms of social sanction, and both produce a sense of shame, which is usually met by a vigorous discharge of anger. But as noted earlier, physical violence should not be displayed. The most common response to an insult is litigation, or legal action calling for a fine. This action is the fastest and least costly way for an injured person to redress his grievances, and it sometimes even results in a net profit. Occasionally the Alorese redirect this hostility into "wealth contests" or "wealth feuds." For example after proving his innocence of charges of having had intercourse with a young girl, a man challenged his accusers by buying a pig from an ally for more than the pig was worth. The accusers then had to buy the pig for over twice its value. To refuse would have meant admitting shameful poverty. Even more costly is the rare battle in which allies of each party provide as much wealth as possible, principally in the form of *mokos*, pigs, and gongs. The party that produces the most is victorious. After an encounter like this, bad feelings between contestants may continue for years. The Alorese are profit-minded and practical, however, so they do not usually resort to such economically nonproductive measures.

"Payoff feasts" are scenes of general hostility. Because they are reluctant to pay off their debts, debtors are dunned over a long period of time with increasing bitterness and with threats of litigation. But even when the resources are assembled, creditors often quarrel with debtors over the value of the payments, while the creditors' own creditors —themselves waiting to claim payment—begin quarrels of their own.

As we observed earlier, older boys often follow young men about on their financial errands and serve them. They are motivated at least in part by the prospect of sharing the meals that are given to the young men. Many older men continue this low self-reliant, semi-dependent relationship by serving as satellites of richer men. In return for being present when a crowd is needed, for demeaning physical labor, and for other services, these satellites receive some loyalty and protection against the more severe pressures of financial dealings. These satellites need not be as self-reliant or independent as their more ambitious peers.

The quest for nurturance starts when the child is very young, around the time when he begins to walk and to receive the casual care customary for babies of his age. At this time, as we have already seen, whenever the mother must go to the fields he is likely to have a violent temper tantrum in an effort to make his mother stay with him. The insecurity and dependency of the Alorese child is heightened when his mother leaves or threatens to leave him. For children, sickness is a time when adults do not begrudge care and sacrifices, and for adults, it is a time when kinsmen rally around them. Adults magnify sickness. They are sure that they are about to die, given any internal complaint. Kinsmen divine for them, and if the omens are unfavorable the patients retire in depression to their dark, smoke-filled homes, where they sometimes refuse to bathe, eat, exercise, or get fresh air for days. Their confinement and passivity probably aggravate some illnesses, but they help the sick person to get attention. A grown son, sibling, or other near kinsman will hold a dying person on his lap in a manner resembling that happy, protected stage of infancy, when the Alorese baby was loved, fondled, and petted.

Some Alorese myths reflect their dependency. Despite the realistic, nonsupernatural orientation of these people, myths concerning Good Beings have a seductive attractiveness, and many people go out of their way to be present when a Good Being is supposed to be on hand. These transformed human beings with magical powers are expected to end death and sickness as well as the financial obligations accompanying death and disease. In the myths associated with them, however, Good Beings tend to be the objects rather than the sources of nurturance.

About twenty years ago, a man who owed a *moko* of small value refused to pay it. In response, his creditors stole his daughter. When the father cried and begged for his child, his creditors said he must repay the debt with exactly the same type of *moko* he had received, which was rather rare. He did not have such a drum, and the creditors did not give him time to seek one. Instead they sold the child to a distant village for a three-dollar *moko*. Had the father wished, he could have gone to the village and repurchased his daughter for about four dollars, but rather than doing this he declared her dead from violence, an act to be revenged by a head purchased for about sixty dollars. Headhunting and child stealing no longer occur in Alor, but the attitude displayed by the father, to whom vengeance and prestige were more important than his daughter, have not suddenly become strange to the Atimelangers.

This anecdote reveals how limited many Alorese are in their capacity to form strong or enduring emotional attachments. They are an emotionally unresponsive or insulated people. Moreover, Rorschach ("inkblot test") analysis reveals a people who approach human relationships with suspicion, greed, cunning, calculation, fear, and defensiveness; child drawings reveal feelings of aloneness and self-centeredness, superficial interpersonal relationships, and an inability to come into warm, affective contact with others. Alorese are so distrustful of others that most people assume as a matter of course that the other person is lying, and those who assert the contrary may be reprimanded: "Don't talk that way; we don't know what people have in their hearts" (DuBois 1944): 66). Kardiner (1945: 170) says of the Alorese: "the basic personality in Alor is anxious, suspicious, mistrustful, lacking in [self] confidence, with no interest in the outer world. There is no capacity to idealize parental image or deity. The personality is devoid of enterprise, is filled with repressed hatred and free-floating aggression over which constant vigilance must be exercised. Cooperation must be at a low level and a tenuous social cohesion can be achieved only by dominance-submission attitudes, not by affection and mutual trust."

Children have little opportunity to develop a sense of positive self-esteem. Teasing, ridicule, and casual, whimsical treatment of their property prove to children that others have little concern for their feelings. Adults say of children, sometimes with contempt and sometimes in a matter-of-fact way:

"He is only a child; he doesn't think yet," or "He hasn't a heart yet" (meaning he is an empty person). For one adult to call another adult a "child" is a grave insult. Limited opportunities do exist in Atimelang for small children to gain a sense of being valued, but such opportunities must seem bewildering in their inconsistency. A small child attempting to do an adult dance may on occasion receive encouragement and friendly adult attention; on other occasions his efforts are met with derisive laughter.

Adult self-esteem, too, is vulnerable, and in order to save face, insults must be retaliated quickly with litigation or even stronger measures. Married men who have given feasts should not be compared openly with each other—no matter how obvious the differences may be—because, as one young man said, "If anyone heard that I had said he was less rich, less industrious, or less handsome, he would be ashamed and would want to fight with me. He would be angry" (DuBois 1944: 117). If they permit others to slight them, then all will hear and believe the worst, because within themselves the Atimelangers hear the worst. A man who has gone on an unsuccessful dunning trip must be given a small *moko* to carry back to his village to help him save face, even if a small boy has to return it to its owners the next day.

The principal goal in a man's life is to execute financial maneuvers with such cleverness that he becomes both wealthy and influential. Real success at achieving this goal is limited to a few middle-aged men, but almost every mature male must participate to a fair extent in financial transactions, making repeated payments on his marriage and paying for the feasts given to satisfy ghosts. Only two males (one of them a retardate) in the five villages forming the Atimelang complex do not participate in the competitive wealth-status system. Social, sexual, and personal pressures combine to force men to participate, and once involved, a man cannot easily withdraw. Thus the dominant motive of Alorese male society is achievement in the competitive system, but one may enter the competition for many reasons. Many men become satellites of richer men, thereby easing the pressure to perform. Only a few men have skills in activities other than finances, and standards of excellence in these endeavors are low—carvings, for example, are crude, tooth blackening and tattooing impermanent, and music relatively undeveloped. The Alorese are emotionally unstable. As small children, Alorese are prone to tantrums, but, as among their elders, older children alternately comfort and scold the smaller children in their charge. A slap may be followed rapidly by apologetic feeding, an attempt to comfort by impatient anger. Any feeling of shame produces quick anger, and every feast is the scene of excited quarrels. In their rage, adults hit their dependent kin on the head with weapons, utter insults for which they will be fined, and shout uncontrolled curses that later have to be ceremonially removed. The people rarely carry grudges, however. The Alorese say that the rancor behind a sudden outburst of rage is not deep enough to be permanent. Being emotionally unstable, the Alorese are pushed easily into angry outbursts, but the stimulus is rarely grave enough to remember for very long.

The Alorese view the world as a negative place, and the natural environment is seen as periodically frustrating. The dry season, for example, is known as the "hungry time," despite the fact that food is abundant, although not of the preferred sort. Alorese world view is amplified below in the discussion of expressive systems—including Alorese religion, medical beliefs, myths, witchcraft, and aesthetics.

Alorese Expressive Systems

In their religion, even the benevolent and powerful Good Beings are portrayed as objects who attack, and people who were one's closest kinsmen become, after death, the most malignant ghosts. Each person must manipulate and placate—but only when necessary—the evil but wealth-bringing and familiar spirits. The countryside is covered with places where offended spirits cause disease and bad crops. At an early age, Alorese children absorb information and emotions toward the supernatural, and they learn that many deaths are associated with supernatural malignancy. Spirits are everywhere, impossible to avoid. One can only hope not to offend them. The Alorese supernatural world is filled with aggression and violence. Their myths, too, involve violence. Even though the Alorese believe in witches, witchcraft is not developed as a means of expressing aggression. Similarly the Atimelangers do not seem overly concerned with the prospects of aggression from ghosts, whose death feasts the people delay as long as the ghosts do not cause trouble. The laying of curses is the most common form of symbolically malignant activity. Curses are a public declaration of hostility, showing that interpersonal relationships between two persons have reached the breaking point. In their more impersonal form, curses are used in gardens to warn potential thieves to stay away, or a curse may be erected after one has already been victimized—in the belief that the unknown vandal will contract a disease. Most Atimelangers seem to relieve their anger through less symbolic channels. Rather than using curses to protect their fields or fruit trees, for example, the Alorese more often erect mechanical guards.

Finances are intimately associated with religion. The dedication of a lineage house may require so much wealth as to delay building the house for several years; a series of burial feasts to placate one of the family's dead may drag on a generation or more until occasional illnesses motivate the family to hold an expensive burial feast. Smaller investments are required for sacrifices when, for instance, the village guardian spirit is snared and dragged into a carving erected especially for it, when a familiar spirit is placated, when at different stages of gardening the good will of the souls of previous gardeners is solicited, or when, at the new corn harvest, sacred lineage hearths are "fed." Sacred hearths belonging to lineages are kept in lineage houses and are "fed" once a year. The sacrifice requires that the hearth owner abstain from certain foods before the sacrifice. Taboos for quiet periods of one day are connected with the feeding of certain hearths, and vigorous work, shouting, and quarreling during such periods is prohibited; any infraction of this prohibition results in a fine.

Personal familiars are inherited or acquired through visions. Many familiars bring good fortune if they are kept satisfied, but a spirit who brings good fortune to one person may bring evil to another. The goodness or badness of the spirits depends on one's relationship with them.

Death incurs burial obligations, a series of all-night, gong-beating memorials, and two death feasts, which are supposed to dismiss the souls of the dead from the vicinity of the village. Special observances are held for victims of certain dread diseases or accidents, as well as for those who die violent deaths. For protection against the ghost of the deceased, a spouse must leave the immediate vicinity, and with an unsheathed knife stand guard without sleeping for two days. At the burial, the mourner severs his relationship with the deceased by cutting a string—thus preventing the ghost from returning to him—but as a precaution he continues to carry the knife for two or three months. A dead person has two souls, one which goes under the village unless the death was a violent one, and one which loiters nearby to cause trouble. The latter spirit is not banished until after three death feasts have paid off the debts incurred by the burial. These payoff feasts are generally given only with reluctance, under fear of an illness in the family or of poor crops.

Most illnesses and misfortunes are caused by spirits or ghosts who want to be cared for. The cure is to placate the supernaturals, but the treatment of spirits varies. One woman continues to neglect spirits who have sent her warnings repeatedly in dreams; another man neglects his familiars until an illness occurs, but a third regularly feeds his tutelaries. Most Alorese are on the neglectful side, because even though they believe that the supernatural can cause harm and that illness is caused by offended ghosts and spirits who must be placated, they do not depend on spirits for either protection or for vengeance. Religious practices are not regarded as a form of insurance in Alor. In fact, as Kardiner (1945: 167) aptly stated: "the image of the deity is modeled after the bad creditor."

Alorese aesthetics are rudimentary and found mainly in connection with financial affairs. Gong playing and versification are the major art forms of Alor. All-night dances are held before feasts, and verses are improvised between set choruses. The few adult men who are good singers gain some prestige from their skill, but people snicker behind the backs of those who perform poorly. The verses are mainly concerned with finances. Long, steady gong beating marks burials, lineage house building, and other ceremonies. This uncreative, simple playing is usually turned over to boys and young men; older men experiment with new rhythms and patterns for combining gongs and *mokos* of different sizes.

LOVE AND REJECTION IN THE TWO SOCIETIES: A COMPARISON

Two societies have been described. The Papago are warm and nurturant toward their children; the Alorese are hostile, neglectful, and rarely warm. These differences in parental behavior are associated with expectable differences in personality between the two peoples, as well as with a variety of maintenance system differences (see Chapter Three).

In Alor, mothers are assigned the major responsibility for both child care and food production, but Papago women are uninvolved in heavy agricultural and herding activities, even though they perform many other food-preparing tasks such as husking, shelling, and parching corn. Since the Papago grandmothers can delegate housework to their daughters and daughters-in-law, they have even more time for children than the mothers have. Papago grandmothers thus relieve the mothers of the heavy double burden of both child care and major subsistence contributions by taking control of the older children and by helping with the younger. They do not simply care for their grandchildren, but they care for them with affection. Alorese mothers and grandmothers, on the other hand, do not cooperate in child rearing. Even though they may assume child-care chores, Alorese grandmothers often form alliances with the children, even taking a child's side against his mother. This results in mothers becoming antagonistic toward both the rebellious children and the trouble-making grandmothers.

Alorese mothers view children as a great burden and try to prevent their conception. As DuBois (1944: 38) writes: "the

Alorese mother has economic responsibilities that may make her welcome the birth of a child less cheerfully, and care for it with less solicitude than she might in another culture." Both in Alor and among the Papago, however, penalties for abortion are lenient. Papago mothers, on the other hand, want children, and children are viewed as darling creatures and as supports for old age. After birth, mothers in both societies give infants as much attention as they can, but this is not much among the Alorese, who must return to the fields a few weeks following parturition. Papago mothers always keep their babies on their hips or in a hammock nearby. When the child can walk or after another baby arrives, the Alorese toddler is neglected, whereas among the Papago the grandmother and siblings become important alternate sources of warmth, so that even though the mother becomes less important as a caretaker the child is never neglected. In both social systems fathers fondle at least their young children, but Papago fathers and grandfathers are genuinely important sources of affection: they are warmly supportive; they speak in baby talk rather than mocking a child's mistakes in speech, as do the Alorese; they give the child what he wants rather than teasing him. Papago fathers do not amuse themselves by frightening their children as in Alor. On the contrary, they and the women in the household foster the impression that the father is a powerful protector who can make harmless such frightening things as evil spirits. Papago fathers and grandfathers not only make a point of fondling small children but they also take an interest in the moral development of children over four years old. Lectures on obedience, industry, honesty, and peacefulness are important paternal child-training responsibilities.

Among the Papago, girls who take care of children usually get along well with their charges. Alorese child nurses, however, must often be coerced into caring for little children, and at times they abandon the younger children. Alorese child nurses frequently become impatient and slap their young siblings, and they tease and frighten babies just as adults do. Children's desires in Alor are neglected, and their possessions may be seized or destroyed at the whim of an older person. Moreover, Alorese children are the butt of many aggressive jokes. Small Papago children, however, can have whatever they want. Their wishes come before those of older people. They are viewed as being persons with full rights—with allowances made for their lack of social understanding.

These differences between the two societies in socialization practices are associated with significant differences in personality functioning. The rejection-acceptance theory described in Chapter Two predicted that rejected children and adults the world over will be, in comparison to accepted persons, more hostile and aggressive or passive aggressive (or have more problems with the management of hostility and aggression), will be more dependent, evaluate themselves more negatively, will be less emotionally responsive, less emotionally stable, and will have a more negative world view. To what extent do these predictions hold true among the Papago, who so clearly nurture their children, and among the Alorese, who reject them? And what are some of the other personality likenesses and differences between these two peoples?

Both Alorese and Papago avoid open physical conflict between adults. Papago men fight only when they are drunk, but the Alorese are continuously but often indirectly aggressive, as shown in their continual quarrels and litigations and in their lying, teasing, deception, and chicanery. Alorese women may engage in large-scale brawls, but there is no counterpart to this display among Papago women. Tantrums and sulks are rare among Papago children, and open physical attacks are equally unusual. Alorese children, on the other hand, pinch and run, and they have long, violent tantrums before they are six.

Papago children are independent in that they rarely overtly seek affectionate attention, support, approval, or comfort from their elders. These children make few dependency bids, presumably because their needs for affection have been met. Papago youth are also self-reliant. They frequently leave the reservation for extended periods of time to work for wages. Papago adolescents look forward to the independence and self-reliance of off-reservation work. Self-reliance is encouraged among the Papago by having children make their own decisions. All this is very unlike Alorese children, who receive little warmth, who make many dependency bids, and who are neither particularly self-reliant nor encouraged to be so: small Alorese children kick and scream when their mothers leave them for the fields; older boys follow young men on business trips, and many adult males rely on rich men to protect them from the pressures of financial dealings; the sick retire in depression to the dark of their homes with the hope that relatives will make a fuss over them when they give up the pressures of active adult life for an infantlike, dependent helplessness.

Dependence revealed in interaction with the supernatural also differs between these two societies. Papago do not spend much time trying to make the gods or God care for them. They try not to offend the spirits, but if they do, they use a ritual to clear the offense. They approach the fatherly Christian god with the same attitude: if he sends rain and keeps away sickness, they will handle the rest. The Alorese spend some time manipulating and placating their spirits to make them give aid, but the major indication of dependence is in their reaction to the Good Beings, whose stories make up most of their mythology. When it is predicted that Good Beings, who are transformed humans with powers that can be used benevolently, are going to visit an area, people come from all around to have their youth restored and their troubles ended. Inevitable disappointments are slow to destroy their faith.

The Papago are also unlike the Alorese in emotional stability. The Papago maintain a calm reserve that is difficult to disturb except in laughter, and they are generally capable of dealing calmly with stress and change. The Alorese, however, place little value on a cool demeanor. They anger easily and lose their composure under mild stress, and they quarrel violently over debts and as a result of jealousy and slights to their dignity.

Even though they are reserved, the Papago are also emotionally responsive, capable of making warm, lasting friendships, and among themselves they are able to express their affection spontaneously. They are an outgoing, sociable people who enjoy visiting. Women are expected to restrict most of their visits to kinsmen, but men maintain friendships throughout the reservation. Strong ties unite the extended family, which is always ready to aid its members. Little girls try to be friends with their teachers, and all the children mention specific persons with pleasant rather than unpleasant experiences even when they are asked what makes them mad or angry.

Warm, lasting, nondefensive relationships are a rarity among the Alorese. Men respond to their wives with physical desire, jealousy, and anger, but not spontaneous affection. Marriage is full of discord, but so are other interpersonal relationships. Results of Rorschach analyses, children's drawings, and observed behavior all show the Alorese to be suspicious, fearful, and cunning in human relationships.[3] Moreover, the Alorese are often petty, mean, and grasping, and they are rarely generous. The Papago, on the other hand, positively value generosity and cooperativeness.

Achievement motivation seems to be higher in Alor than among the Papago, and it is highest among the Alorese men, who work hard to amass wealth. Some Alorese men, however, associate themselves with high "achievers" rather than strive to compete on their own. Among the Papago, individual achievement strivings are discouraged by the belief that people should not attempt to stand out conspicuously.

The Papago see their environment as dangerously full of spirits and animals which can cause disease and drought. Medicine men, however, are believed to be capable of handling supernatural problems. The Alorese view all human and supernatural relationships with suspicion, fear, and calculation. Although they are less concerned than the Papago with the supernatural, their environment is as filled with disease-causing supernaturals. Even their powerful, benevolent spirits, the Good Beings, are under constant attack in their myths. The dangerous environment of the Papago, however, has not made them into suspicious or bitter people. To the contrary, they are confident that other people, at least relatives, can be trusted. The Alorese, on the other hand, are so full of suspicion that they are not sure they can depend on anyone. In their childhood they played one adult against another, and as adults men play one financial exchange associate against another. Similarly, their supernaturals are either manipulated or ignored, but in neither case do the supernaturals provide security.

The religious beliefs of these two populations mirror, if somewhat imperfectly, both their maintenance systems and their prevailing personality dispositions. Papago religion is as flexible and self-reliant as the worshippers, and like the worshippers it is not, for the most part, organized beyond the village level. The people run their own Sonoral Catholic, Roman Catholic, Presbyterian, and traditional religious rituals, and they are able to delay or advance a fiesta one day or more to suit their own convenience. Should a drought come, they combine rituals from all religions to help solve the problem. Rituals control the supernaturals that menace people, but, unlike the Alorese, the Papago do not divine an inauspicious result and then give up. Their divinations are intended to find a cure, not to discover whether a cure exists or whether the cure is worth attempting. Also unlike the Alorese, who are constantly frustrated in their search for a Good Being, the Papago through ritual and the power of a medicine man have constant access to a reliably benevolent power coming from I'itoi, the Trinity, and from San Francisco Xavier (Saint Francis Xavier).

Alorese religion reveals the hostility, dependence, and manipulativeness of the people themselves. Spirits everywhere are angered by trespassers, and they attack with disease. Each person has connections with a number of personal spirits which can cause good or harm, but usually only when the spirits cause harm or when the person wants something do the spirits receive care and proper sacrifice. Alorese religion also reflects their social structure in its lack of organization beyond the village level and in its entanglement with finances. One must engage in finances to pay off death feasts, to placate ghosts, and to make sacrifices placating other spirits. Alorese religion also differs from Papago religion in that while village-level ritual exists, rituals are usually not enacted, and thus ceremonies for uniting the members of the village are neglected. This fact probably reflects the high degree of competitiveness and mutual distrust generated in part by the financial system. The village is a unit only by accident, when financial alliances chance to make it one. In summary, then, the religions of both societies are more concerned with malevolent occurrences than with the benign or benevolent, and evil forces play a major role in each. It is no surprise, however, that of the two, Papago cosmology has stronger and more reliably benevolent forces than the Alorese world view.

The proper study of mankind is man.
POPE

CHAPTER SIX

Epilogue: How Does It All Add Up?

Throughout this volume we have advocated a point of view regarding the proper study of human behavior, at least for those students who wish to know something about *human* behavior as distinguished from the behavior of some native population studied by anthropologists, or from the behavior of Americans studied by sociologists, or of undergraduate students used in so much of psychology. This point of view asserts that with care, attention to the best standards of behavioral science, and the special perspective that comes from an extended immersion in cross-cultural materials—as well as the materials of the other sciences—it is fully possible to establish verifiable "principles" of human behavior: generalizations that either hold true across our species regardless of culture, physical type, or other bounding conditions or that hold true in certain contexts or situations wherever they occur.

The universalist approach is an outgrowth of a renewed curiosity about the longstanding questions: "What does it mean to be a human being? " or "What are we like as members of the species Homo sapiens?" These questions ask about the "nature of human nature," about man's shared species characteristics. They ask: "How much do we share in common developmental tendencies and other capacities and dispositions?" As baldly stated here, these questions are impossible to answer within the bounds of science, because they are basically philosophical questions, not scientific

164

questions. For this reason many academic scholars have shied away from the universalist approach, arguing that it is hopeless to try to deal with anything so complex. Some behavioral scientists even feel that the questions are slightly "indecent." Fortunately, other scholars insist that the universalist issue is scientifically respectable and that, even though the questions are indeed complicated, the quest for principles is worth the effort.

The universalist approach assumes the truth of two basic but presently untestable assumptions about man. The first assumption states that all normal (i.e. nonpathological) humans are subject to the same developmental tendencies. The second states that at birth all normal men share the same general capabilities for thought, feelings, and action. Together these two assumptions comprise what anthropologists call the psychic unity of mankind.

Probably all universalist research requires an adequate anthropological perspective. It requires a profound familiarity with the reality of culture and a genuine understanding of the force of culture learning. The perspective implies a worldwide, comparative orientation; it implies an endorsement of the concept of cultural relativity, but a rejection of radical relativism; and while it asks for a recognition of the anthropological concept of functionalism, it rejects the extreme functionalist argument.

Moreover, the universalist approach requires a recognition, at least at some level, of the biological bases of human behavior. In other words, when one asks about the "nature of human nature" or about man's shared species characteristics, he is usually asking about the biological substrates of behavior, in that most behavior which holds true across our species is likely to have a biological or genetic base rather than being solely the product of learning. By implication, then, man's several million years of common biological evolution must be involved to account for the specieswide distribution of a behavioral constant. Thus a good deal of universalist research implicates the phylogenetic perspective.

The phylogenetic perspective does not dismiss the influence of experience or learning. In fact, the perspective requires a synthesis of biological and learning theory approaches. It recognizes that man is not limitlessly plastic or modifiable through experience, as much of anthropology and psychological theory—especially learning theory—assume. This assumption of indefinite modifiability has its roots in British empirical philosophy, but the position was elaborated in psychology most notably by Robert I. Watson, who argued that children are capable of being limitlessly shaped through the application of conditioning procedures. The truth is, however, that mankind has certain limiting biological and genetic dispositions—endogenous regulatory mechanisms, so to speak—but that these proclivities can be modified through experience, at least within narrow ranges. Experience interacts with these endogenous regulatory mechanisms to produce what seem at times to be limitless worldwide variations in culture and individual behavior.

Even though the phylogenetic perspective emphasizes species uniformities, it does not overlook the fact that each human is also unique. To illustrate: it is probably true that all humans share the same repertoire of basic emotions—fear, anger, sadness, joy, etc. We all share the same neurophysiological elements of rage, for example. This is a biological-evolutionary constant in man. But individuals can learn what to get mad at, and they learn how to manage and express their anger when the emotion is felt (see Boucher 1974: 7). Within limits, each individual is uniquely different in the management of his own emotional life.

The phylogenetic viewpoint is clearly implicated in our work on the worldwide causes and consequences of parental acceptance-rejection. It seems increasingly clear that parental rejection has "malignant" effects for all humans. But why should this be so? From the point of view of the phylogenetic perspective, we argue that all humans have a profound, but generalized, need for positive response from the people who are important to us. This need for positive response is rooted in man's psychosocial and morphological evolution, and when we are denied love, esteem, and other forms of positive response, "pernicious" things happen to us.

This assumption of "malignancy" is the very thing we are trying to test. What evidence is there that the withdrawal of love has such effects throughout our species, and what is known about the "causes" of acceptance-rejection? We are not going to summarize the details presented in this volume. Rather we will highlight several of its most conspicuous conclusions. Different scholars require different forms of evidence before they are willing to risk the conclusion that a "principle" of human behavior has indeed been established. We will leave it to each reader to decide for himself how convincing the various sources of data are for drawing the conclusion that parental rejection-acceptance has species-wide consequences for personality development and functioning, and that certain conditions are universally predictive of what parents are likely to do to their children with respect to warmth, hostility, and neglect.

It is our view that the universalist, multimethod research strategy outlined in Chapter One is adequate for confirming or rejecting purported universalist "principles." Briefly, the universalist research strategy presumes the minimum standards of scientific inquiry: generalizations coming from the research must be able to withstand scientific scrutiny; they must be supported by empirical evidence collected in an objective, impersonal manner; and the procedures used must be open to public review and replication. In addition, the research design must incorporate adequately operationalized and transculturally equivalent variables. Moreover, the design requires a comparative orientation, especially a worldwide sampling design, but also, under some circumstances, cross-species comparisons. The idea here is that investigators must be able to show that the purported "principles" can indeed be generalized beyond the sample, population, or cognate populations from which the conclusions were originally derived or discovered. The presumption of a universalist principle cannot be accepted until the proposition has withstood the rigors of adequate pancultural testing, thus affirming that the generalizations are not simple artifacts of some special circumstance or unique situation. One's confidence in the generalizability of a proposition is increased insofar as the same conclusions emerge after using multiple research operations and methodologies. Using the multimethod research strategy, one gains confidence that his results genuinely relate to the phenomenon under study, that they are not an artifact of the method(ology) used.

Most of these methodological requirements of the universalist approach are based on the idea of a "probability" model. We assume that exceptions to generalizations will occur. The best that we can generally hope for in behavioral science is to make predictions with tolerably few exceptions. This is a matter of statistics, or of the probability of an event happening, or of two or more events co-occurring. Hence, at least until behavioral science has undergone a major paradigmatic revolution (cf. Kuhn 1970), our most powerful conclusions are likely to be in the form of statistically significant regularities, not exceptionless uniformities. In keeping with these ideas, our research on the worldwide causes and consequence of parental acceptance and rejection is reported within the framework of a probability model.

The evidence discussed in the three components of our research, using the logic of the "triangulation of methodologies," converges on the conclusion that parental rejection in children, as well as in adults who were rejected as children, leads to: hostility, aggression, passive aggression, or problems with the management of hostility and aggression; dependency; probably emotional unresponsiveness and negative self-evaluation (negative self-esteem and negative self-adequacy); and, probably, emotional instability as well as a negative world view. Firm evidence in one or more methodologies is yet to be marshaled for some of these characteristics, but overall, the direction of evidence is so clear and so overwhelmingly consistent that there seems to be little doubt that these personality dispositions can be elevated to the level of "principles" of human behavior—at least at a gross level and subject to possible qualification when data come in from the community study component.[1]

The universal generalizability of other behavioral characteristics and correlates of parental acceptance-rejection is less clear, because even though information is available in one or sometimes two components (i.e. methodologies), the evidence is yet to be tested in the third component. A reasonable amount of information is available in psychological research regarding the effects of "maternal" deprivation and child abuse, for example, and the relationship between parental rejection and certain behavior disorders, conduct problems, and forms of psychopathology is fairly clear. But little cross-cultural fieldwork has been done on most of these issues, and no holocultural study has yet addressed any of them.

What else is known about the causes and consequences of parental acceptance-rejection, especially about the antecedents of acceptance-rejection? Psychological research in America focuses principally on the personality and behavioral outcome of parental rejection. Holocultural studies and community studies inform us about this outcome, but they also inform us about specific psychological, environmental, and maintenance systems conditions under which parents everywhere accept or reject. These sources of data also give information about the expressive systems correlates of parental behavior.

Cross-cultural survey data in Chapter Four and the ethnographic data in Chapter Five converge on several conclusions regarding the antecedents of parental acceptance-rejection—as well as on the personality and expressive systems outcomes of acceptance-rejection. Both holocultural and ethnographic evidence support the general hypothesis that mothers who are unable to escape the intensity of continuous interaction with their children are more likely to reject their offspring than are mothers who can get away from time to time, even if only briefly.

More specifically, evidence in these two components supports the hypothesis that the more important fathers are as alternate caretakers, and the more accessible fathers are to their children, the more likely children are to be accepted. Alternatively, one can say that the minimal presence of fathers in the home is predictive of greater rejection. Grandparents, too, have emerged cross-culturally as significantly nurturant agents. The cross-cultural research of Minturn and

Lambert (1964) and Whiting (1961) reinforces these conclusions about the importance of alternate caretakers. Alorese fathers, for example, devote little time to their children, and little is expected of them. "It is definitely the less busy—that is, less important—father who has time to be a good mother substitute" (DuBois 1944: 38). Papago fathers, on the other hand, are warm and concerned about their children; the men spend as much time with their children as they can. A double burden is placed on Alorese mothers, who are not only expected to be the primary caretakers of children but are also so heavily involved in subsistence activities that they have little time and little energy left to care for their children —even if they wanted to. Nonetheless it is also true that Alorese grandmothers and siblings are available, at least to a limited extent, as alternate caretakers.

Both sources of evidence—cross-cultural survey data and case-study material—also support the conclusion that the more children are wanted before they are born, the more they are loved after parturition. In this instance, experimental evidence in the United States helps confirm the worldwide generalizability of this proposition (see Sears, Maccoby, and Levin 1957). Moreover, both holocultural and the case-study data support the conclusion that parents who are concerned about reducing such drives in their babies as hunger, thirst, and unidentified discomforts are also likely to give these children more love when they grow older than are parents who fail to attend to these infantile needs as nurturantly. In general, the conclusion seems warranted that parents who indulge their babies and who consistently and solicitously reduce their discomfort are also prone to nurture their children when they mature beyond the infancy stage. The conclusion also seems warranted that accepted children form warmer and less hostile peer group relations than rejected children. This is not surprising, given the "malignant" personality consequences of rejection already discussed. Two personality characteristics not mentioned above deserve comment here. Holocultural data show that adults who were accepted as children are more generous and more responsible than those who were rejected. Both of these dispositions seem to be supported by data among the Papago and the Alorese, but they have not yet been adequately tested psychologically in North America.

Many institutionalized expressive systems are closely connected to the socialization practices of a people. The supernatural world is viewed as being malevolent in societies where children are rejected—as we have seen in Alor—but the supernatural is conceived as more benevolent in societies where parents accept their children, as among the Papago. The idea that these expressive systems can be reliable indicators of internal psychological processes is demonstrated by the fact that adults around the world who believe in malevolent supernaturals are often themselves hostile and cheerless people. Witness the Alorese.

Data in the three components of this research do not always converge on the same results, and, as already noted, in many instances data drawn from one methodology or component are untested in the other two. It is also true, of course, that some kinds of questions that can be asked using one methodology simply cannot be assessed within the framework of a second. Thus many loose ends are inevitably left, and a great deal is yet to be done before a tested theory of the worldwide causes and consequences of parental acceptance-rejection is approximated. No doubt some of the most productive questions are yet to be asked, but right now there seem to be at least three complementary classes of questions that require extensive work in the universalist study of parental love: (1) the personality outcome of acceptance-rejection, including the expressive systems correlates of this behavior (2) the psychological, social, and environmental antecedents to such behavior, or the conditions under which parents accept or reject, and (3) parents' differential treatment of their children. We amplify briefly on each of these.

Regarding the personality and expressive systems outcome of parental acceptance-rejection, we have shown that rejection has "malignant" effects throughout our species—and in terms of "personality," perhaps even in other species, such as apes and monkeys. We are not yet able to say what all these "pernicious" effects are, however. Equally important is the fact that, in the measures used here, some children do not seem to show the expected results of rejection. The fault does not lie so much in rejection-acceptance theory as in measures that are too unrefined. For example it is often not sufficient simply to know that parents reject their children —we must also assess the *form* of rejection (e.g. hostile rejection or rejection in the form of neglect), who rejects the child and under what condition, for how long, and in what intensity. How old is the child, and what were his prior experiences? Inadequate controls for these and other factors undoubtedly reduce the magnitude of the correlations between a global measure of rejection-acceptance and, let us say, aggression.

The second and related class of questions is the one of the psychological, social, and environmental conditions under which parents give or withhold love. At least three other interrelated issues lie within this topic: (a) What personality characteristics distinguish rejecting parents from accepting parents? This question is likely to lead investigators into a query about the parents' own developmental experiences as accepted or rejected children. Other factors, however, are also relevant. Is it true, as rejection-acceptance theory predicts, for example, that parents who are achievement oriented (e.g. "professionally" oriented) in terms of nonfamily activities are more likely to find child raising constraining, frustrating, and less satisfying than parents, for example mothers, who enjoy the home-making role? And are not these frustrated adults then more likely to withdraw warmth than parents who get satisfaction from parenting? This is partly a question about the effects of personality differences between accepting and rejecting parents and partly a question about "role gratification." A second issue within the topic of "psychosocial-environmental antecedents" of parental behavior relates to (b) the "social-environmental" part of the chain. Questions here pertain to "structural" factors, such as the influence of crowding on parent-child interaction, the adult/child ratio within a family, and the parents' freedom to get away from their children from time to time. Probably the most important question within this larger issue is the one about (c) an interaction between the "psychological" part of the chain and the "social-environmental" part. For example not all mothers who live in crowded isolation with their children are rejecting. What personality (i.e. psychological) characteristics distinguish rejecting mothers from accepting mothers under these social-environmental or "structural" conditions?

Finally, the third but complementary class of questions relates to a study of parents' differential treatment of their children—both in terms of causes and consequences of parental behavior. A more refined look needs to be taken at parental acceptance-rejection in terms of different styles of behavior, i.e. aggression or neglect, and in terms of sex differences in children, age differences in children, and the interaction between sex of parent and sex of child—namely, the effects on sons and on daughters of *paternal* rejection versus *maternal* rejection. In order to test for the level of worldwide generalizability of results coming from any single set of procedures all these questions should, of course, be assessed within the framework of the universalist approach.

The work of this volume represents only the beginning of the quest for specieswide "principles" of human behavior. Clearly we are not ready to give answers to the multitude of specific questions contained in the guiding question: "What does it mean to be a human being?" The future may show some of the conclusions reached here to be incorrect. Other conclusions may later be solidly confirmed, and no doubt many new and currently unsuspected relationships are yet to be discovered. One fact seems to stand out clearly, however. The withdrawal of warmth has "malignant" effects throughout our species. Parental love and the loss of love have implications permeating throughout both personality and the entire social system—and perhaps even across the species.

Definition and Operationalization of Personality Characteristics

INTRODUCTORY

The first eight personality characteristics cited here were defined and coded in the cross-cultural survey component of the Rejection-Acceptance Project. The remaining four traits were originally defined and coded elsewhere. It is important to keep in mind with the following definitions that we as individuals are not, for example, either dependent or independent, but that all of us are dependent (or independent) to a certain extent or in varying degrees. (This continuumlike quality of the personality traits discussed below is not emphasized in the definitions, but the fact of variability among individuals should not be overlooked.

HOSTILITY, AGGRESSION OR PASSIVE AGGRESSION, AND PROBLEMS WITH THE MANAGEMENT OF HOSTILITY AND AGGRESSION

Hostility and (Active) Aggression

Hostility is an emotional (internal) reaction or feeling of anger, enmity, or resentment directed toward another person or situation or toward oneself. Hostility is expressed behaviorally (externally) in the form of aggression, an act which is intended to hurt someone or something, usually another person, but sometimes oneself.[1] Active aggression may be manifested *verbally*, for example, in such forms as bickering, quarreling, "telling someone off," sarcasm, or by making fun of someone, criticizing him, humiliating him, cursing him, or saying thoughtless, unkind, or cruel things to him. Aggression may be revealed *physically* by fighting, hitting, kicking, biting, scratching, pinching, throwing things, or by some other form of destructiveness.

Passive Aggression

Passive aggression is a less direct expression of aggression, manifested in such forms as pouting, sulking, procrastination, stubbornness, passive obstructionism, bitterness, vindictiveness, irritability, and temper tantrums.

Problems with the Management of Hostility and Aggression

Sometimes an individual—adult or child—has conscious (recognized) or unconscious (unrecognized) difficulty coping with or managing his feelings of hostility, and he may also have trouble expressing these feelings. In some social systems, in fact, adults are expected to inhibit almost all forms of aggression. Nonetheless these feelings are likely to be expressed, at least in disguised or symbolic forms, such as worried preoccupation about aggression, aggressive fantasies or dreams, anxiety over one's own real or fantasied aggression, unusual interest in hearing or talking about violent incidents, or by an unusual concern about the real or threatened aggression of others.

DEPENDENCE

Dependence is the *emotional* reliance of one person on another for comfort, approval, guidance, support, reassurance, or decision making. Independence is the essential freedom from such *emotional* reliance.[2]

The goal of dependency behavior among *children* is usually the elicitation of warm, affectionate attention from an adult. Indicators of dependency among children include clinging to their mother (or other major caretaker); attention seeking; becoming anxious, insecure, unhappy, weepy, or

whiney when they are separated from their mother; or waiting for or demanding the nurturant response of someone else
(i.e. succorance).

Indicators of dependency among *adults* (as well as among
children) include frequent seeking of comfort, nurturance,
reassurance, support, approval, or guidance from others,
especially those who are important to the individual, such as
friends and family members including major caretakers. The
dependent person attempts to solicit sympathy, consolation,
encouragement, or affection from friends when he is troubled
or having difficulty. He often seeks to have others help him
when he is having personal problems, and he likes to have
others feel sorry for him or make a fuss over him when he is
sick or hurt.

The independent person, on the other hand, does not rely
heavily on others for emotional comfort, support, encouragement, or reassurance. He does not feel the need to evoke
sympathy from his friends or family when he is troubled, and
he does not often feel the need to seek reassurance, support,
comfort, nurturance, or guidance.

SELF-EVALUATION (SELF-ESTEEM AND SELF-ADEQUACY)

Self-evaluation consists of feelings about, attitudes toward,
and perception of oneself, falling on a continuum from positive to negative. Self-evaluation consists of two related dimensions, self-esteem and self-adequacy:

Self-esteem. Self-esteem is a global, emotional evaluation
of oneself in terms of *worth*. Positive feelings of self-esteem
imply that a person likes or approves of himself, accepts himself, is comfortable with himself, is rarely disappointed in
himself, and perceives himself as being a person of worth, or
worthy of respect. Negative self-esteem, on the other hand,
implies that a person dislikes or disapproves of himself, is
uncomfortable with himself, is disappointed in himself, devaluates himself, perhaps feels inferior to others, and perceives himself as being essentially a worthless person or as
being worthy of condemnation.

Self-adequacy. Self-adequacy is an overall self-evaluation of one's competence to perform daily tasks adequately, to cope satisfactorily with daily problems, and to satisfy one's own needs. Positive feelings of self-adequacy imply that a person views himself as being a capable person, able to deal satisfactorily with his daily problems, and feels that he is a success or is capable of success in the things he sets out to do; he is self-assured or self-confident and feels socially adequate.

Negative feelings of self-adequacy, on the other hand, imply that a person feels he is an incompetent person, unable to meet or cope successfully with the demands of day-to-day living. He lacks confident self-assurance, often feeling inept, and he sees himself as a failure and as being unable to compete successfully for the things he wants.

EMOTIONAL RESPONSIVENESS

Emotional responsiveness refers to a person's ability to express freely and openly his emotions, for example feelings of warmth, affection, and other positive emotions. Emotional responsiveness is revealed by the spontaneity and ease with which a person is able to respond emotionally to another person. Emotionally responsive people have no difficulty forming warm, intimate, involved, and lasting attachments. Their attachments are not troubled by emotional constriction or defensiveness. They are able to show spontaneous affection toward their friends and family, and they are able to act out easily their sympathy and other feelings on appropriate occasions. Interpersonal relations of emotionally responsive people tend to be close and personal, and such persons have no trouble responding emotionally to the friendship advances of others.

Emotionally unresponsive or insulated people, on the other hand, are able to form only restricted or defensive emotional involvements. They may be friendly and sociable, but their friendships tend to be impersonal and emotionally unexpressive. Emotionally unresponsive people may be cold, detached, aloof, or unexpressive, and they may lack spontaneity. They often are unable or find it difficult to give or receive normal affection, and under extreme conditions they may be apathetic or emotionally bland or flat.

EVALUATION OF THE WORLD (WORLD VIEW)

World view is a person's often unverbalized global or overall evaluation of life and the universe as being essentially a positive or negative place, that is as being basically a good, secure, friendly, happy, unthreatening place having few dangers (positive world view), or as being a bad, insecure, threatening, unpleasant, hostile, or uncertain place full of dangers (negative world view). World view refers to a person's conception of and feelings about the basic nature of the cosmos and of life itself; it does not refer to his empirically derived knowledge of the economic, political, social, or natural environment in which he lives.

EMOTIONAL STABILITY

Emotional stability refers to an individual's constancy or steadiness of mood and to his ability to withstand minor setbacks, failures, difficulties, or other stresses without becoming emotionally upset. An emotionally stable person is able to maintain his composure under minor emotional stress. He is not easily or quickly excited or angered, and he is fairly constant in his basic mood.

Emotionally unstable people, on the other hand, are subject to fairly wide, frequent, and unpredictable mood shifts, which swing from such poles as cheery to gloomy, happy to unhappy, contented to dissatisfied, or friendly to hostile. Such persons are often upset easily by small setbacks or difficulties, and they tend to lose composure under minor stress. Oftentimes emotionally unstable people also tend to be excitable or to get angry easily and quickly.

ACHIEVEMENT

Achievement-oriented behavior is the tendency to evaluate one's behavior and that of others with reference to standards of excellence and to strive to behave in such a way as to rise as high as possible on one's scale of excellence. Achievement motivation refers to any active attempt to attain individual standards of excellence, and although it may include competitiveness, it is not limited to competition. Indicators of achievement orientation include efforts to attain or maintain high standards of excellence in the performance of such tasks as hunting, athletic events, academic performance, or aesthetic activities. Achievement-oriented behavior is frequently encountered in the same context as independence and self-reliance, but it should not be confused with either of these.

SELF-RELIANCE

Self-reliance includes unsupervised, goal-directed behavior (see note 2). An individual meets his own instrumental (i.e. action- or task-oriented) needs without relying on or asking for the help of others. Children are self-reliant when they learn to be independent of the assistance of other people in satisfying their instrumental needs and wishes. Indicators of self-reliance among young children include a child's dressing himself, feeding himself, playing away from home without supervision, acquiring or preparing his own food, and bathing himself. The child who says, "I'll do it myself," when asked if he needs help is behaving self-reliantly. Indicators of self-reliance among adults include all responses wherein an adult relies on his own skills or resources to execute a task. An adult who willingly takes the initiative to accomplish some novel task without seeking guidance, supervision, or support is acting in a self-reliant manner.

GENEROSITY

No formal definition of generosity is provided in Bacon, Child, and Barry (1963), but presumably the concept is used in the conventional sense of "liberality in giving."

NURTURANCE

Barry, Bacon, and Child (1967) define nurturance in the following way:

Murray [Murray, Henry A., et al., *Explorations in Personality* (New York, Oxford University Press, 1958)] defines nurturant behavior as follows: "to give sympathy and gratify the needs of a helpless one: an infant or anyone that is weak, disabled, tired, inexperienced, inferior, defeated, humiliated, lonely, dejected, sick, mentally confused. To assist an O in danger. To feed, help, support, console, protect, comfort, nurse, heal." Other nurturant acts described include giving of medicine, food, candy, money, toys, etc., or to inhibit narcissistic needs in presence of an inferior O, to refrain from bothering or annoying an O, to be lenient and indulgent, to give freedom, to condone, or to become indignant when children are maltreated [Barry, Bacon, and Child 1967: 297].

CONFLICT OVER NURTURANT BEHAVIOR

The same authors combine the conceptualization of nurturance given above with the notion of "conflict." Conflict is defined as follows:

. . . : a function of the extent to which the positive learning (together with anxiety about non-performance) on the one hand, and anxiety about performance on the other hand, are both strong and of approximate equality. The rating of conflict, while based on this general reasoning, was made intuitively as a judgment of the extent to which conflict should arise from the pattern of training described, rather than by a quantitative formula [Barry, Bacon, and Child 1967: 296].

RESPONSIBILITY

Barry, Bacon, and Child define responsibility as follows:

"Responsible behavior" refers to the performance of tasks, duties, or routines which are demanded by the culture. It includes economic tasks, such as participation in farming and animal husbandry, collecting food and fuel, carrying water, cooking, serving, and washing; going to school or otherwise submitting oneself to formal training; saying prayers or participating in rituals as an obligation. The emphasis here is on work or effortful or time-consuming behavior which it is an obligation to perform, and which are probably thought of as required for the good of the family or community. Insofar as the tasks are done solely for the benefit of the child himself (self-reliance) or for a specific person in a state of need (nurturance), they are excluded from consideration here. Also excluded is inhibition, as for example acceptance of toilet and sexual inhibitions, aggression restraint, taboos, etc.

An extreme of responsibility in this sense would be found in the *willing* performance of *laborious* duties or tasks, which the child has come to carry out on his own at the proper time and can be trusted to do. It can be contrasted with high obedience, where the child may passively do what he is told on any occasion, but has not himself learned to perform duties without immediate instruction [Barry, Bacon, and Child 1967: 296].

The Meaning of Correlation Coefficients, Chi-Square Test of Association, and Probability

CORRELATION COEFFICIENTS

A correlation coefficient (r) gives information about the extent to which one variable increases (or decreases) as a second variable increases (or decreases). To illustrate, let us say that we want to know what the relationship is between parental rejection-acceptance as one variable and adult emotional stability as the second variable. The scattergram in Figure A-1 shows that parental rejection-acceptance ranges from rejection (2) to acceptance (10) and that adult emotional stability ranges from low stability (2) to high stability (10). The scattergram also shows a certain amount of variability in emotional stability at any given degree of rejection-acceptance. Looking at point 2 on the rejection-acceptance dimension (horizontal axis or abscissa), we see that two societies fall at point 2 on the stability scale (vertical axis or ordinate) and that one society falls at point 3. We also note that at point 10 on the rejection-acceptance scale, one society on the emotional stability scale falls at point 8 and one at point 9. In general, the scattergram shows that as parents in different societies become increasingly affectionate toward their children, adults tend to become more emotionally stable; alternatively we could say that as parents are more rejecting, adults become less emotionally stable. This is shown in the scattergram by the fact that as the numbers on the rejection-acceptance axis increase—go from 2 toward 10—the numbers on the emotional stability axis also tend to increase.

Using a standard formula available in most statistics books, it is possible to compute a correlation coefficient (r) between parental behavior and emotional stability and thereby mathematically determine the strength of the relationship between these traits. A correlation coefficient merely shows mathematically the extent to which the dependent variable (e.g. emotional stability) increases or decreases as the independent variable (e.g. parental rejection-acceptance) increases or decreases. If emotional stability were to increase by a unit of one each time rejection-acceptance increased by a unit of one, we would have a perfect positive relationship,

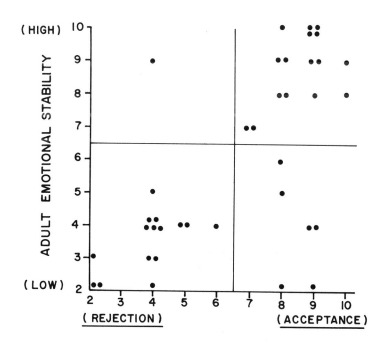

PARENTAL ACCEPTANCE-REJECTION

FIGURE A1. Correlation Between Parental Acceptance-Rejection and
Emotional Responsiveness in Adulthood

or a correlation of $r=1.00$, as shown in Figure A-2. If, on the other hand, the dependent variable were to decrease by a unit of one each time the independent variable increased by a unit of one, we would have the perfect negative relationship shown in Figure A-3, below. Such a correlation is written $r=-1.00$.[1] A negative correlation of $r=-.48$ between parental

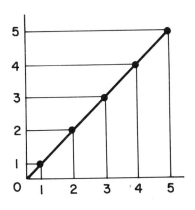

FIGURE A2.   Illustration of a Perfect
Positive Correlation

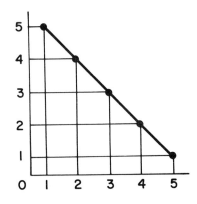

FIGURE A3.   Illustration of a Perfect
Negative Correlation

rejection-accetance and child hostility was discussed in Chapter Four. This negative relationship means that as parents become *increasingly* warm, children tend to become *less* hostile; one could also say that as parents become *less* nurturant, children become *more* hostile. A negative correlation, then, is one where one variable increases in magnitude while the second decreases; in positive correlations, on the other hand, both variables increase or decrease together.

The maximum value or strength that a correlation coefficient can have is $+1.00$ or -1.00. Rarely are such strong relationships achieved. Coefficients more typically fall between perfect positive or negative (i.e. $r=\pm1.00$) on the one

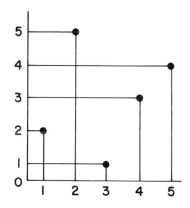

FIGURE A4.   Illustration of a Zero Correlation
(Approximate)

hand, and zero or no correlation (i.e. $r=0.00$) on the other. A correlation of $r=0.00$ means that as the independent variable increases by a unit of one, the dependent variable fluctuates haphazardly or randomly. In other words, absolutely no relationship exists between the two variables. Such a correlation coefficient is approximated in Figure A-4.

Returning now to Figure A-1, we saw in Chapter Four that the correlation between parental rejection-acceptance and adult emotional stability is $r=.62$. This correlation is considered by behavioral scientists to be fairly strong. The meaning of the number is not directly obvious, however, except to those who have had a fair amount of experience with statistics. The nature of correlation coefficients becomes more understandable if we explain that the square of the coefficient (.62) tells us the amount of variability (technically, the "variance") in the dependent variable (e.g. emotional stability) that is explained by the independent variable (e.g. rejection-acceptance). That is (.62)^2 is .38, meaning that 38 percent of the variability found in emotional stability in societies around the world can be explained by knowing how children are treated in terms of parental acceptance-rejection. The remaining portion of the variability is to be explained by other, unknown life experiences.

CHI-SQUARE (X^2) TEST OF ASSOCIATION; PROBABILITY

One of the great advantages of a correlation coefficient is that it takes into account every item of available information. In other words, all the variation found in a trait such as rejection-acceptance is used in calculating the correlation. This is not true of other statistics, such as the chi-square (X^2) test, where the full range of variability that may characterize a trait is ignored. Instead, the variable is collapsed into two or more mutually exclusive categories. For example rejection-acceptance is no longer treated as a continuum from 2-10, but, as shown by the intersecting lines in Figure A-1, discrete categories of acceptance *and* rejection are developed by calling points 2-6, rejection, and points 7-10, acceptance. In the same way, the full range of variability characterizing emotional stability is ignored by dividing that scale into low emotional stability (points 2-6) and high emotional stability (points 7-10). One may collapse data in this way if one wishes to know simply whether acceptance is related significantly to high emotional stability and whether rejection is related significantly to low emotional stability. The chi-square test tells whether two or more classes of variables are associated significantly with each other, but it says nothing about the strength of this relationship.

Sometimes one has no choice but to use discrete variables

rather than continuous scales. Such would be the case if we wanted to know about the relationship between sex and formal political affiliation in the United States. Only two sex choices are possible, male and female, and one has but a limited number of discrete options regarding political affiliation—e.g. Democrat, Republican, Independent, and the like. We cannot speak of degrees of sex such as "more male" or "less male," and we cannot speak of degrees of "Democratness." Both of these categories are generally mutually exclusive and self-contained, and the chi-square test is an appropriate statistical procedure for measuring whether these two variables are related significantly to each other.

FIGURE A5.   Relationship Between Parental Acceptance-Rejection and Emotional Stability in Adulthood

Emotional Stability	*Parental Acceptance-Rejection*	
	Rejection	*Acceptance*
High	1	16
Low	15	6

$X^2 = 16.56$
1 df
$p < .0001$

These points can be made clearer by referring back to Figure A-1, where the scattergram is divided by two intersecting lines into four quadrants or cells. It is now possible to transform Figure A-1 into the format shown in Figure A-5. Figure A-1 shows that one society falls in the upper left-hand cell —the cell labeled high emotional stability/rejection in Figure A-5. Similarly, we can count the number of societies in each quadrant in Figure A-1 and record these societies in the appropriate cell of Figure A-5. Reading down the left column of Figure A-5, we see that adults tend to be emotionally unstable in fifteen of the sixteen societies in the sample where children are rejected; the right-hand column shows that adults tend to be quite emotionally stable in sixteen out of the twenty-two societies where children are accepted. We now ask whether the distribution of societies in the four cells of Figure A-5 is different significantly from what one would expect if nothing more than pure chance were operating. In effect, we are asking what the odds are of being wrong if the hypothesis is accepted that rejection leads to low emotional stability in adults and that acceptance leads to high emotional stability. The chi-square test of association provides a statistical answer to this question.

We will not go into the logic of probability or into the computational procedures for chi-square, because instruction on these issues can be found in almost any textbook on elementary statistics. We will mention, however, that from a practical viewpoint the value (number) one gets from a chi-square test is essentially meaningless until one looks up the associated probability (p) level of the X^2 value in a statistical table usually called "distribution of chi-square." One can see in Figure A-5, for example, that $X^2 = 16.56$. As revealed in the statistical table "distribution of chi-square," at one degree of freedom (df, a concept explained in almost any discussion of chi-square), this chi-square value reaches a probability level of $p < .0001$, meaning that the probability of rejection being associated with adult emotional stability (as shown in Figure A-5) purely on a chance basis is less than one in ten thousand.[2] From this evidence, one concludes that a genuine relationship exists between emotional stability and rejection-acceptance.

Before concluding this Appendix, we should note that behavioral scientists generally accept hypotheses that reach the 5 percent level of significance, i.e. where probability is .05 or less (e.g. $p = .02$, $p = .01$, $p = .005$, etc.). Any hypothesis that does not reach the 5 percent level of significance should be rejected. Occasionally in this book, however, we report results that achieve the 10 percent level of significance $(p = .10)$; these may be viewed as nonsignificant trends.

Methodology in the Holocultural Component of the Rejection-Acceptance Project

This appendix reviews the methodological procedures used in the cross-cultural survey component of the Rejection-Acceptance Project (RAP). Specifically, the appendix deals with four major issues in holocultural methodology: (1) the cross-cultural sample and its characteristics, including problems of sampling bias; (2) definition and operationalization of variables; (3) the coding process and code characteristics, including problems of coder bias; and (4) problems of ethnographer bias (data quality control).

THE SAMPLE AND ITS CHARACTERISTICS

The Sample

The cross-cultural survey component of the RAP was initiated in 1960. Several pilot studies were done between 1960 and 1966, when the final sample used today was drawn. Sampling procedures included the following: a bibliography was compiled of all ethnographies in the English language believed to have at least some information on socialization and personality. This procedure resulted in a list of approximately 235 sources. The list has since been inadvertently discarded. Without having all bibliographic references accessible for inspection, an effort was made to determine, by referring to published and other sources, which of the ethnographies on the list described specific communities localized in space by definable geographic coordinates and anchored in a delimited time period. Such communities, pinpointed in space and time, form the basic sampling unit in this research. Ethnographies were deleted from the list when preliminary screening revealed that either (a) an ethnographer had worked in a community intermittently over a period of years (e.g. a few weeks each summer for thirty years) or (b) an ethnography described a large region rather than a local community or a defined subpopulation within the region. These procedures resulted in a sampling universe of approximately 200 societies.

The final sample drawn from this universe is based on four stratification criteria. First, the world was divided into six major geographic regions, following Murdock (1957: 666; 1962: 113-15); each region was then subdivided into ten culture areas, again following Murdock (1957: 666; 1962: 113-15); to the extent possible, four societies were then drawn from each culture area following Murdock's (1967: 112-13) "three-degree" or "200-mile" rule. According to this rule, societies within 200 miles of each other should not be included in a sample because of their geographic propinquity and the possibility of historical influence. Finally, in those cases where more than four societies within any given culture area were available for inclusion in the sample—within the limits of the 200-mile rule—four were randomly selected.

Several deviations from this sampling design were required: (1) approximately six sample ethnographies were not available for coding. Randomly selected substitutions were made for these when possible. (2) Approximately three societies were deleted because they were seriously inconsistent with the unit-definition requirements specified above. The preliminary screening failed to show that the ethnographies actually encompassed large areas rather than local communities or at least a definable subpopulation within larger regions. (3) Approximately four ethnographies were substituted for ethnographies that were dramatically superior in extensiveness and quality of ethnographic reporting to the originally drawn ethnographies. Table A1 at the end of the appendix charts the worldwide distribution of the 101 societies in the final sample. The ethnographic references used with time and space notations of the local communities are included in Table A2, also at the end of this appendix, and Table A3 lists the page numbers where information was found in the ethnographies relevant to the coding of each variable in each society.

Sampling Bias (Galton's Problem)

Systematic stratification procedures in sampling may alleviate the problem of diffusion, of migration, or of historical contact between populations, but they cannot rule out the possibility of historical influence. For this reason, the possibility is raised that the variables being measured in cross-cultural survey research may not be independent of each other. Rather, relevant variables in any two societies may co-occur not as a result of some postulated universal causal-functional relationship but as a result of historical contact between populations. This issue is generally known in holocultural research as Galton's problem. More precisely, it is one type of sampling bias. The stratification criteria outlined above help assure that the sample is representative of the world's "cultures," but use of these criteria cannot by themselves guarantee that the units of the sample are independent of one another, as they must be in a valid sample.

Two different tests assessing the effects of sampling bias were run on data in the RAP. The first test used D'Andrade's (Naroll and D'Andrade 1963) matched pair technique on data from two sets of hypotheses. In both sets, the historical/diffusion hypotheses were rejected. In other words, diffusion or historical contact did not account for the positive relationship between the variables (see Pugh 1967). We shall not elaborate further on this set of tests. A more conclusive test was made using Naroll's (1964) linked pair method on the entire sample of 101 societies, as well as on the subsample of 90 societies coded for rejection-acceptance.[1] Only the linked pair test for the subsample of 90 is reported here.

The general characteristics of the linked pair test are provided in Naroll (1964); only the general features of the procedure are detailed here.[2] Table A4 shows a rank ordering (by societal proximity) of all 101 societies in the sample. The Mende were arbitrarily selected as the point of origin for the ordering. The nearest society in the sample to the Mende are the Tallensi, who are listed second. Similar measurements were made for the Tallensi and its nearest neighbor in the sample. This procedure was followed throughout the entire sample, each society being juxtaposed with its closest neighbor.

The linked pair method requires that adjacently listed societies be scored in the following way: if the society listed second has a value for some variable (e.g. rejection-acceptance) above the mean value for all listed societies (i.e. the total mean), the first-listed society is scored Y_2; if the second-listed society has a value below the total mean, the first-listed society is scored Y_1. The second-listed society is similarly scored Y_1 or Y_2, depending on whether the value of the third-listed society is above or below the total mean. The society listed last is not scored. Table A5 presents the results of scoring the societies coded for rejection-acceptance.

As shown in Table A6, the total mean for this array is 7.14. The mean for societies scored Y_1 is 7.0, but the mean for societies scored Y_2 is 7.24. A t-test on these Y_1 and Y_2 means is nonsignificant (t=.80; p=ns). Thus, the t-test version of the linked pair method reveals that adjacent societies in the sample are sufficiently dissimilar in their parental warmth codes to reject the null hypothesis of nonindependence among the units of the sample. That is, diffusion or historical contact does not explain the occurrence of rejection-acceptance in the arrayed societies.

Regional Testing

Results in holocultural research should, in principle, be capable of replication in each of the major geographic regions of the world as well as on a worldwide basis. Genuine causal-functional relationships should not generally hold true in North America but fail to hold true in East Eurasia, for example. Thus another methodological issue related to Galton's problem is the one of regional testing of hypotheses. The basic assumption underlying regional testing is that even though some diffusion may occur across continental boundaries, it is highly unlikely that two culture traits will diffuse together to all the major geographic regions of the world. Given this assumption, if a statistically significant association is found between two variables in six regions of the world, then one may usually infer that the association reflects the operation of factors other than diffusion. A statistically significant relationship within a single region may reflect either diffusion or a causal-functional relationship, but it is improbable that the replication of a significant association across six separate regions reflects simple diffusion, migration, or historical contact. In general, then, one gains confidence in the universal generalizability of one's conclusions insofar as they hold up within the major geographic regions of the world.

Following this logic, four RAP hypotheses were chosen because they could be measured on a sample of sixty or more societies. All other hypotheses relating parental behavior to personality were based on fewer than sixty cases, thus creating serious statistical problems in the regional test because of the resulting small sample size where, if the societies were evenly distributed geographically, the largest sample in any region could be only ten societies. Accordingly, regional tests were run only on the relationship between rejection-acceptance and: (a) child hostility (b) adult hostility (c) adult emotional responsiveness, and (d) adult world view. The results of these tests are detailed in Ness and Rohner (1974).[3] They are not elaborated here, because to do so would require an inappropriately lengthy discussion. Overall, however, the results are mixed. A majority of the regional tests emerged as nonsignificant, because the regional samples were very small—even though only tests based on sixty or more societies were used. Almost 80 percent (i.e. nineteen out of twenty-four) of the tests were based on samples having fewer than fifteen cases within any region; no region had more than eighteen cases. Therefore a Pearsons correlation coefficient of $r \geqslant .51$ would be required to produce a statistically significant relationship at the 5 percent level. These essentially negative results seem to be more a matter of inadequate sample size within the geographic regions than a disconfirmation of the hypothesized causal-functional relationship between pairs of traits. This interpretation is strengthened in view of the fact that the linked pair test was run on all five traits (i.e. rejection-acceptance, child hostility, adult hostility, adult emotional responsiveness, and adult world view) within each of the six regions. Only one trait in one region, viz. adult hostility in South America ($p < .05$), is possibly affected by diffusion (see Ness and Rohner 1974).

DEFINITION AND OPERATIONALIZATION OF VARIABLES

A central problem in the holocultural method is that of adequately defining theoretical concepts and then operationalizing them. Concepts or variables in cross-cultural research must be generalizable transculturally, and they must be equivalent conceptually across cultural boundaries. Indicators of variables should have direct face validity.

The personality concepts used in the RAP are defined and operationalized in Appendix 1; the concepts of rejection-acceptance, parental warmth, parental hostility, and parental neglect are discussed in detail in Chapter Two, but the operationalization of rejection-acceptance used in the holocultural component is given below. All variables were coded on a five-point scale. Each of the five points on the rejection-acceptance scale was defined as follows:[4]

1. *Rejection.* The parent-child relationship is characterized by rejection, i.e. by the absence of warmth and affection on the part of the parents toward the child. Physical punishment may be frequent and severe, but punishment per se is relevant to this scale only insofar as it is an expression of hostility toward the child. (See Acceptance, point 5 on the scale.)

2. *Usually rejecting.* The parent-child relationship is characterized by significant elements of rejection, i.e. by fre-

quent or significant withdrawal of warmth and affection on the part of the parents toward the child. Parents may be indifferent toward the child (lack interest in his development), and they may be hostile or aggressive toward him, but at least minor signs of warmth and affection are also present.

3. *Equal acceptance and rejection.* The parent-child relationship is characterized by an approximately equal emphasis on acceptance and rejection. Manifestations of this type of behavior include fundamental signs of ambivalence or inconsistency on the part of the parents toward the child. Ambivalence is an emotional orientation which is characterized by warmth and affection mixed with elements of hostility toward the child. Inconsistency is a behavioral response wherein the parents sometimes behave in a warm and affectionate manner toward the child, and at other times withdraw warmth and affection, behaving in an indifferent, hostile, or aggressive manner toward the child.

4. *Usually accepting.* The parent-child relationship is typically characterized by acceptance (warmth and affection), but minor indications of ambivalence or inconsistency toward the child are present.

5. *Acceptance.* The parent-child relationship is characterized by warmth and affection on the part of the parents toward the child. Parents give love without qualification, but not necessarily with great demonstration. Warmth and affection may be manifested by doing things to please the child, playing with him, enjoying him, fondling him, cuddling him, praising him, singing lullabies to him, caressing and hugging him, or demonstrating love in words or other actions. Routine caretaking and amusing the child as part of a schedule or as a matter of felt duty or responsibility are not to be considered as automatically indicating emotional warmth and affection. Spontaneous signs of warmth and affection should weigh more heavily in this rating than warmth and affection that are solicited by the child. Discipline may take such forms as moderate physical punishment or scolding, and it may be fairly frequent. Discipline as such, however, has little bear-

ing on the rating unless it is an expression of hostility toward the child.

CODING PROCESS AND CODE CHARACTERISTICS

The five-point code scale and the definitions of variables were pretested for their adequacy in several pilot studies before the final sample was drawn. Detailed "Raters' Instructions . . . " were also pretested before coding was initiated in the final sample. These raters' instructions are given in Table A7, at the end of the appendix, along with the code sheets (Tables A8 and A9) used by the raters. Prior to initiating their final codes, two independent raters were trained on a small sample of ethnographies that were not part of the RAP sample. Subsequently the raters completed two sets of codes for the final sample, viz. uncorrected codes and corrected codes. *Uncorrected* codes refer to the codings made independently by the two raters. Periodically the raters conferred on their work, with the objective of reconciling differences in codes within each society. The raters were instructed to try to reconcile all coding differences of two points or more. For example if rater *one* coded child hostility 5 in society *A*, but rater *two* coded child hostility 3 in that society, the coders returned to the ethnographic source for society *A* to review and discuss the bases for their respective coding. Occasionally simple errors were discovered, such as when one rater overlooked relevant material in an ethnography that was used for coding by the second. After conferring, the raters often agreed on the code to within one point or less. Rater *one* might recode child hostility 4, for example, while rater *two* continued to code it 5, or both raters might recode the variable 4. On other occasions, however, the two raters continued to disagree by two or more points. Under such circumstances, the variable in that society was deleted from the research. These revised codes are identified as *corrected* codes. Raters were also instructed to indicate their level of confidence in their codes (see Table A7 for an explanation).

Statistical tests in the RAP are based on the nine-point scale created by summing the corrected codes of the two independent raters, i.e. by creating a single scale ranging from two to ten points for each variable. As revealed in the "Raters' Instructions . . ." (Table A7), provisions are also allowed for coding any exceptional cases that extend beyond this nine-point scale. The final code for each variable in each society is presented in Table A10, at the end of this appendix.

Coder Bias (Validity and Reliability of Codes)

Coder bias occurs when raters consistently make errors in one direction, for example when one or both raters skew the codes to favor or disfavor the hypotheses being tested. Rohner and Katz (1970) present a set of procedures for assessing the extent to which the variance present in codings drawn from ethnographic sources reflects actual variation in the traits themselves, reflects rater bias, or reflects trait-rater interaction. Ideally, rating scales should reveal nothing more than the amount of variability in the traits themselves, but a significant portion of the variance in ethnographic coding results from rater error. The validity of codes is most seriously affected by trait-rater interaction, which occurs when both raters code some variables spuriously high and others spuriously low.

The procedures recommended by Rohner and Katz require that each trait coded by the first rater be correlated with each trait coded by the second, and all the codings of a single rater are intercorrelated with each other. The results are presented in multitrait-multirater matrices. From these matrices it is possible to determine interrater reliability and discriminant validity of traits, in addition to a higher order concept based on pairs of traits (see Rohner and Katz 1970; Campbell and Fiske 1959).

Interrater reliability refers to the extent of agreement between two independent raters; discriminant validity refers to the distinctiveness of traits and implies that two variables are distinguished from each other. Operationally this means that the raters' codings of two separate variables should not correlate as highly with each other as their codings of the same variable. A given variable might display interrater reliability and still be spuriously correlated with one or more other variables. For example interrater reliability could be high for two traits, ambitiousness and industriousness, but raters could still fail to respond to differences in the operationalized definitions of these two variables. For this reason, the trait-pair would lack discriminant validity, and the utility of employing separate names for these variables could be questioned. From these matrices it is also possible to assess convergent validity of the relations between variables. Convergent validity implies that agreement exists between different measures of the same variable.

Turning now to the problem of coder bias in the RAP, the correlations in Tables A11, A12, and A13 result from the judgments made by two independent raters, each of whom coded from eleven to eighty-five societies for each of fourteen traits. The rectangular matrix (Table A11), which contains the uncorrected correlations of trait codings between rater *one* and rater *two*, is termed the heterorater matrix; the two triangular matrices (Tables A12 and A13), containing each rater's uncorrected trait-correlations, are termed the monorater triangles.[5] The negative diagonal of monotrait correlations (i.e. correlations in parentheses) in the heterorater matrix is termed the reliability diagonal. The reliability diagonal in Table A11 reveals interrater reliability, but Table A14 contains complete reporting of interrater reliability for both the uncorrected and corrected codes in this research.

A formal, step-by-step analysis of the data in Tables A11, A12, and A13 is too complex to report here; a full analysis is presented in Rohner and Ness (1975).[6] Briefly, however, the multitrait-multirater technique shows that in a matrix of ninety-one pairs of variables (i.e. Tables A11 through A13), two pairs emerge as having only equivocal discriminant validity: (a) adult emotional stability and adult self-evaluation; and (b) adult dependence and adult self-evaluation. In addition, the discriminant validity of one other pair—child self-evaluation and adult self-evaluation—was questioned, but to a lesser extent. Why these pairs of traits are not discriminated clearly by the coders is not known. The possibility that the raters failed to perceive or respond to differences in the operational definition of the first two pairs is remote, since the definitions are unambiguously distinct (see Appendix One). Regarding the trait-pair "child self-evaluation/ adult self-evaluation," we should note that the two traits are strongly correlated in a positive manner in both monorater triangles. This suggests that both raters tended to code each society the same way for both child and adult self-evaluation. It is not possible to be certain why the raters independently coded societies similarly on these two traits. However, one plausible explanation is that the apparent lack of discriminant validity between these traits reflects the fact that the raters accurately coded two variables whose values tended to be strongly correlated universally. RAP theory would in fact expect adult and child self-evaluation to be manifested similarly in any given society.

Investigators may be satisfied that their traits exhibit reasonable interrater reliability and discriminant validity; the specific variables coded may each appear to be uniquely responsible for a substantial amount of coding variability. The extent to which any two of these traits are related, however, is also of interest. Thus, if the theory being tested predicts a negative relationship between variables X and Y, the investigator will want to assess the convergent validity of the relationship between these variables. Operationally, this means that if both monorater correlations between the two traits are statistically significant ($p \leq .05$) in the same direction, then the relationship between the two traits X and Y may be regarded as having convergent validity if, at the same time, both heterorater coefficients involving these traits are also significant ($p \leq .05$) and in the same direction as the correlations in the monorater triangles.

Eleven of fifteen pairs of traits predicted in RAP theory to be significantly related emerged from this analysis with adequate convergent validity. Three of the four "questionable" pairs involved "dependence:" rejection-acceptance and child dependence, rejection-acceptance and adult dependence, and child dependence and adult dependence. The fourth relationship having questionable convergent validity is between rejection-acceptance and adult world view. No explanation for these apparent exceptions to RAP theory is offered now.

ETHNOGRAPHER BIAS (DATA QUALITY CONTROL)

Ethnographer bias refers to any systematic error occurring in the ethnographic reporting process. The general issue is often discussed under the label "data quality control." We do not give a complete analysis here of the problems of ethnographer bias in the RAP, because this has been published elsewhere (see Rohner, DeWalt, and Ness 1973). In this section, we merely summarize the results of tests for ethnographer bias.

Ethnographer bias becomes a serious problem in cross-cultural survey research if ethnographers in different societies make the same "mistakes," i.e. if they have similar or consistent biases. Naroll (1962: 88-89), for example, found that ethnographers who live in the field for a year or more tend significantly more often than "short stayers" to report the presence of witchcraft. If reports on warfare are biased in the same way, with "long stayers" being more likely to report the presence of warfare than "short stayers," then holocultural researchers may find a statistically significant but spurious cross-cultural relationship between the incidence of witchcraft and the incidence of warfare. The true relationship between witchcraft and warfare would, in this way, be obscured because of a systematic "error" (i.e. bias) in the ethnographic reporting process.

In order to detect the presence of ethnographer bias, a series of *control variables* which may affect the data collecting and reporting processes is enumerated. These control variables are measured in each sample ethnography, and they are then correlated with the *substantive variables* of theoretical interest. The substantive variables in this case are rejection-acceptance and the personality characteristics of children and adults. If a data quality control variable is significantly related to a pair of substantive variables, for example to both rejection-acceptance and adult achievement, then that control variable must be taken into account in the interpretation of the relationship between parental behavior and adult achievement. More specifically, if the control variable "total months of fieldwork" is related to both parental acceptance-rejection and to adult achievement, then the investigator must determine whether the relationship between these two substantive variables continues to be statistically significant after controlling for the effect of the control variable, "total months of fieldwork." If the correlation between parental warmth and adult achievement is no longer significant after controlling for "months of fieldwork," then the researchers must reject the hypothesis that a causal-functional relationship exists between the two substantive variables.

Our task here is to determine if the magnitude of the correlations in Table 1, Chapter Four, remains substantially unchanged after controlling for the effects of a series of quality control variables. In order to detect the influence of ethnographer bias, two independent coders measured certain characteristics of the ethnographers themselves—their fieldwork procedures and their written work. Table A15, at the end of this appendix, provides a list of the control variables used, along with the raters' instructions for coding and the definition of the control variables; Table A16 is a facsimile of the raters' data quality control code sheet; Table A17 presents the codes for the data quality control variables in each society; Table A2, cited earlier, gives a list of the ethnographic references coded by the raters. Table A18 shows that interrater reliability for all control variables is high, the lowest reliability coefficient being $r = .84$.

In order to assess the effects of ethnographer bias on RAP data, the following sequence of steps was employed: (a) an intercorrelation matrix of control variables was prepared; (b) the matrix was factor analyzed in order to reduce the control variables to a manageable number; (c) factor scores for each ethnographer were computed in order to determine each ethnographer's position on every *control factor* obtained in step *b*; (d) every ethnographer's factor scores for each control factor were correlated with all substantive variables; (e) the resulting correlation matrix was examined for patterns of statistically significant relationships between the ethnographer's factor scores for each control factor and the substantive variable; (f) controlling statistically for the possible effect of the *control measures* (i.e. the control factors as well as the control variables that were retained in the analysis, even though they did not load significantly on any control factor), an assessment was made of the relationship between the substantive variables. In effect, the question was asked: "What is the relationship between parental acceptance-rejection and the other personality variables after partialing out or controlling for the effects of the data quality control measures?" Does ethnographer bias "cause" any relationship between the pairs of substantive variables in Table 1, Chapter Four, to appear when in fact no genuine causal-functional relationship actually exists?

The statistical analysis of these data employed the method of "correlation of residuals," which is based on multiple regression. Effectively, this procedure subtracts from the scores of any pair of substantive variables the part of the score that is accounted for by the control measures. The remainder, the *residual*, is free from the possible contaminating influence of the control measures and may be regarded as a "true" score. The final step in the correlation of residual procedures is to correlate the residual score for all relevant pairs of substantive variables. The resulting coefficient is free from any measured ethnographer bias.

Comparing the residual correlations, which control for the effects of the data quality control measures, with the original correlations in Table 1, Chapter Four, one can see in Table A19 that four of the "original" correlations (see *original correlation* in Table A19) are affected by ethnographer bias: two coefficients that had been statistically significant previously (i.e. the correlation between rejection-acceptance and child self-evaluation and that between rejection-acceptance and adult achievement) are no longer significant statistically; two relationships which had been nonsignificant previously now emerge as being significant (i.e. the relationship between rejection-acceptance and child achievement and that between rejection-acceptance and child self-reliance).

As suggested in Chapter Four, RAP theory made no advance predictions about the relationship between rejection-acceptance and child self-reliance, rejection-acceptance and child achievement, or rejection-acceptance and adult achievement. Therefore, the fact that ethnographer bias seems to affect the true relationship between these sets of variables does not influence the universalist theory presented in this book. The fact that the reported relationship between rejection-acceptance and child self-evaluation is affected by ethnographer bias does, however, seem to influence RAP theory. In view of the substantial supporting evidence for this relationship reported by psychologists in the United States (see Chapter Three), it is unclear why the theoretically expectable association between rejection-acceptance and child self-evaluation should fail to be substantiated. It is worth nothing, however, that the sample size on which the original and residual correlations were based is unusually small (n=11).

Failure to confirm the relationship between rejection-acceptance and child self-evaluation could, therefore, be due to sampling error. It could also be due to coder bias, since children's self-evaluation is difficult to measure in holocultural research. (In this context, see the discussion of child self-evaluation in the preceding section regarding coder bias.) The original correlation between rejection-acceptance and child self-evaluation may possibly be unreliable because of either or both of these responses. We are therefore reluctant to make a firm interpretation about the effects of ethnographer bias on this relationship. All other causal-functional relationships postulated in RAP theory are validated in this analysis of ethnographer bias.

The Bias of Romanticism in Anthropological Research

Even though they do not affect significantly the relationship between parental warmth and the personality characteristics, several control measures are related to the reporting of acceptance-rejection and certain personality traits. These measures seem to form a constellation which can be labeled

the "bias of romanticism" in anthropological research (see
Rohner, DeWalt, and Ness 1973).

Ethnographers who employ a variety of verification efforts
in their socialization research also report more parental rejection and more "negative" personality characteristics than
ethnographers who do not use these procedures. More specifically, in comparison with ethnographers who do not employ
systematic verification procedures, ethnographers who administer tests or questionnaires, or who make repeated observations on different families' socialization practices also
report more parental rejection (r=−.21, p<.05), and less child
achievement (r=−.39; p<.05) and, among adults, less achievement (r=−.21; p<.05), more hostility (r=.24; p<.05), more
dependency (r=.29; p<.05), and greater emotional unresponsiveness (r=.29; p<.05).

It seems likely that these facts are expressive of a kind of
"moral commitment" which anthropologists as a group have
to think well of the people with whom they work. This commitment to see "their people" in a positive light, along with
an uncompromising belief in cultural relativity and in the
functionalist interpretation of ethnographic data, have produced a subtle tendency for many anthropologists to roman-
ticize mankind (see also Chapter One). Thus very often ethnographers simply do not see "negative" features in their
people's life-style or personalities unless these features are
forced upon their attention through the use of objective tests,
through repeated and structured observations, or through
formal interviewing of multiple informants. Researchers who
do make use of these multiple verification efforts are more
likely to become confronted with the reality of certain "negative" aspects of their hosts' social systems and personalities.
For these reasons, an unknown portion of ethnography is
confounded by a systematic error, an error we call the bias of
romanticism.

TABLE A1. Distribution of Societies in the Rejection-Acceptance Project Sample

Geographic Region	*Culture Area*	*Society*
Africa	African Hunters	Naron
	South African Bantu	Bechuana
		Sotho (Basuto)
		Umbundu (Mbundu)
	Central Bantu	Lambas
		Ngoni
	Northeast Bantu	Gusii
		Nyakyusa
		Soga
	Guinea Coast	Ashanti
		Fon (Dahomeans)
		Mende
		Yoruba
	Western Sudan	Tallensi
	Nigerian Plateau	Tiv
	Upper Nile	Nuer
Circum-Mediterranean	Muslim Sudan	Arab Sudanese
	North Africa	Egyptians
	South Europe	Greeks, Modern
	Overseas Europeans	Americans
		Australians (rural)
		Canadians, French
		Jews, East European
	Northwest Europe	Dutch
		French (Anjou)
		French (Vaucluse)
	East Europe	Serbs
	Semitic Near East	Lebanese
East Eurasia	Arctic Asia	Chukchee
	East Asia	Chinese (Shantung Province)
		Japanese
		Okinawans
		Taiwanese
	Himalayas	Lepcha
	North and Central India	Indians
		Indians (high-caste Hindus)
		Indians (Rajputs)
	South India	Muria
	Indian Ocean	Andamanese
		Tanala
	Southeast Asia	Cambodians
		Malays
		Thai

(*Continued on Next Page*)

Table A1. Continued

Geographic Region	Culture Area	Society
Insular Pacific	Philippines and Formosa	Filipinos
		Ilocos
	Western Indonesia	Balinese
		Javanese
	Eastern Indonesia	Alorese
	New Guinea	Kwoma
		Wogeo
	Micronesia	Chamorros
		Woleaians (Ifaluk)
		Palauans
		Trukese
	Western Melanesia	Dobuans
		Manus
		New Irelanders
		Siuai
	Eastern Melanesia	Fijians (Vanua Levu)
		Malekula
	Western Polynesia	Samoans
		Tikopians
	Eastern Polynesia	Maori
North America	Arctic America	Eskimo, Alaskan
		Eskimo, Greenland
		Kaska
		Potawatomi, Prairie
	Northwest Coast	Hupa
		Kwakiutl
	California	Klamath
	Great Basin and Plateau	Kutenay
		Paiute (Harney Valley)
	Plains	Cheyenne
		Crow
		Mandan
		Sioux (Teton-Dakota)
	Prairie	Ojibwa
		Wichita
	Southwest	Apache, Chiracahua
		Apache, Western
		Hopi
		Navaho
	Northwest Mexico	Papago
	Central Mexico	Mixtecans
		Tepoztecans

Table A1. Continued

Geographic Region	Culture Area	Society
South America	Central America	Guatemalan Indians
	Carribean	Carriacou
		Colombian Mestizo
		Jamaicans
		Puerto Ricans
	Interior Amazon	Siriono
		Tukuna
		Yaguans
	Andes	Aymara
	Chile and Patagonia	Araucanians (Mapuche)
	Gran Chaco	Paraguayans
	Mato Grosso	Akwe-Shavante
		Camayura
	Eastern Brazil	Sherente
		Tenetehara
		Timbira, Eastern

TABLE A2.

Ethnographic References Used in the Cross-Cultural Survey
Component of the Rejection-Acceptance Project

001 *AKWE-SHAVANTE* in the vicinity of town of São Domingo (13°30'S, 51°30'W) in 1958.

Maybury-Lewis, David

1967 *Akwe-Shavante society*, London, Oxford University Press.

002 *ALORESE* in the community of Atimelang (8°30'S, 124°30'E) from 1937-38.

DuBois, Cora

1944 *The people of Alor: a social-psychological study of an East Indian island*, Minneapolis, University of Minnesota Press.

003 *AMERICANS* in Orchard Town (42°30'N, 71°30'W) in 1954.

Fischer, John L., and Ann Fischer

1966 "The New Englanders of Orchard Town, U.S.A.," *Six Cultures Series, Vol. 5*, New York, John Wiley and Sons.

004 *ANDAMANESE* in vicinity of Aka-Bea tribe of South Andaman Island (12°N, 93°E) from 1906-08.

Radcliffe-Brown, A.

1922 *The Andamanese Islanders*, Cambridge, Cambridge University Press.

005 *APACHE, CHIRICAHUA* in Chiricahua proper in southeastern Arizona (32°N, 109°30'W), 1931-37 (two years).

Opler, M. E.

1941 *An Apache life-way*, Chicago, University of Chicago Press.

006 *APACHE, WESTERN* in east-central Arizona (34°N, 110°W) from 1929-30.

Goodwin, G.

1942   *Social organization of the Western Apache*, Chicago, University of Chicago Press.

007 *ARAB SUDANESE* in the community of Buurri Al Lamaab (15°N, 32°E) from April 1959 to March 1960.

Barclay, Harold B.
1964   *Buurri Al Lamaab: a surburban village in the Sudan*, Ithaca, Cornell University Press.

008 *ARAUCANIANS* in the southern part of Cautín Province and the northern part of Valdivia Province (40°S, 73°W) from November 1946 to April 1947.

Hilger, M. Inez
1957   "Araucanian child life and its cultural background," *Smithsonian Miscellaneous Collections 133.*

009 *ASHANTI* in the state of Kumasi (7°N, 1°30'W) in 1922.

Rattray, R. S.
1923   *Ashanti*, Oxford, Clarendon Press.
1927   *Religion and art in Ashanti*, Oxford, Clarendon Press.
1929   *Ashanti law and constitution*, Oxford, Clarendon Press.

010 *AUSTRALIANS (RURAL)* in Mallee Town in the northwest corner of Victoria (35°S, 141°30'E) in about 1950.

Oeser, O. A., and F. E. Emery
1954   *Social structure and personality in a rural community*, London, Routledge and Kegan Paul.

011 *AYMARA* in community of Chucuito, Peru (15°S, 70°W) from March 1940 to June 1942.

Tshopik, Harry
1951   "The Aymara of Chucuito, Peru, part 1, magic," *American Museum of Natural History, Anthropological Papers Vol. 44, part 2.*

012 *BALINESE* in community of Bajoeng Gede (8°30'S, 115°E) from March 1936 to March 1938 and February to March 1939.

Bateson, Gregory, and Margaret Mead
1942   *Balinese character*, New York, New York Academy of Sciences.

013 *BECHUANA* in BaKgatla Reserve (24°S, 27°E), 1929-34 (fourteen months).

Schapera, I.
1940   *Married life in an African tribe*, London, Faber and Faber.

014 *CAMAYURA* in community of Tuatuari (12°S, 54°W) from June 1948 to August 1948.

Oberg, Kalervo
1953   "Indian tribes of northern Mato Grosso, Brazil," *Smithsonian Institution, Institute of Social Anthropology, Publication 15.*

015 *CAMBODIANS* in the whole country (13°N, 105°E) during 1950s.

Steinberg, David J., et al.
1957   *Cambodia, its people, its society, its culture*, New Haven, HRAF Press.

016 *CANADIANS, FRENCH* in community of St. Denis (47°30'N, 70°W) from July 1936 to June 1937.

Miner, Horace
1963   *St. Denis, a French-Canadian parish*, Chicago, University of Chicago Press.

017 *CARRIACOU* in West Indian Island of Carriacou (12°N, 61°W) from June 1953 to July 1953.

Smith, M. G.

1962 *Kinship and community in Carriacou*, New Haven, Yale University Press.

018 *CHAMORROS* in community of Chalan Kanoa (15°N, 145°E) from July 1947 to January 1948.

Joseph, Alice, and Veronica F. Murray

1951 *Chamorros and Carolinians of Saipan: personality studies*, Cambridge, Harvard University Press.

019 *CHEYENNE* in southeastern Montana (46°N, 104°W) from 1935-36.

Hoebel, E. A.

1960 *The Cheyennes: Indians of the Great Plains*, New York, Holt, Rinehart and Winston.

020 *CHINESE (SHANTUNG PROVINCE)* in community of Taitou (36°N, 120°E)—author was born and raised there.

Yang, Martin C.

1945 *A Chinese village: Taitou, Shantung Province*, New York, Columbia University Press.

021 *CHUKCHEE* between the coast of Chaun Bay and the Kolyma Mountains and River (69°N, 165°E) from 1919 to 1921.

Sverdrup, Harald Ulrik

1938 *With the people of the Tundra* (HRAF translation).

022 *COLOMBIAN MESTIZO* in community of Aritama (10°N, 74°W) during 1950s.

Reichel-Dolmatoff, Gerardo, and Alicia Reichel-Dolmatoff

1961 *The people of Aritama, the cultural personality of a Colombian Mestizo village*, Chicago, University of Chicago Press.

023 *CROW* on reservation south of Billings, Montana (45°N, 108°W) in "field seasons" of 1907, 1910 to 1916.

Lowie, Robert H.

1935 *The Crow Indians*, New York, Farrar and Rinehart.

024 *DOBUANS* on Tewara Island and Dobu Island (10°S, 151°E), 1927-28 (six months).

Fortune, R. F.

1932 *Sorcerors of Dobu*, New York, Dutton.

025 *DUTCH* in community of Anderen (52°N, 6°E) from September 1951 to June 1952.

Keur, John Y., and D. L. Keur

1955 "The deeply rooted: a study of a Drents community in the Netherlands," *American Ethnological Society Monograph 25*, New York, J. J. Augustin.

026 *EGYPTIANS* in community of Silwa (24°30′N, 33°E) in 1950.

Ammar, Hamed

1954 *Growing up in an Egyptian village*, London, Routledge and Kegan Paul.

027 *ESKIMO, ALASKAN* in community of Napaskiak (60°N, 163°W) in 1956.

Oswalt, Wendell

1963 *Napaskiak, an Alaskan Eskimo community*, Tucson, University of Arizona Press.

028 *ESKIMO, GREENLAND* southeastern coast of Greenland (66°30′N, 40°W) in about 1884.

Mirsky, Jeannette
1937   "The Eskimo of Greenland," in Margaret Mead, ed., *Cooperation and Competition among Primitive Peoples*, New York, McGraw-Hill: 51-81.
029 *FIJIANS* in community of Nakoroka (16°30'S, 179°E) from 1935-36.
Quain, Buell
1948   *Fijian village*, Chicago, University of Chicago Press.
030 *FILIPINOS* in community of Guinhangdan (11°N, 123°E) from December 1955 to July 1956.
Nurge, Ethel
1965   *Life in a Leyte village*, Seattle, University of Washington Press.
031 *FON* of the city and environs of Abomey (7°N, 2°E) from March 1931 to August 1931.
Herskovits, Melville J.
1938   *Dahomey; an ancient West African kingdom*, New York, J. J. Augustin.
032 *FRENCH (ANJOU)* in community of Chanzeaux (48°N, 0°) in 1957, summers 1962 to 1965.
Wylie, Laurence
1966   *Chanzeaux: a village in Anjou*, Cambridge, Harvard University Press.
033 *FRENCH, VAUCLUSE* in the community of Peyrane (44°N, 5°E) from 1950-51.
Wylie, Laurence
1957   *Village in the Vaucluse*, Cambridge, Harvard University Press.
034 *GREEKS, MODERN* in community of Vasilika (38°N, 22°E), 1955-56, summer of 1959, and July of 1961.
Friedl, Ernestine
1962   *Vasilika; a village in modern Greece*, New York, Holt, Rinehart and Winston.
035 *GUATEMALAN INDIANS* in community of San Pedro de La Laguna (15°N, 91°W) in 1941.
Paul, B. D.
1950   "Symbolic sibling rivalry in a Guatemalan Indian village," *American Anthropologist 52:* 205-18.
Paul, B. D. and L. Paul
1952   "The life cycle," in Sol Tax et al., eds., *Heritage of Conquest: The Ethnology of Middle America*, Glencoe, Illinois, The Free Press: 174-92.
036 *GUSII* in community of Nyansongo (0°, 35°E) from April 1956 to May 1957.
LeVine, Robert A., and Barbara B. LeVine
1966   "Nyansongo: a Gusii community in Kenya," *Six Cultures Series, Vol. 2*, New York, John Wiley and Sons.
037 *HOPI* in communities of New Oraibi and Hotavila on Hopi Reservation (36°N, 111°W) in summers of 1937 and 1938.
Dennis, Wayne
1940   *The Hopi child*, New York, Appleton-Century.
038 *HUPA* on Hupa reservation along Trinity River in northwestern California (40°30'N, 123°30'W) from 1945 to 1946.

Wallace, W. J.
1947 "Hupa child training—a study in primitive education," *Educational Administration and Supervision 33:* 13-25.

039 *ILOCOS* in community of Tarong Barrio (17°N, 121°E) in 1954.

Nydegger, William F., and Corinne Nydegger
1966 "Tarong: an Ilocos Barrio in the Philippines," *Six Cultures Series, Vol.* 6, New York, John Wiley and Sons.

040 *INDIANS (HIGH-CASTE HINDU)* in community of Deoli (26°N, 75°E) from 1951 to 1952.

Carstairs, G. Morris
1957 *The twice born,* London, Hogarth Press.

041 *INDIANS (RAJPUTS)* in community of Khalapur (20°N, 77°E) in 1954.

Minturn, Leigh, and John T. Hitchcock
1966 "The Rajputs of Khalapur, India," *Six Cultures Series, Vol. 3,* New York, John Wiley and Sons.

042 *INDIANS* in community of Shamirpet (17°N, 78°E) from 1951 to 1952.

Dube, S. C.
1955 *Indian village,* London, Routledge and Kegan Paul.

043 *JAMAICANS* in communities of Patentville, Orange Grove, and Sugartown (18°N, 77°W) from 1947 to 1949.

Kerr, Madeline
1952 *Personality and conflict in Jamaica,* Liverpool, University Press.

044 *JAPANESE* in community of Takashima of southern Okayama prefecture (35°N, 133°30'E) from 1917 to 1926 and June 1950 to April 1951.

Norbeck, Edward
1954 *Takashima; a Japanese fishing community,* Salt Lake City, University of Utah Press.

Haring, D. G.
1948 "Aspects of personal character in Japan," in D. G. Haring, ed., *Personal Character and Cultural Milieu,* Syracuse, Syracuse University Press: 396-407.

045 *JAVANESE* in community of Modjokuto (8°S, 113°E) from May 1953 to October 1954.

Geertz, Hildred
1961 *The Javanese family: a study of kinship and socialization,* New York, The Free Press of Glencoe.

046 *JEWS, EAST EUROPEAN* in a kibbutz called Kirijat Yeddim (32°N, 35°E) from 1951 to 1952.

Spiro, Melford E.
1958 *Children of the kibbutz,* Cambridge, Harvard University Press.

047 *KASKA* around the Upper Liard and Dease River (60°N, 131°W) in 1944.

Honigmann, J. J.
1954 "The Kaska Indians: an ethnographic reconstruction," *Yale University Publications in Anthropology No. 51.*

048 *KLAMATH* on Klamath Reservation (42°30'N, 122°W), 1947 (summer).

Pearsall, M.
1950 "Klamath childhood," *University of California, Anthropological Records 9:* 5.

049 *KUTENAY* around the Kootenay River (49°N, 116°30'W) from June 1939 to September 1939, July 1940 to August 1940.

Turney-High, Harry H.
 1941   "Ethnography of the Kutenai," *Memoirs of the American Anthropological Association, Article 56.*
050 *KWAKIUTL* in community of Gilford (51°N, 126°30'W) from September 1962 to August 1963, June 1964 to July 1964.
 Rohner, R. P.
 1965   "The people of Gilford: a contemporary Kwakiutl village," *National Museum of Canada, Bulletin 225.*
051 *KWOMA* in a hamlet called Rumbina among the Hongwam subtribe (4°S, 142°30'E) from October 1936 to April 1937.
 Whiting, John W. M.
 1941   *Becoming a Kwoma,* New Haven, Yale University Press.
052 *LAMBAS* in Mushili district (13°S, 28°E) from 1914 to 1921.
 Doke, Clement
 1931   *The Lambas of Northern Rhodesia,* London, George Harrap.
053 *LEBANESE* in city of Beirut and Beqaa Valley (34°N, 35°30'E) in 1959.
 Prothro, Edwin T.
 1961   "Child rearing in the Lebanon," *Harvard Middle Eastern Monographs 8.*
054 *LEPCHA* in community of Lingthem in Sikkim (27°30'N, 89°E) in 1937.
 Gorer, Geoffrey
 1938   *Himalayan village,* London, Michael Joseph.
055 *MALAYS* in community of Rusembilan (7°N, 101°E) from February 1956 to September 1956.
 Fraser, Thomas M., Jr.
 1960   *Rusembilan: a Malay fishing village in Southern Thailand,* Ithaca, Cornell University Press.
 1966   *Fishermen of South Thailand: the Malay villagers,* New York, Holt, Rinehart and Winston.
056 *MALEKULA* an island in New Hebrides (16°S, 167°E) from January 1926 to March 1927.
 Deacon, A. Bernard
 1934   *Malekula: a vanishing people in the New Hebrides,* London, George Routledge and Sons.
057 *MANDAN* in Fort Berthold reservation (47°N, 101°W) in 1930.
 Bowers, A. W.
 1950   *Mandan social and ceremonial organization,* Chicago, University of Chicago Press.
058 *MANUS* of Peri Village (2°S, 147°E) in 1929.
 Mead, Margaret
 1930   *Growing up in New Guinea,* New York, William Morrow.
 1948   "Age patterning in personality development," in D. G. Haring, ed., *Personal Character and Cultural Milieu,* Syracuse, Syracuse University Press.
059 *MAORI* in community of Rakau (38°30'S, 177°E) in summers of 1954 and 1955.
 Ritchie, James E.
 1956   "Basic personality in Rakau," *Monographs on Maori Social Life and Personality 1, Victoria University College Publications in Psychology 8.*
060 *MENDE* near town of Bo (8°N, 12°W) from 1945 to 1946.
 Little, K. L.

1951 *The Mende of Sierra Leone*, London, Routledge and Kegan Paul.
061 *MIXTECANS* in community of Juxtlahuaca (17°N, 98°W) in 1955.
Romney, A. K., and Romaine Romney
1966 "The Mixtecans of Juxtlahuaca, Mexico," *Six Cultures Series, Vol. 4*, New York, John Wiley and Sons.
062 *MURIA* in Bastar State, India (19°N, 81°E) from 1935-42.
Elwin, V.
1947 *The Muria and their Ghotul*, Bombay, Oxford University Press.
063 *NARON* on the Kalahari Desert (23°S, 21°E) in 1920s.
Schapera, I.
1930 *The Khoisan peoples of South Africa*, London, Routledge and Kegan Paul.
064 *NAVAHO* in Shiprock, Ramah, and Navaho Mountain Reservations (37°N, 110°W) from 1942 to 1943.
Kluckhohn, Clyde, and Dorothea Leighton
1946 *The Navaho*, Cambridge, Harvard University Press.
Leighton, Dorothea, and Clyde Kluckhohn
1947 *Children of the people*, Cambridge, Harvard University Press.
065 *NEW IRELANDERS* in community of Lesu (3°S, 152°E) from March 1929 to March 1930.
Powdermaker, Hortense
1933 *Life in Lesu*, New York, W. W. Norton.
066 *NGONI* in northern Malawi (12°S, 34°E), 1935 to 1939 (three-and-one-half years).
Read, Margaret
1960 *Children of their fathers, growing up among the Ngoni of Nyasaland*, New Haven, Yale University Press.
067 *NUER* in the Nilotic Sudan (8°N, 32°E), 1930 to 1936 (one year).
Evans-Pritchard, E. E.
1951 *Kinship and marriage among the Nuer*, Oxford, Clarendon Press.
068 *NYAKYUSA* near the communities of Mwaya and Masoko (9°30'S, 34°E) from 1934 to 1938.
Wilson, Monica
1951 *Good company: a study of Nyakyusa age-villages*, London, Oxford University Press.
069 *OJIBWA* principally on Red Lake Reservation, Minn. (48°N, 95°W) in summers of 1932, 1933, 1935, 1938-40.
Hilger, M. I.
1951 "Chippewa child life and its cultural background," *Bulletin of the U.S. Bureau of American Ethnology 146*.
070 *OKINAWANS* in community of Taira (26°N, 128°E) in 1954.
Maretzki, Thomas W., and Hatsumi Maretzki
1966 "Taira: an Okinawan village," *Six Cultures Series, Vol. 7*, New York, John Wiley and Sons.
071 *PAIUTE* in community of Burns, Oregon (43°30'N, 119°W) in summers of 1936 to 1938.
Whiting, Beatrice
1950 "Paiute sorcery," *Viking Fund Publication, 15*.

072 *PALAUANS* on island of Babeldaob (7°N, 135°E) from 1947-48.
Barnett, Homer
    1960   *Being a Palauan*, New York, Holt, Rinehart and Winston.
073 *PAPAGO* in Baboquivari, Hickiwan, and GuVo districts (31°N, 112°W) from 1942-43.
Joseph, Alice, R.B. Spicer, and Jane Cheskey
    1949   *The desert people: a study of the Papago Indians*, Chicago, University of Chicago Press.
074 *PARAGUAYANS* in community of Tobati (25°S, 57°W) from 1948-49.
Service, Elman R., and Helen S. Service
    1954   *Tobati Paraguayan town*, Chicago, University of Chicago Press.
075 *POTAWATOMI (PRAIRIE)* in northwest Kansas on the reservation (39°30'N, 96°W) from June 1964 to August 1964.
Searey, Ann McElroy
    1965   "Contemporary and traditional Prairie Potawatomi child life," Kansas University, *Potawatomi Study Research Report 7.*
076 *PUERTO RICANS* in community of Valle Cana (18°N, 66°W) in 1951.
Landy, David
    1959   *Tropical childhood*, New York, Harper and Row.
077 *SAMOANS* in Tau Island of Manu'a Archipelago (14°S, 169°30'W) in mid-1920s.
Mead, Margaret
    1928   *Coming of age in Samoa*, New York, William Morrow.
078 *SERBS* in community of Orasać (43°N, 18°E) from 1953-54.
Halpern, Joel Martin
    1958   *A Serbian village*, New York, Columbia University Press.
079 *SHERENTE* around the Rio Tocantins (10°S, 48°W) in 1930 and 1937.
Nimuendaju, Curt
    1942   "The Sherente," *Publications of the Frederick Webb Hodge Anniversary Publication Fund, Vol. 4.*
080 *SIOUX (TETON-DAKOTA)* in Kyle, Wanblee, and Pine Ridge Town Reservations (43°30'N, 103°W) from August 1942 to June 1943.
MacGregor, G.
    1946   *Warriors without weapons*, Chicago, University of Chicago Press.
081 *SIRIONO* near the Rio Blanco (14°30'S, 63°30'W) from 1940-41.
Holmberg, A. R.
    1950   *Nomads of the long bow: the Siriono of eastern Bolivia*, Washington, D.C., Government Printing Office.
082 *SIUAI* in communities of Mataras, Kieta, and Turunom on southwestern Bougainville Island (7°S, 155°30'E) in 1938.
Oliver, Douglas L.
    1955   *A Solomon Island society*, Cambridge, Harvard University Press.
083 *SOGA* around communities of Busamburi and Kaliro (1°N, 33°E) from November 1950 to July 1952.
Fallers, Lloyd A.
    1956   *Bantu bureaucracy; a study of integration and conflict in the political institutions of an East African people*, Cambridge, W. Heffer and Sons.

084 *SOTHO (BASUTO)* in Basutoland (29°S, 28°E) from 1935-36.
Ashton, H.
1952 *The Basuto*, London, Oxford University Press.
085 *TAIWANESE* in community of Hsin Hsing (24°N, 120°E) from 1957-58.
Gallin, Bernard
1966 *Hsin Hsing, Taiwan: a Chinese village in change*, Berkeley, University of California Press.
086 *TALLENSI* in southcentral part of Upper Volta (10°30′N, 0°30′W) in 1934.
Fortes, Meyer
1959 *Web of kinship among the Tallensi*, London, Oxford University Press.
087 *TANALA* of Menabe subtribe in mountainous areas of Madagascar (20°S, 48°E) in 1927.
Linton, Ralph
1939 "The Tanala of Madagascar" and "Analysis of Tanala culture," in A. Kardiner, ed., *The Individual and his Society*, New York, Columbia University Press: 251-351.
088 *TENETEHARA* along the Pindaré River (4°30′S, 45°W) in 1941.
Wagley, C., and E. Galvao
1949 *The Tenetehara Indians of Brazil*, New York, Columbia University Press.
089 *TEPOZTECANS* in community of Tepoztlan (19°N, 99°W) in 1944.
Lewis, Oscar
1951 *Life in a Mexican village: Tepoztlan restudied*, Urbana, University of Illinois Press.
090 *THAI* in community of Bang Chan (14°N, 101°E), 1948 and 1956-58 (three years).
DeYoung, John E.
1955 *Village life in modern Thailand*, Berkeley, Institute of East Asiatic Studies, University of California.
Phillips, Herbert P.
1965 *Thai peasant personality. The patterning of interpersonal behavior in the village of Bang Chan*, Berkeley, University of California Press.
091 *TIKOPIANS* in community of Matautu (12°30′S, 168°30′E) from 1928-29.
Firth, Raymond
1936 *We, the Tikopia*, London, Allen and Unwin.
092 *TIMBIRA* mostly among the Ramkokamekra subtribe in the community of Ponto (6°30′S, 45°30′W) from 1929 to 1936.
Nimuendaju, Curt
1947 "The Eastern Timbira," *University of California Publications in American Archaeology and Ethnology, 41*.
093 *TIV* in Benue Province (7°N, 9°E) from July 1949 to August 1950, 1951-52.
Bohannan, Laura, and Paul Bohannan
1953 *The Tiv of Central Nigeria*, London, International African Institute, Hazell, Watson & Viney.
094 *TRUKESE* on island of Romonum (7°N, 152°E) for four years: 1947+.
Gladwin, T., and S. B. Sarason
1953 "Truk, man in paradise," *Viking Fund Publication in Anthropology 20*.

095 *TUKUNA* in Brazil along the Solimões River (4°S, 69°W) from 1941-42.
    Nimuendaju, Curt
        1952 "The Tukuna," *University of California Publications in American Archaeology and Ethnology 45.*
096 *UMBUNDU* in Benguela Highlands of Central Angola (12°S, 16°30'E) from 1933-38.
    Childs, G. M.
        1949 *Umbundu kinship and character,* London, Oxford University Press.
097 *WICHITA* in community of Anadarko, Oklahoma (35°N, 98°W) from 1949-50.
    Schmitt, Karl, and Iva Schmitt
        n.d. *Wichita kinship—past and present,* Norman, Oklahoma, University Book Exchange.
098 *WOGEO* islanders of the Wonevara district (3°S, 144°E) in 1934.
    Hogbin, Ian
        1935 "Native culture of Wogeo," *Oceania 5:* 308-37.
        1943 "New Guinea infancy: from conception to weaning in Wogeo," *Oceania 13:* 285-309.
        1946 "A New Guinea childhood: from weaning till the eighth year in Wogeo," *Oceania 16:* 275-96.
099 *WOLEAIANS* in Ifaluk atoll in the Caroline Islands (7°N, 147°E) in 1948.
    Burrows, E. G., and M. E. Spiro
        1953 *An atoll culture: ethnography of Ifaluk in the Central Carolines,* New Haven, HRAF.
100 *YAGUANS* in northeastern Peru between Putumayo and Amazon Rivers (3°S, 72°W) from December 1940 to August 1941.
    Fejos, Paul
        1943 "Ethnography of the Yagua," *Viking Fund Publication in Anthropology 1.*
101 *YORUBA* in southwestern part of Nigeria (8°N, 4°E) from October 1930 to November 1934.
    Ward, Edward
        1936 "The parent-child relationship among the Yoruba," *Anthropological Quarterly 9:* 56-64.

TABLE A3.

Ethnographic Page References for Codes in the Cross-Cultural Survey Component of the Rejection-Acceptance Project

Part I: Adult Personality Characteristics

IBM Society #		Adult Personality Characteristics				
	Hostility	Self-Evaluation	Dependency	Emotional Responsiveness	World View	Emotional Stability
001 Akwe-Shavante	179-89, 86, 103, 304, 306, 274, 305	142		148, 86, 207	103, 287, 102, 275, 276	
002 Alorese	118, 119	151, 150, 188, 181	152, 186-88	150, 178, 79, 115	151, 169, 68, 79, 165, 189	152, 153, 157, 159, 190, 115, 118, 154
003 Americans	15, 21, 30-32, 43	144	77	18, 23	31, 35, 36	
004 Andamanese	48, 49, 50, 84, 86		47, 257, 258, 263-64, 328, 273, 322	82, 83, 240	139, 168, 299, 301, 328, 300, 327	
005 Apache, Chiricahua	406, 407, 33		75	74	213, 234, 238, 254, 29, 235, 43	
006 Apache, Western	228, 384-96, 554, 555	562	123, 125, 181	123	123, 180, 560	
007 Arab Sudanese	100, 108, 109	226		63-67, 273	137, 211	
008 Araucanians (Mapuche)	45, 69, 68, 245	66, 53		43, 62, 47, 63, 245	112, 143, 110, 140, 36	248, 124, 125

(*Continued on Next Page*)

Table A3. Continued

IBM Society #	Hostility	Self-Evaluation	Adult Personality Characteristics Dependency	Emotional Responsiveness	World View	Emotional Stability
009 Ashanti	121, 327, 135	79	366		163, 5, 26, 29, 103, 188, 16, 100, 191	326
010 Australians (rural)		42	23	25, 105		
011 Aymara	170, 180, 173, 156, 166, 161, 162	160, 171, 182	173, 182, 171	167, 172	163, 173, 174, 170, 172	173, 174, 162, 163, 157
012 Balinese	10	9		32, 84	35, 38, 13	5, 27
013 Bechuana	35, 36, 277, 278, 19			115, 173, 178, 277, 278, 146, 167	76	
014 Camayura	8, 9, 51	46	52	9	52, 54	
015 Cambodians	7, 102	316, 317			263, 268, 293	268
016 Canadians, French	41, 58, 68		72	144	99, 103, 100	137
017 Carriacou	201				144, 146	

018 Chamorros	210, 226, 227, 295, 299	226	226, 228	225	67	223, 224, 225, 226
019 Cheyenne	90, 91, 28, 54	90			85	
020 Chinese (Shantung Province)	151, 164, 63-67, 55, 163, 159, 160, 80			151, 13	45, 53, 130	
021 Chukchee	379, 142, 144, 339	144, 145	348	359, 347	415, 379, 400, 402, 417, 404	142, 145, 140, 379
022 Colombian Mestizo	106, 107, 186, 193, 189, 190, 48, 195	185, 449	212, 261	xvii, 99, 195, 191	77, 99, 102, 439, 441, 94, 212	47, 332, 259, 353, 48, 49
023 Crow	192, 62, 59, 60, 228, 215, 218-20	185	25	42, 108, 90, 172	70, 329, 334, 69, 70, 239	243, 244, 329-34
024 Dobuans	279, 137	279, 232	277, 279	278	278	
025 Dutch	167, 162, 164, 101	164, 141	100, 105, 108, 112	110, 146, 164, 168	145	140, 168, 146
026 Egyptians	63, 847			56, 51	36, 38, 84	84
027 Eskimo, Alaskan	46, 118, 37	46	78	13, 51, 50, 78, 31, 39, 607	144-46	46
028 Eskimo, Greenland	62, 65, 70, 68			62	62	
029 Fijians (Vanua Levu)	204, 248, 330, 255, 300, 203, 36, 339, 405, 6	325	244, 326, 321	135, 136, 260, 294, 295, 296, 179, 263	302, xii, 151, 281	

(Continued on Next Page)

Table A3. Continued

IBM #	Society	Hostility	Self-Evaluation	Dependency	Emotional Responsiveness	World View	Emotional Stability
				Adult Personality Characteristics			
030	Filipinos	97, 94, 111, 126		91, 92, 109		126, 127	
031	Fon (Dahomeans)	343			240, 299, 88	209	
032	French (Anjou)	87	316	156, 157, 331, 305	143, 190, 308	289	
033	French (Vaucluse)	196, 197, 212, 194		331, 205	9, 204, 205	208, 163, 214	338
034	Greeks, Modern	60, 53, 76	86, 42, 69		74, 14, 49, 84	31, 75, 42, 77, 78	
035	Guatemalan Indians		211, 190		191	211, 212, 176-80, 183	
036	Gusii	4, 11, 15, 23, 39, 74, 75, 77, 80, 91, 113, 24, 36		21, 22, 23, 77, 78	36, 64, 77, 187	40, 39, 57, 11, 63, 77, 187, 188	
037	Hopi	22	27	18		35	
038	Hupa						
039	Ilocos	53, 54, 63		48, 49, 51, 63	13, 53, 56, 57, 103, 104	57, 58, 59, 70	
040	Indians (high-caste Hindus)	46, 40, 42, 45, 68	215		39, 40, 43, 44, 49, 56, 42	48, 54, 105, 151, 40, 57, 89, 104	44, 46, 106, 215, 259, 315

041 Indians (Rajputs)	14, 15, 55, 56, 25, 23, 49, 52	12, 14, 37		32, 34, 33, 45, 85, 86	70, 71, 79, 106	
042 Indians	134, 141, 144, 145, 181, 183, 200			182, 153	93, 94, 90, 124	127, 128
043 Jamaicans	193, 204, 205	116, 172, 195, 107, 108, 193, 167, 168	116	63	116, 167	190, 191
044 Japanese	51, 116, 117, 402, 403	118, 405	47, 404	51, 83, 88, 115	123, 139, 128, 161, 119, 130, 404	162, 405
045 Javanese	136, 153, 291, 52	123	123, 125	26, 23		
046 Jews, East European	45-47	39	22, 39	38-40, 318	13	
047 Kaska	267, 278	258, 252, 306, 251	280-84	287, 311, 251		
048 Klamath				344	345	
049 Kutenay	154, 155, 126, 128, 162	32	127, 134	125, 121, 124	34	
050 Kwakiutl	112, 109, 156, 220, 229, 230, 41, 159, 218		231, 173, 232	113, 126, 112, 155	111, 152	266, 79
051 Kwoma	145, 164, 165		114	154		139, 40, 137
052 Lambas	28				243, 244	
053 Lebanese	133		133	33		

(Continued on Next Page)

Table A3. Continued

IBM Society #	Hostility	Self-Evaluation	Adult Personality Characteristics			
			Dependency	Emotional Responsiveness	World View	Emotional Stability
054 Lepcha	365, 133, 134, 135, 10, 162, 163, 275, 140	273	268, 365	256	16, 305, 111, 208, 313	269, 270
055 Malays				80, 141, 39	168, 178, 189, 169, 170, 177	
056 Malekula	44		48	36, 40, 520	45, 46	
057 Mandan	100			23, 49, 50		100
058 Manus	128, 126	15, 38		61, 62, 98	16, 68, 75, 70	37
059 Maori	89, 63	82, 89, 141	85	90, 78	100	100, 79, 96
060 Mende	36			74		
061 Mixtecans	68, 69, 111, 21, 71, 64, 67		42, 68, 41, 70	41, 68	20, 67	22
062 Muria	400, 448			xii, 69, 447, 68, 67, 367	138, 147, 180, 181, 146	170, 172, 181
063 Naron	156, 158, 154			92, 93, 75	166, 171, 178, 189, 191, 192, 289	
064 Navaho	95, 96, 396, 170, 169		171	96, 51	125, 126, 223, 127, 128, 147, 223	96, 111, 113, 170, 173
065 New Ire-landers		297	331		324	59

	1	2	3	4	5	6
066 Ngoni	152, 170		152, 62, 65	155, 156	64	170
067 Nuer	133, 143, 2, 52, 54				42	
068 Nyakyusa	136-51, 14, 56, 80, 89, 103, 108	11, 133, 28		66, 163, 196, 68, 75	91, 57, 74, 78, 92, 163, 104	133
069 Ojibwa	97, 99, 100			109, 43, 114, 113, 35, 97, 112	9, 44, 60, 78, 107, 61, 72, 73	
070 Okinawans	55, 87, 23, 39, 45, 86		68, 75, 55	22, 23, 47, 50, 5	7, 66, 74, 67	36, 5, 77, 82, 83
071 Paiute (Harney Valley)	69-70	74, 69, 81, 94	68, 31	73	33	70
072 Palauans	13	15, 16, 17	12, 15	14, 5, 13	10, 11, 5	15, 13
073 Papago	100, 77, 103, 90, 166	226	52, 53, 54, 198, 226	56, 65, 167	77, 78, 80, 202, 204, 205	27
074 Paraguayans	212, 207, 246			202, 201	249, 250, 246	
075 Potawatomi, Prairie						
076 Puerto Ricans	56, 57, 67, 114	48, 97, 233	65, 81, 80, 94, 223, 91	169, 194	40, 96, 39, 194	69
077 Samoans			78	215, 10, 73	92, 93	207, 208, 157, 206

(*Continued on Next Page*)

Table A3. Continued

IBM Society #	Hostility	Self-Evaluation	Dependency	Adult Personality Characteristics Emotional Responsiveness	World View	Emotional Stability
078 Serbs	285	292, 293, 284		160, 285, 293	232	
079 Sherente	75, 50, 80	32, 91	85		84	
080 Sioux (Teton-Dakota)	84, 156	120	57, 58	54, 55, 201	89	204, 190
081 Siriono	39, 60, 61, 62, 49, 57		98	98, 36, 38	86, 44, 90	
082 Siuai	411	79	239	36, 333	74, 66	
083 Soga	78, 82	807	81	78		
084 Sotho (Basuto)	18, 94, 280, 69, 90	113		69, 88-90	113-15, 119, 289, 129	
085 Taiwanese	171, 189			58, 59, 171, 172, 173, 201	173, 174, 175	174
086 Tallensi	33, 37, 83, 127		79, 89, 147, 171, 172	37		
087 Tanala	275, 277, 280, 279, 281, 256, 265, 276, 329, 300, 314			265	266, 267, 288, 272, 274, 337	291, 298, 286, 287
088 Tenetehara	24		30	15	30, 98, 99, 102	
089 Tepoztecans	293, 294, 295, 296	49, 302, 303	48, 49, 58, 59, 297	287, 289, 310, 292, 297	275, 292, 297, 302	295, 313, 314, 302

090 Thai	187, 174, 80, 172	75, 155, 184, 202	23, 78, 86, 157, 181, 206	32, 38, 88, 54, 90, 91, 27, 23, 26, 40, 67, 79	143, 38, 31	206, 176
091 Tikopians	18, 50, 75, 74, 53	18		17, 18, 64, 128, 189		
092 Timbira, Eastern	113, 119, 159, 130		84	101, 100, 104		
093 Tiv	25			48	82, 85, 86	
094 Trukese	14, 8-50, 228, 238, 95, 145, 148, 224	137, 234, 235, 46	47, 139, 146, 147, 226, 237, 145	228, 242	149, 145, 69, 149	145, 146, 225, 229
095 Tukuna	50-57, 64, 65			53	70, 52, 53	30-51, 53
096 Umbundu (Mbundu)	56, 57, 130, 124, 125, 60, 128, 13, 60		39	128, 129, 32		124
097 Wichita	47			47, 49		
098 Wogeo	317, 328, 314, 315		320, 317	194, 317	330, 327	314, 330
099 Woleaians (Ifaluk)	278, 281, 282, 121, 122	121	159	164	121, 213	172, 171
100 Yaguans	81, 83	106, 111		87, 110	96, 97	108, 89
101 Yoruba						

TABLE A3.

Ethnographic Page References for Codes in the Cross-Cultural Survey Component of the Rejection-Acceptance Project

Part II: Rejection-Acceptance and Child Personality Characteristics

IBM #	Society	Rejection-Acceptance Overall	Child Personality Characteristics		
			Hostility	Self-Evaluation	Dependency
001	Akwe-Shavante	67, 69, 70	68, 71, 73		
002	Alorese		48, 54, 51, 40, 41, 43, 47, 178	52, 181-83	46, 51, 177, 181
003	Americans		31, 52, 90, 94, 102, 103, 76, 101, 104		97, 102
004	Andamanese				
005	Apache, Chiricahua	32, 33, 155, 74			
006	Apache, Western			452	
007	Arab Sudanese	225	108, 109	226	
008	Araucanians (Mapuche)		53-55	53, 244	
009	Ashanti				
010	Australians (rural)				
011	Aymara	164, 165	166, 164, 165	166	164, 182, 183
012	Balinese		33, 40, 13		33, 41
013	Bechuana		248		19, 247
014	Camayura		64, 68	63	

No.	Society				
015	Cambodians	263			
016	Canadians, French	170			
017	Carriacou	94, 99			
018	Chamorros	63, 65	63		
019	Cheyenne				
020	Chinese (Shantung Province)				
021	Chukchee	452	144, 452	144	
022	Colombian Mestizo		87, 97, 98, 92, 102		98, 97
023	Crow				
024	Dobuans			274	274
025	Dutch	91	88	91	
026	Egyptians	111, 166	109		
027	Eskimo, Alaskan	42	37, 42		
028	Eskimo, Greenland	72, 75	72, 75		
029	Fijians (Vanua Levu)	282, 284	308		316
030	Filipinos	79	79		73, 72, 82
031	Fon (Dahomeans)			274	
032	French (Anjou)				
033	French (Vaucluse)		49, 54, 50		54
034	Greeks, Modern	78, 79	79		

(Continued on Next Page)

Table A3. Continued

IBM #	Society	Rejection-Acceptance Overall	Child Personality Characteristics		
			Hostility	Self-Evaluation	Dependency
035	Guatemalan Indians	184	208		208
036	Gusii		137, 134		134, 135, 145, 127
037	Hopi		190	190	83
038	Hupa	17			17
039	Ilocos		136, 138, 141	139	139, 138, 145
040	Indians (high-caste Hindus)	158	157		
041	Indians (Rajputs)		136, 137, 138		130
042	Indians	148, 193	194		
043	Jamaicans		71, 50, 51		68-70
044	Japanese	168	51, 168, 169 170		402
045	Javanese		117	111, 113, 152	34
046	Jews, East European	438, 70, 71	76, 77, 87, 92, 74		73, 74, 78, 431, 213-17
047	Kaska		187, 184	307, 310, 311, 189	308, 188, 309
048	Klamath		342		
049	Kutenay	116, 118, 128			
050	Kwakiutl		161, 169, 168, 197	37, 62	
051	Kwoma		36, 58, 59		34, 52

052	Lambas	65, 66, 70			
053	Lebanese				136
054	Lepcha	302, 306, 400		254	
055	Malays				
056	Malekula				
057	Mandan		50, 51, 49		
058	Mamus		60, 78, 123	15, 38	52, 75, 38
059	Maori		94	78, 149, 129	41
060	Mende				
061	Mixtecans			109	105, 106
062	Muria	76			76
063	Naron	117			
064	Navaho		3, 35, 42, 176, 36, 97	33	32, 36, 38
065	New Irelanders	90	84, 85, 86, 82, 87	89, 297, 305	
066	Ngoni		84, 85-87, 82		
067	Nuer				
068	Nyakyusa				
069	Ojibwa		99		28, 29
070	Okinawans	94	109, 111, 113, 128, 118, 115, 127		109, 110, 111, 121

(*Continued on Next Page*)

Table A3. Continued

IBM #	Society	Rejection-Acceptance Overall	Child Personality Characteristics		
			Hostility	Self-Evaluation	Dependency
071	Paiute (Harney Valley)		68-71		105, 31
072	Palauans	4-5	4-7		4, 5, 7
073	Papago		200, 133, 161		139, 226
074	Paraguayans	222, 223, 219	222, 223		
075	Potawatomi, Prairie		37, 48, 50, 140, 38, 39, 40		56, 38
076	Puerto Ricans		114, 115, 161, 163, 164, 116, 241		94, 99, 141, 223 120, 138, 65
077	Samoans	209	27		59, 25, 63
078	Serbs	174	176	175	
079	Sherente				
080	Sioux (Teton-Dakota)	56, 182	137, 138, 194		
081	Siriono	95	77		98
082	Siuai		190	191	191-93
083	Soga		82, 83		82, 81
084	Sotho (Basuto)	35, 43	38, 35, 37, 46		46
085	Taiwanese	188			
086	Tallensi		247		172, 245, 190
087	Tanala				263

No.	Group				
088	Tenetehara	75, 76			
089	Tepoztecans		378, 344, 337, 379, 199, 333, 377		333, 418
090	Thai	54	35		85
091	Tikopians	143	158		142
092	Timbira		111		
093	Tiv				
094	Trukese	234	84, 85, 235, 262, 260	235	235, 260, 237
095	Tukuna		50, 5, 72		
096	Unbundu (Mbundu)		124, 128		98
097	Wichita	47, 48	50		
098	Wogeo		291	280, 286	291, 292
099	Woleaians (Ifaluk)	257, 274, 275, 258	258, 263, 271, 276, 272, 275		258, 275, 272
100	Yaguans		72		
101	Yoruba				

TABLE A4. Rank Ordering by Distance of 101 Societies in the Rejection-Acceptance Project Sample

Society	Geographical Region*	Cultural Area	Distance in Statute Miles between Societies
1. Mende	A	Guinea Coast	
			695
2. Tallensi	A	Western Sudan	
			230
3. Ashanti	A	Guinea Coast	
			205
4. Fon (Dahomeans)	A	Guinea Coast	
			520
5. Tiv	A	Nigerian Plateau	
			1,520
6. Nuer	A	Upper Nile	
			500
7. Arab Sudanese	CM	Muslim Sudan	
			615
8. Egyptians	CM	North Africa	
			540
9. Jews, East European	CM	Overseas Europeans	
			150
10. Lebanese	CM	Semitic Near East	
			1,875
11. Yoruba	A	Guinea Coast	
			1,000
12. Gusii	A	Northeast Bantu	
			215
13. Soga	A	Northeast Bantu	
			670
14. Nyakyusa	A	Northeast Bantu	
			245
15. Ngoni	A	Central Bantu	
			1,060
16. Tanala	EE	Indian Ocean	
			1,380
17. Lambas	A	Central Bantu	
			815
18. Umbundu (Mbundu)	A	South African Bantu	
			775
19. Naron	A	African Hunters	
			1,130
20. Bechuana	A	South African Bantu	
			320
21. Sotho (Basuto)	A	South African Bantu	
			4,705
22. Greeks, Modern	CM	South Europe	
			380
23. Serbs	CM	East Europe	
			660
24. French (Vaucluse)	CM	Northwest Europe	
			395
25. French (Anjou)	CM	Northwest Europe	
			270
26. Dutch	CM	Northwest Europe	
			8,505
27. Indians (Rajputs)	EE	North and Central India	
			230
28. Muria	EE	South India	
			275
29. Indians (high-caste Hindu)	EE	North and Central India	
			590
30. Indians	EE	North and Central India	
			845
31. Lepcha	EE	Himalayas	
			1,205
32. Andamanese	EE	Indian Ocean	
			625
33. Malays	EE	Southeast Asia	
			485
34. Cambodians	EE	Southeast Asia	
			375
35. Thai	EE	Southeast Asia	
			1,490
36. Taiwanese	EE	East Asia	
			540
37. Okinawans	EE	East Asia	
			810

Table A4. Continued

Society	Geographical Region	Cultural Area	Distance in Statute Miles between Societies
38. Chinese (Shantung Province)	EE	East Asia	850
39. Japanese	EE	East Asia	1,630
40. Ilocos	IP	Philippines and Formosa	455
41. Filipinos	IP	Philippines and Formosa	1,400
42. Balinese	IP	Western Indonesia	370
43. Javanese	IP	Western Indonesia	1,095
44. Alorese	IP	Eastern Indonesia	1,470
45. Kwoma	IP	New Guinea	140
46. Wogeo	IP	New Guinea	995
47. Palauans	IP	Micronesia	700
48. Woleaians	IP	Micronesia	645
49. Chamorros	IP	Micronesia	725
50. Trukese	IP	Micronesia	745
51. Manus	IP	Western Melanesia	430
52. New Irelanders	IP	Western Melanesia	305
53. Siuai	IP	Western Melanesia	395
54. Dobuans	IP	Western Melanesia	1,355
55. Tikopians	IP	Western Polynesia	255
56. Samoans	IP	Western Polynesia	270
57. Malekula	IP	Eastern Melanesia	695
58. Fijians	IP	Eastern Melanesia	1,300
59. Maori	IP	Eastern Polynesia	1,905
60. Australians (rural)	CM	Overseas Europeans	8,090
61. Araucanians	SA	Chile and Patagonia	1,150
62. Paraguayans	SA	Gran Chaco	670
63. Siriono	SA	Interior Amazon	310
64. Aymara	SA	Andes	1,020
65. Camayura	SA	Mato Grosso	210
66. Akwe-Shavante	SA	Mato Grosso	350
67. Sherente	SA	Eastern Brazil	235
68. Timbira	SA	Eastern Brazil	255
69. Tenetehara	SA	Eastern Brazil	1,600
70. Tukuna	SA	Interior Amazon	215
71. Yaguans	SA	Interior Amazon	860
72. Colombian Mestizo	SA	Carribean	900

(*Continued on Next Page*)

Table A4. Continued

Society	Geographical Region	Cultural Area	Distance in Statute Miles between Societies
73. Carriacou	SA	Carribean	535
74. Puerto Ricans	SA	Carribean	710
75. Jamaicans	SA	Carribean	750
76. Guatemalan Indians	SA	Central America	505
77. Mixtecans	NA	Central Mexico	140
78. Tepoztecans	NA	Central Mexico	1,120
79. Papago	NA	Northwest Mexico	170
80. Apache, Chiricahua	NA	Southwest	285
81. Apache, Western	NA	Southwest	160
82. Hopi	NA	Southwest	100
83. Navaho	NA	Southwest	325
84. Cheyenne	NA	Plains	470
85. Wichita	NA	Prairie	570
86. Sioux	NA	Plains	370
87. Crow	NA	Plains	810
88. Mandan	NA	Plains	425
89. Ojibwa	NA	Prairie	640
90. Potawatomi, Prairie	NA	Arctic America	600
91. Canadians, French	CM	Overseas Europeans	280
92. Americans	CM	Overseas Europeans	2,070
93. Eskimo, Greenland	NA	Arctic America	3,300
94. Chukchee	EE	Arctic Asia	1,230
95. Eskimo, Alaskan	NA	Arctic America	1,250
96. Kaska	NA	Arctic America	570
97. Kwakiutl	NA	Northwest Coast	430
98. Kutenay	NA	Great Basin and Plateau	470
99. Paiute (Harney Valley)	NA	Great Basin and Plateau	160
100. Klamath	NA	California	240
101. Hupa	NA	Northwest Coast (California)	

Geographical Region
A = Africa
CM = Circum Mediterranean
EE = East Eurasia
IP = Insular Pacific
NA = North America
SA = South America

TABLE A5. Linked Pair Test: Societal Scores

Society	R/A Value	Y Score
1. Tallensi	8	Y_1
2. Fon (Dahomeans)	7	Y_2
3. Nuer	10	Y_2
4. Arab Sudanese	9	Y_1
5. Egyptians	5	Y_1
6. Jews, East European	7	Y_1
7. Lebanese	6	Y_2
8. Yoruba	10	Y_1
9. Gusii	5	Y_2
10. Soga	9	Y_2
11. Ngoni	8	Y_2
12. Tanala	8	Y_2
13. Umbundu (Mbundu)	8	Y_2
14. Naron	10	Y_1
15. Bechuana	7	Y_1
16. Sotho (Basuto)	2	Y_1
17. Greeks, Modern	7	Y_2
18. Serbs	10	Y_2
19. French (Vaucluse)	9	Y_2
20. Dutch	9	Y_1
21. Indians (Rajputs)	4	Y_2
22. Muria	9	Y_1
23. Indians (high-caste Hindu)	4	Y_1
24. Indians	6	Y_1
25. Lepcha	6	Y_2
26. Andamanese	9	Y_2
27. Malays	8	Y_2
28. Cambodians	8	Y_2
29. Thai	8	Y_1
30. Taiwanese	7	Y_2
31. Okinawans	8	Y_2
32. Chinese (Shantung Province)	10	Y_1
33. Japanese	4	Y_1
34. Ilocos	3	Y_2
35. Filipinos	8	Y_1
36. Balinese	4	Y_2
37. Javanese	9	Y_1
38. Alorese	4	Y_1
39. Kwoma	5	Y_2
40. Wogeo	9	Y_1
41. Palauans	2	Y_1
42. Woleaians	2	Y_1
43. Chamorros	4	Y_1
44. Trukese	4	Y_1
45. Manus	6	Y_2

(*Continued on Next Page*)

Table A5. Continued

Society	R/A Value	Y Score
46. New Irelanders	8	Y_2
47. Siuai	8	Y_1
48. Dobuans	4	Y_2
49. Tikopians	10	Y_2
50. Samoans	8	Y_2
51. Fijians	10	Y_1
52. Maori	4	Y_2
53. Australians (rural)	10	Y_2
54. Araucanians	10	Y_2
55. Paraguayans	10	Y_1
56. Siriono	6	Y_1
57. Aymara	2	Y_2
58. Camayura	8	Y_2
59. Akwe-Shavante	8	Y_1
60. Sherente	7	Y_2
61. Timbira	8	Y_2
62. Tenetehara	8	Y_1
63. Yaguans	7	Y_1
64. Colombian Mestizo	2	Y_1
65. Puerto Ricans	5	Y_2
66. Jamaicans	8	Y_1
67. Guatemalan Indians	4	Y_1
68. Mextecans	7	Y_1
69. Tepoztecans	4	Y_2
70. Papago	10	Y_1
71. Apache, Chiricahua	7	Y_1
72. Apache, Western	7	Y_2
73. Hopi	8	Y_2
74. Navaho	8	Y_2
75. Cheyenne	9	Y_2
76. Wichita	9	Y_2
77. Sioux	8	Y_2
78. Crow	8	Y_2
79. Mandan	9	Y_1
80. Potawatomi	6	Y_2
81. Canadians, French	10	Y_1
82. Americans	7	Y_2
83. Eskimo, Greenland	10	Y_2
84. Eskimo, Alaskan	9	Y_1
85. Kaska	5	Y_2
86. Kwakiutl	9	Y_2
87. Kutenay	8	Y_2
88. Paiute	9	Y_2
89. Klamath	8	Y_2
90. Hupa	8	—

Total mean = 7.14

TABLE A6. Linked Pair Test: Mean Values for Y_1 and Y_2

39 Y_1 *Societies' values*		50 Y_2 *Societies' values*		
8	Total Y_1 value = 273	7	8	Total Y_2 value = 362
9		10	8	
5	Y_1 mean = 7.0	6	7	Y_2 mean = 7.24
7		5	6	
10	N = 39	9	10	N = 50
10		8	5	
7		8	9	
2		8	8	
9		7	9	
9		10	8	
4		9		
6		4		
8		6		
10		9		
4		8		
8		8		
9		7		
4		8		
9		3		
2		4		
2		5		
4		6		
4		8		
8		4		
10		10		
10		8		
6		4		
8		10		
8		10		
7		2		
2		8		
8		7		
4		8		
7		5		
10		4		
7		7		
9		8		
10		8		
9		9		
		9		

TABLE A7.   Raters' Instructions for the Analysis of Socialization Practices
Relating to Parental Rejection and Acceptance, and Their
Consequences for Personality Development

GENERAL INSTRUCTIONS

All ratings are to be made on a five-point scale. In general, the scales
are designed to measure the amount or intensity of some phenomenon,
where a rating of *1* means low and a rating of *5* means high (e.g. self-
reliance, where *1* means low self-reliance and *5* means high self-reliance).
If an exceptionally deviant case appears after standards are well set, it
should be given a rating lower than *1* (e.g. *0*, −*1*) or higher than *5* (e.g.
6, 7).

Each entry should be marked with one of two degrees of confidence.
Reasonably satisfactory evidence can be recorded by a plain entry, e.g. *4*.
Doubtful, ambiguous, or inconsistent evidence should be recorded by
placing parentheses around the entry, e.g. *(4)*. If insufficient information
is available to make a rating, record the letter *N* (None).

Write in clarifying remarks whenever they appear useful. Expanded
notes may be recorded on the back of the code sheet. Also record the
page number(s) where information for each rating occurs. Write the major
bibliographic sources used for each set of ratings on the back of each
code sheet. Be sure to include the date of publication and, whenever possible, the time period during which fieldwork was conducted. When
possible, you should also record the major community (or specific area)
where the fieldwork was carried out. When using the HRAF, identify the
author according to his discipline and evaluation of the source (identification is given in code at the top of the HRAF file slip).
Use the following format:

Author
date *Title*, place of publication
Fieldwork: (dates)
Community: (specify name or at least general location)
Identification: (discipline of author and evaluation of his work)

Following is an example of this format:

Bateson, Gregory, and Margaret Mead
1942 *Balinese Character*, New York; New York Academy of Sciences.
Fieldwork: 1938-1940
Community: Bajoeng Gede
Identification: E-5

PARENTAL REJECTION AND ACCEPTANCE

The rating emphasis for the rejection-acceptance (R-A) dimension is to
be placed on early childhood, i.e. the period from approximately two to
six years or for as long before two or after six years as the treatment of
the child remains approximately constant. Infancy (approximately the first
two years) and later childhood (approximately seven years and older) are
not to be emphasized in the rating. If a child is given warm, affectionate
attention during the first part of early childhood and then, later during the
period, the parents withdraw warmth and affection—the parent-child

Table A7. Continued

relationship becoming more or less consistently marked by rejection—the major emphasis is to be placed on the later time period.

Two sets of scales are provided for rating parental behavior:

I. *Parental Behavior* (Scale I, Variables 1-4)

In some societies parents behave differently (in terms of R-A) toward their sons and daughters. Some mothers, for example, tend to accept their sons but not their daughters; the same may be true of fathers as well as other socializing agents (specify which). Wherever such differences are found, make the appropriate rating in the cells provided (Variables 1-3).

Often no clear distinction can be made in the behavior of mothers toward their sons and daughters; the same may be true regarding fathers and other caretakers. In such cases you should record a rating in the column marked *both* (Variables 1-3); otherwise this column should not be used.

Ethnographers sometimes write about *parental* behavior toward children, boys and girls; they do not distinguish the behavior of mothers from the behavior of fathers, but they do distinguish *parental* behavior toward sons from *parental* behavior toward daughters. In these cases, you are to mark your rating in the *boys-girls* cells provided for variable 4 (overall rating).

You will find that in many cases no sharp distinction can be made between maternal and paternal behavior toward either boys or girls. In order to maintain consistency throughout the ratings you should make an overall rating (variable 4) in the column marked *both* for every society. This rating represents the average or typical (global) behavior of *parents* toward their *children*.

II. *Importance of Socializing Agent* (Scale II, Variables 5-7)

The relative importance of each parent—and any other significant caretaker, e.g. older sibling—as socializing agent is to be rated on a five-point scale where a rating of *1* means *negligible* and a rating of *5* means *exclusive*.

The same general procedures are to be followed in Scale II as in Scale I. Wherever possible, rate mothers, fathers, and others (specify) individually for their importance as socializing agents for boys *and* for girls. Use the column marked *both* only in those cases where no clear distinction can be made regarding the importance of these caretakers as socializing agents for their sons *and* daughters.

The importance of mothers as socializing agents can usually be discriminated from the importance of fathers and others. If insufficient evidence is available to make a rating for the latter two, write the letter *N* in the columns marked *both*.

III. *Child Development* (Scale III, Variables 8-12)

Each of the five variables in Scale III is described in "Definition of the Scales." The same general procedures are to be followed in coding this scale as were used in the preceding scales.

IV. *Adult Personality* (Scale IV, Variables 13-20)

Each of the eight variables in Scale IV is also defined in "Definition of the Scales." Again, the same general procedures are to be used in coding this scale as were used in coding the preceding scales.

TABLE A8.   Scales I-III: Parental Behavior and Child Personality

RATER _____

DATE _____

SOCIETY _____

SCALE I.   PARENTAL BEHAVIOR
(Rejection-Acceptance)

boys	girls	both

1. Mother
2. Father
3. Other (specify)
4. Overall rating

SCALE II.   IMPORTANCE OF SOCIALIZING AGENT

5. Mother
6. Father
7. Other (specify)

SCALE III.   CHILD DEVELOPMENT

8. Hostility, aggression, or passive aggression
9. Self-evaluation
10. Self-reliance
11. Achievement
12. Dependence

TABLE A9. Scale IV: Adult Personality

RATER _____

DATE _____

SOCIETY _____

male	female	both		
			13.	Hostility, aggression, or passive aggression
			14.	Self-evaluation
			15.	Self-reliance
			16.	Achievement
			17.	Dependence
			18.	Emotional responsiveness
			19.	Evaluation of the world (world view)
			20.	Emotional stability

TABLE A10. Societies and Variables Coded in the Rejection-Acceptance Project

| IBM No. | Society | Parental Behavior | | | Personality Characteristics | | | | | | | | | | | | |
| | | | | | Children | | | | | Adults | | | | | | | |
		Rejection-Acceptance	Hostility	Neglect	Hostility	Self-evaluation	Self-reliance	Achievement	Dependence	Hostility	Self-evaluation	Self-reliance	Achievement	Dependence	Emotional responsiveness	World view	Emotional stability
001	Akwe-Shavante	8	4	5	9	0	9	0	0	10	9	9	10	0	9	6	0
002	Alorese	4	7	8	7	3	2	0	9	9	2	0	10	9	3	3	3
003	Americans	7	6	5	8	0	6	0	8	5	9	9	9	0	7	7	0
004	Andamanese	9	2	2	0	0	3	8	0	6	0	6	0	8	8	4	0
005	Apache, Chiricahua	7	4	4	0	0	9	0	0	8	0	8	8	0	4	5	0
006	Apache, Western	7	5	5	0	8	3	0	0	8	0	3	8	10	0	4	0
007	Arab Sudanese	9	4	8	8	8	8	0	0	8	10	8	8	0	8	7	0
008	Araucanians (Mapuche)	10	2	2	5	9	3	0	0	5	10	8	8	0	9	8	9
009	Ashanti	0	—	—	0	0	9	0	0	0	0	8	0	0	0	3	4
010	Australians (rural)	10	4	0	0	0	0	8	0	0	8	8	8	0	4	0	0
011	Aymara	2	10	7	9	3	4	0	10	10	3	8	5	10	2	2	2
012	Balinese	4	10	8	7	0	8	0	9	2	0	0	3	9	2	5	4
013	Bechuana	7	5	3	2	0	8	0	2	8	0	0	8	2	8	4	0
014	Camayura	8	3	2	2	0	7	0	0	2	0	7	7	7	10	7	10
015	Cambodians	8	4	4	0	0	0	0	0	3	4	7	8	0	0	6	0
016	Canadians, French	10	0	4	0	0	7	0	0	2	0	4	8	0	8	8	0
017	Carriacou	0	—	—	0	0	0	0	0	4	0	8	4	0	0	4	0
018	Chamorros	4	8	7	10	0	9	9	0	8	2	4	10	10	0	4	3

019	Cheyenne	9	8	9	4	9	7	9	7	4	9	8	0	0	2	3	9
020	Chinese (Shantung Province)	0	7	8	0	10	7	0	8	0	0	4	0	0	4	4	7
021	Chukchee	4	2	8	0	10	10	0	8	0	0	10	0	0	—	—	0
022	Colombian Mestizo	2	2	2	8	7	0	4	10	8	10	9	0	12	10	10	2
023	Crow	0	2	10	0	9	7	0	8	0	10	8	0	0	0	0	8
024	Dobuans	5	3	5	0	8	7	0	10	5	0	5	0	9	0	9	4
025	Dutch	0	0	5	10	8	4	4	5	0	0	4	0	2	4	2	9
026	Egyptians	4	4	8	0	10	4	0	8	0	10	7	0	9	10	7	5
027	Eskimo, Alaskan	0	8	6	0	6	9	0	5	0	0	4	0	3	2	3	9
028	Eskimo, Greenland	10	0	0	0	7	10	0	10	0	0	0	0	0	2	2	10
029	Fijians (Vanua Levu)	0	5	9	9	9	9	8	2	8	0	8	0	2	4	3	10
030	Filipinos	0	8	0	4	3	8	0	5	0	2	4	0	5	4	5	8
031	Fon (Dahomeans)	0	4	0	0	8	4	0	0	0	8	0	0	0	0	0	7
032	French (Anjou)	0	8	10	7	10	9	0	8	2	8	0	0	0	—	—	0
033	French (Vaucluse)	0	3	9	8	0	9	0	7	0	0	10	0	6	5	0	9
034	Greeks, Modern	8	4	3	0	10	8	9	6	0	0	0	0	8	0	6	7
035	Guatemalan Indians	0	3	9	0	8	9	8	8	9	6	8	0	10	5	7	4
036	Gusii	4	3	0	8	4	8	0	8	6	0	5	9	8	7	6	5
037	Hopi	0	5	3	7	7	0	0	3	0	5	6	0	3	3	2	8
038	Hupa	8	0	7	0	0	0	0	0	10	8	8	0	0	2	2	8
039	Ilocos	0	6	8	10	5	4	0	7	0	6	8	0	8	7	5	3
040	Indians (high-caste Hindus)	4	8	2	0	8	9	4	10	0	0	8	0	0	6	6	4
041	Indians (Rajputs)	0	3	10	0	9	3	9	8	8	0	3	0	4	6	7	4
042	Indians	0	3	7	0	8	8	0	9	0	8	0	0	8	5	5	6

(Continued on Next Page)

TABLE A10. Societies and Variables Coded in the Rejection-Acceptance Project

IBM No.	Society	Parental Behavior			Children					Adults							
		Rejection-Acceptance	Hostility	Neglect	Hostility	Self-evaluation	Self-reliance	Achievement	Dependence	Hostility	Self-evaluation	Self-reliance	Achievement	Dependence	Emotional responsiveness	World view	Emotional stability
043	Jamaicans	8	—	—	3	0	3	0	9	7	8	3	8	8	5	5	5
044	Japanese	4	5	7	9	0	4	8	0	4	0	8	8	0	9	8	9
045	Javanese	9	3	2	4	0	0	0	9	6	4	5	8	8	0	0	0
046	Jews, East European	7	6	6	7	0	10	8	10	0	0	4	8	0	0	0	0
047	Kaska	5	5	7	4	10	10	0	9	4	6	10	9	8	2	7	0
048	Klamath	8	0	0	0	0	4	10	0	0	0	0	8	0	8	4	0
049	Kutenay	8	0	0	0	0	10	0	0	4	0	8	8	0	9	0	0
050	Kwakiutl	9	4	7	8	0	9	0	0	7	0	8	4	8	4	0	4
051	Kwoma	5	7	7	8	0	7	8	7	9	0	7	8	6	7	4	4
052	Lambas	0	—	—	0	0	9	8	0	4	0	8	0	0	0	0	0
053	Lebanese	6	5	5	0	0	8	0	4	0	0	0	0	10	8	5	4
054	Lepcha	6	6	5	0	0	6	0	0	4	7	9	4	4	8	5	0
055	Malays	8	2	2	0	0	8	8	0	0	0	10	9	0	8	6	0
056	Malekula	0	—	—	0	0	8	0	0	0	0	3	10	0	8	0	0
057	Mandan	9	2	2	4	0	0	0	0	4	0	5	8	0	8	8	0
058	Manus	6	5	5	8	10	10	0	8	8	0	9	10	0	3	0	10
059	Maori	4	10	8	6	2	8	3	3	8	2	8	2	9	3	8	4
060	Mende	0	—	—	0	0	0	0	0	9	0	8	9	0	8	0	0

061 Mixtecans	7	0	5	3	0	8	0	7	4	0	9	4	8	8	7	0
062 Muria	9	2	2	0	0	9	0	8	4	0	0	0	0	10	8	0
063 Naron	10	2	2	8	0	9	0	0	6	0	8	8	0	8	6	0
064 Navaho	8	6	5	4	0	8	0	8	8	0	6	7	0	5	2	2
065 New Irelanders	8	3	3	4	0	9	6	6	3	9	5	9	5	10	9	8
066 Ngoni	8	3	2	0	0	8	8	0	0	0	6	0	0	10	0	10
067 Nuer	10	3	2	0	0	0	0	0	5	0	6	9	2	0	0	0
068 Nyakyusa	0			6	0	0	0	0	5	0	8	9	0	8	3	0
069 Ojibwa	0			8	0	8	0	8	0	0	10	9	0	8	6	0
070 Okinawans	8	5	5	8	0	10	2	0	3	0	8	7	8	10	4	9
071 Paiute (Harney Valley)	9	8	5	8	0	4	8	8	8	3	5	8	8	0	4	4
072 Palauans	2	6	7	10	0	0	0	10	9	3	2	10	10	2	3	3
073 Papago	10	3	3	3	0	9	2	2	3	0	6	4	4	8	4	8
074 Paraguayans	10	4	3	7	0	9	0	0	7	0	8	5	0	9	0	0
075 Potawatomi, Prairie	6	6	6	6	0	9	7	3	0	0	0	0	0	0	0	0
076 Puerto Ricans	5	6	6	7	8	4	4	10	7	9	8	4	9	5	5	0
077 Samoans	8	0	6	0	0	10	2	8	0	0	0	9	0	8	4	10
078 Serbs	10	2	3	0	0	10	0	0	0	8	8	9	0	7	8	0
079 Sherente	7	0	0	0	0	8	8	0	7	0	8	8	5	5	4	7
080 Sioux (Teton Dakota)	8	4	4	8	0	8	3	0	8	4	0	0	8	4	0	0
081 Siriono	6	3	4	7	0	8	0	8	7	0	9	6	2	4	3	0
082 Siuai	8	3	2	8	0	4	9	10	5	0	7	9	6	6	4	0
083 Soga	9	4	0	8	0	0	0	7	7	0	8	8	0	0	0	0
084 Sotho (Basuto)	2	6	7	0	0	0	8	0	8	0	6	8	0	9	6	0
085 Taiwanese	10	2	2	0	0	6	0	0	0	0	7	8	0	10	4	0

(*Continued on Next Page*)

Table A10. Continued

IBM No.	Society	Parental Behavior Rejection-Acceptance	Hostility	Neglect	Children Hostility	Self-evaluation	Self-reliance	Achievement	Dependence	Adults Hostility	Self-evaluation	Self-reliance	Achievement	Dependence	Emotional responsiveness	World view	Emotional stability
086	Tallensi	8	2	2	6	0	0	0	8	0	0	4	0	8	9	8	0
087	Tanala	8	4	0	0	0	9	0	0	9	0	9	10	0	8	6	6
088	Tenetehara	8	2	3	0	0	9	0	0	0	0	7	0	0	8	4	0
089	Tepoztecans	4	7	6	8	0	4	0	8	8	8	9	5	8	2	4	2
090	Thai	8	2	5	2	0	7	0	0	5	9	10	0	4	7	4	9
091	Tikopians	10	3	3	6	0	8	0	8	5	0	5	8	0	10	0	0
092	Timbira, Eastern	8	3	4	0	0	8	0	0	2	0	5	0	8	8	0	0
093	Tiv	0	—	—	0	0	0	0	0	8	0	8	6	0	8	4	0
094	Trukese	4	6	6	8	4	4	0	9	8	3	9	3	9	3	4	4
095	Tukuna	0	—	—	10	0	9	0	0	10	0	9	0	0	8	3	2
096	Umbundu (Mbundu)	8	4	4	4	0	8	8	2	7	0	6	8	0	10	0	9
097	Wichita	9	0	5	4	0	8	0	0	7	0	8	0	0	8	0	0
098	Wogeo	9	3	2	10	0	9	7	10	10	0	8	9	0	9	7	2
099	Woleaians (Ifaluk)	2	6	8	10	0	9	5	9	2	9	6	4	0	0	0	0
100	Yaguans	7	2	3	2	0	9	0	0	2	8	8	3	0	8	5	7
101	Yoruba	10	2	2	0	0	8	10	0	0	0	0	10	0	0	0	0

KEY TO CODES

"—" means no attempt was made to code the variable.

"0" means unable to code the variable.

TABLE A11. Heterorater Matrix: Uncorrected Ratings

Rater 1

Trait	A_1	B_1	C_1	D_1	E_1	F_1	G_1	H_1	I_1	J_1	K_1	L_1	M_1	N_1
A_2	(.78)	-.59	.68	.09	-.06	-.23	-.45	.43	.02	.16	-.25	.46	.18	.46
B_2	-.39	(.85)	-.44	.10	.35	.30	.54	-.09	.18	.03	.15	-.28	-.30	-.46
C_2	.67	-.69	(.94)	.38	.19	.19	-.65	.80	.02	.77	-.77	.62	.58	.34
D_2	.14	.02	.13	(.67)	-.15	-.26	-.14	-.07	.21	.07	-.09	.10	.13	.15
E_2	.26	.11	.57	.07	(.70)	.04	-.07	-.03	.08	.53	.06	.47	.10	.03
F_2	-.19	.49	.14	-.21	.13	(.52)	.02	.00	-.24	.21	-.05	-.19	-.18	-.56
G_2	-.23	.64	-.53	-.12	.65	.33	(.69)	-.20	.17	.18	.28	-.36	-.30	-.46
H_2	.43	-.46	.95	.10	-.20	-.33	-.66	(.85)	.31	.09	-.48	.64	.48	.66
I_2	.17	.07	.23	.30	.02	.12	-.05	.27	(.54)	.04	-.12	.00	.02	.22
J_2	.29	.18	.47	.14	.68	-.08	.24	.10	-.08	(.69)	.12	.24	-.10	.01
K_2	-.28	.18	-.57	.03	.12	.21	.17	-.51	-.37	.08	(.30)	-.15	-.17	-.45
L_2	.43	-.28	.37	.13	-.02	-.37	-.32	.57	-.26	.15	-.29	(.75)	.20	.52
M_2	.40	-.54	.54	-.03	-.08	-.21	-.39	.33	.00	.11	-.19	.41	(.45)	.74
N_2	.53	-.66	.62	.08	-.33	-.63	-.57	.81	.08	-.02	-.31	.33	.53	(.76)

Variable Number	Name
A	Rejection-Acceptance
B	Children's Hostility
C	Children's Self-evaluation
D	Children's Self-reliance
E	Children's Achievement
F	Children's Dependence
G	Adult's Hostility

Variable Number	Name
H	Adult's Self-evaluation
I	Adult's Self-reliance
J	Adult's Achievement
K	Adult's Dependence
L	Adult's Emotional Responsiveness
M	Adult's World View
N	Adult's Emotional Stability

Note:—Italicized figures, $p < .05$.

TABLE A12. Monorater Triangle One (Rater 1): Uncorrected Ratings

Trait	A_1	B_1	C_1	D_1	E_1	F_1	G_1	H_1	I_1	J_1	K_1	L_1	M_1
A_1													
B_1	−.49												
C_1	.62	−.46											
D_1	.04	.11	.40										
E_1	−.06	.51	.00	−.13									
F_1	−.41	.46	−.10	−.41	.31								
G_1	−.28	.55	−.65	−.09	.43	.16							
H_1	.28	−.08	.92	.23	−.15	−.17	−.40						
I_1	−.02	.03	−.12	.20	−.02	.15	.08	.23					
J_1	.22	.16	.44	.08	.59	.04	.14	.05	−.17				
K_1	−.16	.18	−.31	−.18	.05	.12	.40	−.70	−.15	−.02			
L_1	.39	−.27	.57	.16	−.02	−.35	−.27	.75	−.23	.29	−.49		
M_1	.14	−.34	.57	.21	−.33	−.17	−.39	.51	.07	.02	−.28	.25	
N_1	.51	−.59	.34	.13	−.44	−.75	−.62	.60	.00	.08	−.30	.70	.53

Note:—Italicized figures, $p < .05$. Trait names are identified in Figure 4.

TABLE A13. Monorater Triangle Two (Rater 2): Uncorrected Ratings

Trait	A₂	B₂	C₂	D₂	E₂	F₂	G₂	H₂	I₂	J₂	K₂	L₂	M₂
A₂													
B₂	−.60												
C₂	.77	−.71											
D₂	.03	.06	.30										
E₂	.32	.02	.44	.04									
F₂	−.14	.17	.20	−.11	.00								
G₂	−.41	.66	−.79	−.17	.18	.08							
H₂	.59	−.40	.95	−.10	.10	−.21	−.44						
I₂	.22	.07	.53	.48	.19	−.09	.07	.17					
J₂	.20	.12	.64	.12	.50	.17	.32	.10	.10				
K₂	−.12	−.08	−.44	.01	−.35	.66	−.06	−.52	−.11	.05			
L₂	.51	−.40	.26	.14	.19	−.15	−.44	.42	−.03	.22	.08		
M₂	.46	−.41	.62	.13	.22	−.14	−.46	.54	.06	.17	−.08	.45	
N₂	.66	−.65	.86	−.06	.22	−.26	−.60	.85	.18	.02	−.27	.41	.59

Note:—Italicized figures, $p<.05$. Trait names are identified in Figure 4.

TABLE A14.

Interrater Reliability: Parental Acceptance-Rejection and Personality

	Uncorrected Codes[1]			Corrected Codes[2]		
	r^*	p	n	r^*	p	n
Rejection-Acceptance	.78	.0001	85	.88	.0001	90
Parental Hostility	.73	.0001	79	.84	.0001	80
Parental Neglect	.75	.0001	75	.86	.0001	80
Child Hostility	.85	.0001	50	.92	.0001	62
Self-evaluation	.94	.0005	7	.95	.0001	11
Dependency	.52	.001	34	.92	.0001	43
Adult Hostility	.69	.0001	70	.87	.0001	83
Self-evaluation	.85	.0001	25	.89	.0001	33
Dependency	.30	.05	34	.91	.0001	41
Emotional responsiveness	.75	.0001	70	.90	.0001	83
World view	.45	.0001	70	.83	.0001	77
Emotional stability	.76	.0001	31	.94	.0001	41

[1] Uncorrected codes: Codes before raters conferred on interrater differences in codings.

[2] Corrected codes: Codes after raters came to an agreement on interrater differences in coding.

$*r$ = Pearson's correlations

TABLE A15.

Raters' Instructions and Definitions Used for Coding the Data
Quality Control Variables in the Rejection-Acceptance
Project

GENERAL INSTRUCTIONS AND DEFINITIONS

Each entry in items 5-11 should be marked with one of two degrees of confidence. Reasonably satisfactory evidence can be recorded by a plain entry, e.g. *x, female,* or *89.* Doubtful, ambiguous, or inconsistent evidence should be recorded by placing parentheses around the entry, e.g. *(x), (female),* or *(89).* If insufficient information is available to make a rating, record the letter N (None) on the appropriate line.

Write clarifying remarks in the spaces provided (*Remarks*) for variables 7 and 8 whenever they appear useful. Expanded notes may be recorded on the back of the code sheet. The back of the code sheet may also be used to register explanatory or qualifying statements for other variables where the entry *Remarks* is not provided.

Record the page number(s) on the line marked *Page reference(s)* or *page(s)* where information for each rating occurs for variables 7-11.

VARIABLES 6-11

Number of Pages Related to Child-Training Practices (Variable 6)

The purpose of this variable is to get an accurate estimate (aiming toward a precise count) of the number of pages in each book that relate explicitly to child training. Very often the chapter headings or subheadings cited in the table of contents reflect the amount of space devoted to child training, but you should not rely solely on this as a guide. Authors often describe different aspects of child rearing in chapters on kinship or the family, for example, as well as in chapters on the life cycle. You must review all relevant chapters to make your count. Also, review such sections as the introduction and preface for information that might be pertinent. You should note that pages related to "child-training practices" refer to the period of maternal pregnancy through the marriage of the resulting offspring.

If all or most of a page is devoted to socialization, you should count it as one page; if a few lines to about half the page relate to socialization, you should register it as one-half page. Do not attempt to make finer discriminations than one-half page.

Length of Fieldwork (Variable 7)

Authors often state the length of time they spent in the field collecting data for a given publication in the preface, introduction, or first chapter. Record this information in as much detail as possible. An author sometimes writes: "I spent thirty years among the Crow." From his later descriptions, however, he makes it clear that in fact he visited the Crow each summer for thirty years; he did not live with them continuously for thirty years. Your tabulation should reflect only the time he actually spent in

Table A15. Continued

the field. Qualifying statements may be recorded on the lines marked *Remarks*. You should also indicate on the line marked *Page reference(s)* where you found your information.

Informant Characteristics (Variable 8)

Whenever possible, record the actual age and/or sex of the informant(s) used by an ethnographer. Ethnographers sometimes simply state: "Most of my information comes from Wai Wei, an old Hopi woman." In this case, you should record "old woman" on the code sheet. Also record any other information relevant to the age and sex of informants on the lines marked *Remarks*. You should also record the *page(s)* where you found the information.

Verification Efforts (Variable 9)

Variable 9 measures the extent to which an ethnographer attempts to verify his observations and conclusions regarding child-training practices. A check list is provided in the code sheet for four types of verification efforts: (1) repeated observations of different families' socialization practices (2) the use of multiple informants to collect data on child rearing (3) utilization of tests (e.g. Rorschach, TAT, sentence completion, I.Q.), questionnaires, and other objective or quasi-objective measuring devices. (4) A fourth space is also furnished on the code sheet to record other forms of verification efforts. You should specify what these are.

Variable 9.5 asks you to calculate the number of different types of verification efforts employed by an ethnographer. This is the sum of positive responses recorded in variables 9.1 through 9.4. If the ethnographer made no attempt or only minimal attempts to verify his data regarding child training (e.g. hearsay, a single observation, one informant's report, secondhand reporting), and/or if variables 9.1 through 9.4 were all coded with a negative response, you should place a check mark in code category (0). Otherwise you should use code categories 1 through 5. Qualitatively different kinds of verification efforts recorded in variables 9.3 and 9.4 should be individually counted (e.g. if the ethnographer used the TAT, collected and analyzed children's drawings, and used a questionnaire, you should count each as a separate verification effort).

Language Familiarity (Variable 10)

Variable 10 is a measure of the ethnographer's proficiency in the language of the people he is studying. Three categories of proficiency are supplied in the code sheet: (1) little or no knowledge of the native language (2) some knowledge and understanding of the native language (3) fluency in the native language.

An ethnographer may be considered fluent in the language only when he makes an explicit statement saying that he is. The ethnographer may be considered to have some knowledge and understanding of the language when he makes a statement to this effect or when he is able to follow at

Table A15. Continued

least the gist of most casual conversations without being able to speak the language well enough to converse in it himself, except for phrases of etiquette.

He should be considered to have little or no knowledge of the language when he states that this is the case, when he speaks only English (or whatever his own native language may be) in his fieldwork, or when he relies almost exclusively on interpreters. You should check the cell marked (—) if no information is available regarding an ethnographer's proficiency in the native language or if you cannot make a confident inference.

Community Involvement (Variable 11)

Variable 11 is a measure of the extent to which an ethnographer is involved in everyday community life as an active participant-observer. Three categories of involvement are supplied on the code sheet: (1) limited community involvement (2) intermediate community involvement (3) extensive community involvement. An ethnographer may be considered to be extensively involved in community affairs when he actively involves himself in most aspects of day-to-day village life. He typically lives among the people (with a host family or by himself in or near the village) and spends a great deal of time working with, talking to, and observing the members of the community. He may have specialized interests of his own, but he makes it his business to study most other aspects of community life as well.

An ethnographer is intermediately involved in community affairs when he participates fairly actively (but not intensively) in village life. His participation may often be segmentalized, i.e. he may have a specialized status within the community other than full-time ethnographer, such as missionary, teacher, or government official. His major commitment may be to his specialized interests, but in the process of activating these interests he frequently comes into close, personal contact and interaction with the members of the community.

The ethnographer has only limited involvement when he fails to participate in the major aspects of community affairs. In this case, his interaction with the members of the community is usually restricted or sharply segmentalized. For example he may be a teacher who keeps strictly to his job of instruction, or a government official whose only real involvement with the people is in his official capacity.

You should mark the cell marked (—) if insufficient information is available to make a rating or if you cannot make an inference about an ethnographer's community involvement, because of insufficient information.

TABLE A16.   Data Quality Control Code Sheet

RATER ....

DATE ....

....

SOCIETY

1. Author ....

2. Title ....

3. Date of Publication (i.e. earliest copyright date) ....

4. Place of Publication ....

5. Number of Pages in Book (Count from first arabic numeral to the last. The index is not included; appendixes numbered with arabic numerals are included.) ....

6. Number of Pages Related to Child-Training Practices (period of maternal pregnancy through marriage of the resulting offspring) ....

7. Length of Fieldwork
   From .... to ....
        month   year   month   year
   No or insufficient information ....
   Page reference(s) ....
   Remarks ....

8. Informant Characteristics (see item 9.2)
       Ages (1) ....   Sex (1) ....
              (2) ....   (2) ....
              (3) ....   (3) ....
   No or insufficient information ....
   Page reference(s) ....
   Remarks ....

9. Verification Efforts
   (1) Repeated observations made   (1) No ....
         on socialization practices   (2) Yes ....   Pages..........
                             (−) No or insufficient
                                information ....

   (2) Multiple informants   (1) No ....
                           (2) Yes ....   Pages..........
                           (−) No or insufficient
                           information ....

Table A16. Continued

(3) Tests administered (specify types)

(1) No ....
(2) Yes* ....   Pages ....
(—) No or insufficient information ....

(4) Other verification efforts (specify types)

(1) Absent ....
(2) Present* .... Pages ....
(—) No or insufficient information ....

* Specify type(s) ....

(5) Number of types of verification effort [based on 9.1-9.4, above]

(0) No or only minimal attempts made to verify ....
(1) One type ....
(2) Two types ....
(3) Three types ....
(4) Four types ....
(5) Five or more ....

10. Language Familiarity

(1) Little or no knowledge

....
check

(2) Some knowledge or understanding

....   pages ....
check

(3) Fluent

....
check

(—) No information available or insufficient information

....
check

11. Community Involvement

(1) Limited

....
check

(2) Intermediate

....   pages ....
check

(3) Extensive

....
check

(—) No information available or insufficient information

....
check

Key to Table A17.   Societies and Codes for Data Quality Control Variables

Variable No.	IBM Col. No.	Variable I.D.
1	10-11	Date of publication [last two (2) digits of date]
2	12-14	Number of pages in book
3	15-17	Number of pages on child training
4	18-20	Proportion of book devoted to child training
5	24-25	Year fieldwork began [last two (2) digits of date]
6	26-27	Total months of fieldwork
7	29-30	Age of informants (see code categories)
8	31	Sex of informants (1=male; 2=female; 3=both)
9	32	Number of informants (codes 1 to 5 = 16 or more informants)
10	35	Repeated observations made on same phenomena (1=no; 2=yes)
11	36	Multiple informants (1=no; 2=yes)
12	37	Tests administered (1=no; 2=yes)
13	38	Other verification efforts (1=absent; 2=present)
14	39	Number of types of verification efforts (1 to 5= five or more)
15	40	Language familiarity (1=little or no understanding; 2=some understanding; 3=fluent)
16	41	Community involvement (1=limited; 2=intermediate; 3=extensive)
17	43-44	Index of ethnographer adequacy (decimal from 1.00-2.67)

TABLE A17. Societies and Codes for Data Quality Control Variables

RAP IBM #	Society Name	Variable Number (See Key for Identification)															
		1	2	3	4	5	6	7	8	9	10	11	12	13	14	15	16	17
001	Akwe-Shavente	67	309	50	17	58	14	5	0	5	2	2	1	1	2	2	3	20
002	Alorese	44	375	83	22	37	24	5	1	3	2	2	2	2	5	2	3	24
003	Americans	66	148	93	63	54	10	7	3	5	2	2	2	2	4	3	3	23
004	Andamanese	22	504	18	4	6	24	7	3	5	2	2	1	1	2	2	0	20
005	Apache, Chiricahua	41	482	137	29	31	24	7	0	5	2	2	1	1	2	0	2	20
006	Apache, Western	42	698	175	25	29	22	7	3	5	2	2	0	1	2	3	3	26
007	Arab-Sudanese	64	288	54	18	59	15	7	3	5	2	2	0	0	2	3	2	22
008	Araucanians (Mapuche)	57	257	90	35	46	10	7	3	5	2	2	0	2	3	2	1	17
010	Australians (rural)	54	274	82	33	0	0	7	0	0	2	2	2	2	5	3	1	22
011	Aymara	51	165	6	4	40	27	7	3	5	2	2	0	2	3	1	2	20
012	Balinese	42	281	122	43	0	12	0	0	0	2	2	1	1	2	2	2	20
013	Bechuana	46	342	118	35	29	14	7	3	5	2	2	0	2	3	2	2	22
014	Camayura	53	68	6	9	48	3	7	3	5	2	0	0	0	2	1	3	18
015	Cambodians	59	274	10	4	0	0	0	0	0	0	0	0	0	0	0	0	0
016	Canadians, French	39	290	50	17	36	11	7	3	5	2	2	0	2	3	3	3	23
018	Chamorros	51	350	51	15	47	7	4	2	5	2	2	2	1	5	1	0	17
019	Cheyenne	60	103	15	15	35	0	3	3	0	1	2	1	2	2	0	0	17
020	Chinese (Shantung Province)	47	269	80	29	0	0	0	3	5	2	2	1	1	2	3	3	20
022	Colombian Mestizo	61	460	79	17	0	14	7	3	5	2	2	0	2	4	0	0	25
023	Crow	35	331	30	9	7	0	3	3	5	2	2	1	2	3	2	3	18
024	Dobuans	32	314	35	12	28	6	5	3	5	2	2	1	2	3	2	3	19
025	Dutch	55	190	60	31	51	10	7	3	5	2	2	1	2	5	3	3	21

(Continued on Next Page)

Table A17. Continued

		Variable Number (See Key for Identification)																
RAP IBM #	Society Name	1	2	3	4	5	6	7	8	9	10	11	12	13	14	15	16	17
026	Egyptians	54	307	110	36	0	6	3	1	2	2	2	2	1	5	3	3	20
027	Eskimo, Alaskan	63	163	32	19	55	11	7	3	5	2	2	0	2	4	2	3	22
028	Eskimo, Greenland	37	35	5	14	0	0	0	0	0	0	0	0	2	2	0	0	20
029	Fijians (Vanua Levu)	48	439	50	12	35	10	0	0	5	2	2	1	1	2	2	0	17
030	Filipinos	65	129	52	40	55	8	2	2	5	2	2	1	2	3	2	2	19
031	Fon (Dahomeans)	38	402	82	20	31	6	7	3	5	2	2	0	2	3	1	2	17
033	French (Vaucluse)	57	338	120	36	50	12	5	3	5	2	2	2	2	5	3	3	23
034	Greeks, Modern	62	106	31	29	55	3	0	0	0	2	2	0	0	2	2	3	24
035	Guatemalan Indians	52	18	16	88	41	12	0	0	0	0	0	0	2	3	0	0	25
036	Gusii	66	230	105	46	54	0	7	3	5	2	2	2	1	3	1	3	18
037	Hopi	40	190	158	83	37	6	0	0	0	2	2	1	1	2	0	2	15
038	Hupa	47	12	10	83	45	12	0	0	0	2	0	0	2	2	0	0	20
039	Ilocos	66	177	72	41	54	10	7	3	5	2	2	2	2	4	1	3	20
040	Indians (high-caste Hindus)	57	334	43	13	51	10	4	3	5	2	2	2	0	5	3	3	23
041	Indians (Rajputs)	66	189	66	35	54	10	4	2	5	2	2	2	2	4	1	2	19
042	Indians	55	235	23	9	51	12	7	3	5	2	2	2	2	4	3	2	21
043	Jamaicans	52	211	67	32	47	24	0	0	0	2	2	2	2	5	0	2	23
044	Japanese	54	232	25	11	50	8	7	3	5	2	2	1	2	3	2	1	17
045	Javanese	61	162	50	31	53	15	7	3	5	2	2	1	2	3	3	2	21
046	Jews, East European	58	488	349	72	51	12	7	3	5	2	2	2	2	5	3	3	23
047	Kaska	54	155	20	13	44	8	6	1	3	2	2	1	1	2	3	3	20
048	Klamath	50	11	11	100	47	2	3	3	3	1	2	1	1	1	0	0	12

049	Kutenay	41	193	18	9	39	3	0	3	5	2	2	1	1	2	2	0	15
050	Kwakiutl	67	166	30	18	62	13	0	3	5	2	2	2	2	4	3	3	24
051	Kwoma	41	223	110	49	36	7	5	3	5	2	2	1	1	2	2	1	16
053	Lebanese	61	176	100	56	58	11	2	2	5	0	2	2	2	5	2	2	20
054	Lepcha	38	456	60	13	36	6	0	0	5	2	2	1	1	2	2	0	15
055	Malays	60	256	25	10	56	7	6	3	5	2	2	1	1	2	0	3	18
057	Mandan	50	369	40	11	30	6	3	3	5	2	2	1	1	2	1	0	13
058	Manus	30	215	90	42	20	0	7	3	5	2	2	2	2	5	3	3	23
059	Maori	56	177	31	18	54	7	7	3	5	2	2	2	2	4	0	0	20
061	Mixtecans	66	146	63	41	54	9	7	3	5	2	2	2	2	4	0	3	22
062	Muria	47	669	100	15	35	0	0	0	5	2	2	1	1	2	2	2	17
063	Naron	30	220	21	10	0	0	7	3	5	2	2	0	0	2	0	0	20
064	Navaho	46	238	16	7	0	0	7	3	5	2	2	2	1	5	0	0	20
065	New Irelanders	33	342	83	23	29	11	0	3	5	2	2	1	0	2	2	3	19
066	Ngoni	60	176	87	43	0	42	7	3	5	2	2	2	1	3	0	2	24
067	Nuer	51	194	24	11	30	12	0	3	0	2	2	1	0	2	1	0	15
070	Okinawans	66	172	90	52	54	10	7	3	5	2	2	2	2	4	2	2	21
071	Paiute (Harney Valley)	50	107	10	9	36	9	7	3	5	2	2	2	0	3	3	0	22
072	Palauans	60	85	16	19	47	9	7	3	5	2	2	0	2	3	2	0	20
073	Papago	49	266	121	45	41	0	1	3	5	2	2	2	2	5	2	2	20
074	Paraguayans	54	325	66	20	48	11	7	3	5	2	2	2	0	5	2	3	22
075	Potawatomi, Prairie	65	74	60	81	64	3	7	3	5	2	2	2	0	3	3	1	18
076	Puerto Ricans	59	276	134	49	50	8	7	3	5	2	2	2	2	5	2	2	20
077	Samoans	28	192	58	30	0	9	1	2	5	2	2	2	2	5	3	3	23
078	Serbs	58	313	42	13	53	12	7	3	0	2	2	2	1	4	3	2	20

(Continued on Next Page)

Table A17. Continued

RAP IBM #	Society Name	Variable Number (See Key for Identification)																
		1	2	3	4	5	6	7	8	9	10	11	12	13	14	15	16	17
079	Sherente	42	102	30	29	37	0	0	1	5	2	2	1	1	2	3	3	20
080	Sioux (Teton-Dakota)	46	221	106	48	42	10	1	3	5	0	2	2	2	5	0	0	20
081	Siriono	50	99	20	20	40	12	7	3	5	2	2	0	2	3	3	2	22
082	Siuai	55	488	90	18	38	21	7	3	5	1	2	1	0	2	3	1	17
083	Soga	56	278	5	2	50	21	7	3	5	2	2	0	2	5	2	2	22
084	Sotho (Basuto)	52	345	62	18	34	9	7	3	5	2	2	0	2	5	3	3	20
085	Taiwanese	66	285	31	11	57	16	7	3	0	2	2	1	2	3	2	3	21
086	Tallensi	49	347	146	42	34	0	7	3	5	2	2	0	2	2	0	0	20
087	Tanala	39	100	20	20	26	30	7	3	5	2	2	0	0	2	2	3	26
088	Tenetehara	49	187	32	17	41	9	7	3	5	2	2	0	2	3	1	2	17
089	Tepoztecans	51	494	110	22	43	7	7	3	5	2	2	2	2	5	0	2	20
090	Thai	65	208	14	7	56	22	2	3	5	2	2	2	2	5	2	1	20
091	Tikopians	36	488	188	39	28	17	7	3	0	2	2	1	2	3	3	3	23
092	Timbira, Eastern	46	249	38	15	0	0	0	0	0	2	0	1	1	1	3	0	18
094	Trukese	54	651	235	35	47	7	7	3	5	2	2	2	2	5	2	0	20
096	Umbundu (Mbundu)	49	231	76	33	33	60	7	3	5	2	2	0	2	4	0	0	25
097	Wichita	—	70	22	31	47	25	7	3	5	2	2	0	0	2	3	1	24
098	Wogeo	49	231	76	33	33	60	7	3	5	2	2	0	2	4	0	0	25
099	Woleaians (Ifaluk)	53	323	50	15	47	6	7	1	0	2	2	2	2	4	1	1	16
100	Yaguans	43	110	15	14	40	9	7	3	0	2	2	1	1	3	2	3	19
101	Yoruba	36	9	8	88	30	48	7	3	5	2	2	0	0	2	2	2	24

TABLE A18. Ethnographer Bias: Interrater Reliability

Variable #	Variable Name	r^*	N
1	Date of publication	1.00	92
2	Number of pages in book	1.00	94
3	Number of pages on child training	1.00	94
4	Proportion of book devoted to child training	1.00	94
5	Year fieldwork began	1.00	83
6	Total months of fieldwork	1.00	78
7	Age of informants	1.00	69
8	Sex of informants	1.00	74
9	Number of informants	1.00	72
10	Repeated observations made on same phenomena	1.00	89
11	Multiple informants	100%	88
12	Tests administered	1.00	62
13	Other types of verification efforts	.84	80
14	Number of types of verification efforts	.97	93
15	Language familiarity	1.00	73
16	Community involvement	1.00	69
17	Index of ethnographer adequacy	.99	95

*Note:—Reliability coefficients 1-9 are Pearson's r; coefficients 10, 12, and 13 are Phi coefficients; coefficients 14-17 are Spearman's r_s. No statistical test was possible for variable 11, because all ethnographers used multiple informants. All correlations are significant at the p $<$.001 level.

TABLE A19.
Comparison of Original and Residual Correlations between
Rejection-Acceptance and Personality Characteristics

Personality Characteristics	Original Correlation	p	Residual Correlation	p	N
Child					
Hostility	−.49	.01	−.50	.01	60
Self-evaluation	.72	.01	.13	NS	11
Self-reliance	.16	NS	.19	.05	77
Achievement	−.04	NS	−.29	.05	36
Dependency	−.31	.05	−.28	.05	42
Adult					
Hostility	−.32	.01	−.33	.01	75
Self-evaluation	.40	.05	.41	.05	33
Self-reliance	.08	NS	.10	NS	77
Achievement	.21	.05	.12	NS	77
Dependency	−.41	.01	−.38	.01	40
Emotional responsiveness	.50	.01	.46	.01	75
World view	.29	.05	.26	.05	68
Emotional stability	.62	.01	.61	.01	38

NOTES TO CHAPTER ONE

1. The phrase "the establishment of scientifically derived generalizations about human behavior" is drawn from the Constitution of the Society for Cross-Cultural Research (SCCR), an interdisciplinary and international scientific organization founded in 1971 by George Peter Murdock and Ronald P. Rohner. The objectives of the universalist approach are formally recognized in the Constitution of the SCCR, which states that the "purpose of the Society is to support and encourage interdisciplinary, comparative research that has as its objective the establishment of scientifically derived generalizations about human behavior" (Society for Cross-Cultural Research 1973: 5).

2. In this book we use the term "cross-cultural" to refer generically to worldwide research, including research across different gene pools, natural environments, language groups, cultural systems, and other limiting conditions that might affect human behavior.

3. Malinowski's formula for adequate fieldwork was anticipated earlier by Boas (see Boas 1943: 314), but Boas himself did not implement it in his own research (Rohner 1969).

4. Summarizing the cross-cultural studies of Piagetian theory, Dasen (1972: 23) concluded that the "rate of operational development [rather than being uniform throughout our species] is affected by cultural factors, sometimes to the extent that the concrete operational stage is not reached by large proportions of non-Western samples."

5. In this sentence we speak of the "evolutionary-ethological" argument rather than the "evolutionary-biological-ethological universalist" argument. In this way we can highlight the principal focus of different scholars. The point here is that whereas all these writers are universalist in their perspective, some concentrate on a single element in the chain, e.g. the evolutionary (usually a "Darwinian" or phylogenetic perspective), the biological (genetics and the biological consequences of nutrition, extreme altitude or temperature, disease, crowding, or other stressors), or the ethological (comparative, behavioral ecology; cross-species analogies). Other writers draw on two or all three qualifiers in the chain.

6. Arguments regarding the instinctual basis of aggression are extensively critiqued in Montague (1973).

7. It is likely, however, that the only truly researchable (and therefore scientific) portion of the evolutionary-biological-ethological paradigm regarding human social and emotional be-

havior is the strictly biological portion of the chain, i.e. those questions dealing with actual physiological, nutritional, genetic, and other biological mechanisms and processes in living human populations.

8. In addition to these basic color terms, people everywhere employ a variety of *secondary* color terms, such as, in English, "lemon-colored" (a construct from an object, not a simple, unitary term), or "bay" (a nongeneral term, which, in English, refers to the color of a horse). Unlike secondary color terms, *basic* color terms are general or nonrestrictive in their applicability and are simple monolexemes.

9. The details of the research procedures and tests used in the community study component are given in Rohner's (n.d.[b]) *Field Manual for the Study of Parental Acceptance-Rejection.*

10. In order to measure the parent-child relationship and to assess the personality characteristics of parents and children, a variety of discrete methods are used in the socialization facet of each community study, viz.: parent and child interviews, a parent-child relations questionnaire administered to parents and to sample children, a personality assessment questionnaire administered both to the sample children and to their principal caretakers, and systematic time-sampled and behavior-setting sampled behavior observations. The field team typically is comprised of an anthropologist, who concentrates principally on the ethnographic facet of the research, and a psychologically trained researcher, who focuses on the socialization facet of the research. Many of the same instruments and procedures are also used in the psychological research component.

11. At this writing, two community studies, one in a Turkish peasant village and one in a Newfoundland fishing and mining community, have been completed. The analysis of these studies is not far enough along for reference in this book. Over the next few years we plan to work in about twelve communities around the world, using the community study methodology. As in the Turkish community study, we expect much of this research to be completed by national scholars in their own countries, rather than by teams of American researchers.

12. The biological and evolutionary perspectives of physical anthropology are also likely to contribute positively to the universalist effort.

NOTES TO CHAPTER TWO

1. Enculturation is the process through which an individual gradually learns the culturally prescribed or valued behavior standards of his own society. The concept is roughly equivalent to

"education" in its broadest sense, although the term is probably better interpreted as "culture learning."

2. Some scholars argue that the labels "acceptance" and "rejection" cannot be used to describe behavior in non-Western societies, because the meanings of acceptance and rejection, including their negative associations, are imbedded in our cultural system. These scholars defend their argument by pointing out that people of other societies would probably object to our use of the term rejection when we use it to describe their child-training practices. The problem of using labels such as rejection, which has strong negative overtones in the Western world, to describe non-Western behavior evaporates, however, if we take these concepts outside the context of emotional values and moral judgments and simply say that whenever parents anywhere in the world behave toward their children in a specified manner (described later), we choose to label this behavior as "rejection." By clearly and unambiguously defining the kinds of behavior we include in the concept of rejection, we are operationalizing the definition and are no longer applying an emotionally laden, vaguely defined, and imprecise Western label to behavior in other societies.

3. The rejection process can be very subtle, of course, with the parents themselves not fully aware or able to admit—even to themselves—their true feelings toward their children. The clinical literature in psychiatry and psychology is filled with such cases, as well as cases where parents affirm their love for their children, but where objective observers can discern covert but strongly rejecting tendencies.

4. In the work of this volume, we deal primarily with children from the ages of two through ten. Specifically, in the cross-cultural survey component we measure the characteristics of children from two through six years; and in the community study component we deal with two age groups—three through six and seven through ten. Children of virtually all ages may be included in the psychological research component.

5. We show in Chapter Four how the games people play and how people's religious beliefs and other expressive features of society are related to their childhood experiences.

6. In this work we explicitly reject the classical "social mold" theory of socialization, wherein the child is seen as a passive recipient of parental behavior. Instead, we recognize that the child actively engages in a variety of behaviors that are designed to modify his environment and the people in it. Indeed, a child's basic temperament and other constitutional characteristics affect his responses to parental behavior as well as affecting the type and quality of interaction he initiates with the significant people in his environment (e.g. parents, siblings, peers). We also reject the view that the

parents (especially the mother, as generally emphasized in psychoanalytic theory) are necessarily the most significant influence in a child's life. Anthropological evidence amply documents how culture-bound this "matricentric" view really is.

7. Dependence resulting from rejection seems to be consistent with Bowlby's (1973: 213) concept of anxious attachment.

NOTES TO CHAPTER THREE

1. The Harlows (Harlow and Harlow 1969: 36) observe, however, that: "In a broad sense it is inappropriate to pit the importance of one of these affectional systems [peer affection versus maternal affection] against the other. The fact that either may compensate in whole or in part for deficiencies in the other provides an enormous social safeguard, . . . The biological utility of compensatory social mechanisms is obvious, and that effective social safeguards should have developed over the course of evolutionary development is in no way surprising."

2. Rohner and Turner (n.d.) have prepared an approximately 500-item bibliography on the behavioral correlates of parental acceptance and rejection. The bibliography contains a number of references to the relationship between parental rejection-acceptance and dependency, as well as to the other forms of behavior described in this chapter.

NOTES TO CHAPTER FOUR

1. Readers who would like to have more details than are provided in this chapter about the methodological procedures, codes, and so forth used in the cross-cultural survey research on which this chapter is based should refer to Appendix Three. Rohner (n.d.[a]) will later provide a comprehensive treatment of the methodological problems involved in the holocultural method, including the present research.

2. It was not possible to make confident judgments in the anthropological literature about disguised or symbolic expressions of aggression. Had we been able to reliably identify such behavior, the relationship between hostility and rejection-acceptance reported in Table 1 would probably have been much stronger than $r = -.48$. For a more complete discussion of the meaning of each personality characteristic listed in Table 1, see Appendix One, "Definition of Personality Characteristics."

3. In controlling for the effects of "ethnographer bias" in holocultural research, the statistically significant relationship disap-

pears between rejection-acceptance and children's self-evaluation
(r=.13; p=ns). Why this should be so is unclear, except that the
sample size from which the correlation coefficient is derived is unusually small (n=11). Also, children's self-evaluation is difficult to
measure in cross-cultural surveys, thereby introducing the possibility of coder bias (see Rohner and Katz 1970; Rohner and Ness 1975).
Given the great amount of evidence in psychological research
within the United States and elsewhere linking changes in
children's self-evaluation with parental acceptance-rejection, and
given the possibility of coder bias, etc., we regard these cross-
cultural tests of the relationship between children's self-evaluation
and parental behavior as being inconclusive and possibly unreliable. Until persuasive cross-cultural evidence is marshaled to the
contrary, we continue to regard it as highly likely that parental rejection contributes to negative self-evaluation. (The problem of ethnographer bias is discussed further in Appendix Three). Readers
who do not know how to interpret the numbers (correlation, r; probability, p; number of societies, N) in Table 1 and elsewhere in this
chapter are invited to read Appendix Two, "The Meaning of Correlation Coefficients, Chi-Square Test, and Probability."
    4. Ethnographer bias is discussed at greater length in Appendix
Three. (See also Rohner, DeWalt, and Ness 1973).
    5. This is true for all personality traits except "conflict over
nurturance," which relates to children from about five to twelve
years of age.
    6. Data in cross-cultural surveys do not measure the develop-
ment of children as they grow into adulthood; rather, measurements
are made on the personality of children and adults as they exist at a
single moment in time, as it were. This is the case because anthropologists rarely work in a community for more than a year or
two. Therefore ethnographic descriptions of personality refer to the
behavior of children and adults within a limited time period—not
longitudinally over the span of a generation. Thus these holocultural data could be interpreted to mean that adults who are emotionally unresponsive tend, as parents, to reject their children more
often than emotionally responsive adults (rather than that rejected
children become emotionally unresponsive and·continue to be unresponsive as adults). Indeed, the former conclusion is correct insofar as emotionally insulated adults are unable to give warmth and
affection to their children. We know of no reason, however, to expect dependent adults to be more rejecting than independent
adults, nor to expect adults with a negative world view to be more
rejecting than those with a positive world view. More importantly,
we cannot explain why adults should have the total constellation of
traits that we predict will result from rejection if our data do not, at
least for the most part, reflect a longitudinal continuity of personal
characteristics.

This presumption of continuity is valid only insofar as evidence can be marshaled that the child-rearing practices in the sample societies have maintained reasonable stability over at least two generations—i.e. that the parents themselves were treated in about the same way as they now treat their own children. A careful review of the ethnographic literature shows that about 90 percent of the sample for which measurements could be made had maintained appreciable cultural stability with regard to child-training practices for about twenty-five years prior to the time of fieldwork. With this information, along with the massive supporting evidence regarding the consequences of parental rejection in the psychological literature in America, we conclude that scholars are not in great danger of seriously misinterpreting their data when they conclude that the holocultural relationship between parental behavior and adult personality suggests a basic continuity over time.

7. "Anxiety" here is an average or composite measure of overall "anxiety" experienced by children in terms of oral, anal, sexual, dependence and aggressive behavior.

8. The positive relationship between rejection-acceptance and adult achievement shown in Table 1 disappears when the effects of "ethnographer bias" are controlled. (See discussion of ethnographer bias in Appendix Three.)

9. We thank Robert E. Schongalla for his unpublished work on the relationship between parental behavior and peer group relations.

10. All these questions also inquire about the relationship between socialization practices and some expressive institution.

11. We are indebted to three former students at the University of Connecticut: Jon Allen, James Baily, and Jeanne Willard, for their unpublished research on these tests. We concentrate here principally on the research of Baily and Willard, who measured malevolence and benevolence in terms of the extent to which the gods are predisposed to do man good or evil in terms of health (cure or cause of illness), harvest (good or bad), luck (good or bad), protection from enemies (positive or negative), weather (good or bad). Their work also includes an overall summary measure of malevolence-benevolence of the supernatural.

12. Let us emphasize again that we are dealing in the universalist approach, with a probability model wherein we assume as a matter of course that exceptions to our theories will appear. Exceptions in the cross-cultural survey method can come from a variety of sources, including inaccurate ethnographic reporting, faulty conceptualization of the problem, erroneous coding, and so forth (see Rohner, DeWalt, and Ness 1973). We must try to minimize these exceptions, but we must also account for them when possible.

13. We thank two former students, Meredith Pugh and Jon Allen, for their data on the relationship between the supernatural

world and adult hostility and cheerfulness. We should also note in Table 2 that all societies coded 9 or 10 (extreme acceptance) on a scale ranging from 2 to 10 believe in benevolent deities.

14.   Codes for the complexity of artistic design come from Barry (1952); see also Barry (1957) for other correlates of socialization and the pictorial arts.

15.   A game is defined by Roberts, Arth, and Bush (1959: 597) as a "recreational activity characterized by: (1) organized play, (2) competition, (3) two or more sides, (4) criteria for determining the winner, and (5) agreed-upon rules." Many games of physical skill also have components of strategy as well, such as in fencing or football; chance may also be a factor in some games of physical skill, such as musical chairs. Different elements may also be mixed with the other classes of games.

16.   For additional work relating to these topics, see Roberts, Hoffman, and Sutton-Smith (1965), Roberts, Koenig, and Stark (1969), Roberts and Sutton-Smith (1966), Roberts, Sutton-Smith, and Kendon (1963), Sutton-Smith and Roberts (1964), Sutton-Smith, Roberts, and Kozelka (1963), and Hutchinson and Roberts (1972).

17.   The codes for minimum-maximum presence of fathers within the household came from John Whiting (1959). Whiting identified four types of households, ranging from maximum to minimal presence of the father (Bacon, Child, and Barry 1963: 293-94):

Monogamous nuclear. This household is the usual one in our society. The father, mother, and children eat, sleep, and entertain under one roof. Grandparents, siblings of the parents, and other relatives live elsewhere. The effective presence of the father in the child's environment is thus at a maximum.

Monogamous extended. Here two or more nuclear families live together under one roof. A typical extended family consists of an aged couple, together with their married sons and daughters and their respective families. In such a household, the child's interaction with his father is likely to be somewhat less than in the single nuclear household.

Polygynous polygynous. The polygynous household consists of a man living with his wives and their various children. Here the child is likely to have even less opportunity to interact with his father.

Polygynous mother-child. This type of household occurs in those polygynous societies where each wife has a separate establishment and lives in it with her children. In these societies the father either sleeps in a men's club, has a hut of his own, or divides his time among the houses of his various wives. The husband usually does not sleep in the house of any wife during the two to three years when she is nursing each infant. Thus the mother may become the almost exclusive object of identification for the first few years of life.

18. The relationship between rejection-acceptance and the importance of the father as a socializing agent ($r=.40$; $p=.005$) is, in fact, stronger than the correlation between rejection-acceptance and the importance of the mother ($r=.29$; $p=.005$). It is also pertinent to observe that the earlier the mothers reduce intensive contact with their young infants during the first year, the more likely these mothers are to become rejecting when their offspring reach early childhood ($r=.46$; $p=.025$).

19. In fact, children are accepted in about 90 percent (fourteen out of sixteen) of the societies in our holocultural sample where grandparents are important socializing agents.

20. The *Six Cultures* study (Whiting 1963) is a good illustration of the type of intracultural community studies project we had in mind in Chapter Two, when we wrote about the methodology needed for the universalist approach.

21. The probability level of $p<.07$ is not statistically significant, but since other sources of evidence support the hypothesis that co-wives in the same shelter are likely to mute their expressions of affection toward their children, we are inclined to accept the relationship between co-wife residence and parental behavior as being significant. Since we predicted this relationship before we ran the (two-tailed) test, it is not improper statistically to accept hypotheses, which reach as high as the 10 percent level of confidence.

22. Again, as with the relationship between co-wife proximity and parental behavior, the probability level does not achieve the 5 percent confidence level. Nonetheless, we accept the hypothesis relating parental behavior to economy, because the results were predicted in advance. Moreover the results emerged precisely as predicted: all hunters in the sample accept their children; pastoralists come close to being evenly split in terms of rejection-acceptance, but tend slightly more often to reject. (See in this context, Figure 3, "Model of Expected Relationships between Rejection-Acceptance and Other Features of Society.") Codes for hunting and pastoral economies come from Murdock (1967).

23. We emphasize that pastoralists and other people with a fairly secure food base may reject their children. No argument is made, however, that they necessarily *will* reject their children.

24. Our argument should not be construed to mean that hunters consciously recognize the dangers of rejection or that pastoralists are aware that the effects of rejection are not "lethal" in their type of economy. Rather our "Darwinian" analysis pertains to the unintended and unrecognized interaction between economy and parental behavior.

25. Codes for settlement pattern come from Murdock (1957). Codes for social stratification, which are based on Murdock (1957), come from Bacon, Barry, et al. (1965). Codes for political integration, also based on Murdock (1957), come from Bacon, Child, and Barry (1963). The holocultural tests reported in this chapter were run between 1966 and 1971. They do not include some recent measures of cultural complexity, socialization, and so forth.

26. Codes for "desire for children," "punishment for abortion," "frequency of infanticide," and "sanctions for barrenness" come from Ayres (1954).

27. Codes for "importance of practices to beautify newborn infants" come from Ayres (1954). Codes for "display of affection toward infants" are published in Barry, Bacon, and Child (1967). We should emphasize that these tests and the ones following in the next paragraph show the relationship between parental handling of *infants* during the first year or so and parental treatment of *children* who are two to six years old.

28. Sears, Maccoby, and Levin (1957: 56), however, record a modest but significant tendency for American mothers who say that they were warm toward their infants to also say that they are warm toward the children once they are older ($r=.36$; $p=.01$).

29. Codes for "protection from environmental discomforts," "degree of drive reduction," "immediacy of drive reduction," "consistency of drive reduction," and "over-all indulgence during infancy" are published in Barry, Bacon, and Child (1967).

30. We thank Billie R. DeWalt for his research on the relationship between parental behavior and climate.

NOTES TO CHAPTER FIVE

1. In this chapter, we describe the eastern Baboquivari District and the western Hickiwan and Gu Vo districts. Four related villages, totaling seventy-six households, were studied in the Baboquivari district; in Gu Vo and Hickiwan, the ethnographers studied eight related villages. The description of the Papago is drawn from Joseph, Spicer, and Chesky (1949). The following description is written in the present tense, but the fieldwork for the case study was conducted in 1942-43. References to the east refer to the Baboquivari villages; references to the west are to the villages studied in Hickiwan and Gu Vo.

2. The description of the Alorese is written in the present tense, but fieldwork for the case study was conducted by Cora DuBois (1944) from 1937 to 1939.

3. Papago self-evaluation is not clearly enough described in Joseph, Spicer, and Chesky (1949) to make a meaningful comparison

with the Alorese, who, both as children and as adults, tend to have low self-esteem and feelings of low self-adequacy.

NOTES TO CHAPTER SIX

1. The Papago and Alorese case studies presented in Chapter Five are not, properly speaking, part of the community study methodology, because the data in these communities were not collected using RAP instruments and following RAP research design. These case studies do not reveal the natural variability in behavior that exists within every community. Thus, for instance, it is impossible to tell whether or not the children of more affectionate Alorese are significantly different in behavior or personality from the children of the rejecting Alorese—as predicted in rejection-acceptance theory.

NOTES TO APPENDIX ONE

1. Aggression is to be distinguished from assertiveness. Assertiveness refers to an individual's attempts to place himself in physical, verbal, social, or some other priority over others, for example to dominate a conversation or a group's activities, or to insist upon or stress his will over those of others. An individual may be assertive verbally, physically, or in both ways. Forms of verbal assertiveness include making confident, declarative statements, often without regard for evidence or proof, or pushing forward one's own point of view. Physical assertiveness includes various forms of offensive physical action. But when this offensive action (either physical or verbal) has the intention of *hurting* someone or something, then it becomes aggression, not assertiveness. Thus aggression and assertiveness are often closely related forms of behavior, with the major distinction being the *intentionality* of hurting. Aggression implies such an intention; assertiveness does not.

2. Some scholars (e.g. Beller 1955, Heathers 1955) prefer to distinguish "dependence" from "independence" conceptually. They define the term dependence as we do, but they reserve the term independence for forms of behavior we call self-reliance. The contrast between these usages is essentially one of *emotional* versus *instrumental* reliance (or dependence) of one person upon another, a distinction that is not always easy to make behaviorally. Investigators must be careful not to confuse independence with self-reliance (see definition of self-reliance). Self-reliance includes all behavior that is free from the supervision or guidance of other people (especially older people, for children). It involves a definite tendency to meet one's own *instrumental* (i.e. action- or task-

oriented) needs without relying on or asking for help of others. Thus self-reliance is an *instrumental* response; (in)dependence is an *emotional* response.

NOTES TO APPENDIX TWO

1. A negative sign (e.g. -1.00) is used to report a negative correlation, but a plus ($+$) sign is not used to report a positive correlation. As a matter of convention, all correlations are assumed to be positive—and are therefore not given a "$+$" sign—unless they are marked otherwise.

2. The symbol "$<$" as in $p < .001$ means "less than," and the symbol "$>$" as in $p > .10$ means "greater than."

NOTES TO APPENDIX THREE

1. Eleven ethnographies in the RAP sample of 101 societies could not be coded for rejection-acceptance, but they were coded for personality characteristics.

2. The linked pair test in the Rejection-Acceptance Project was worked out by James W. Jordan (1968).

3. A forty-six-page manuscript describing the logic of regional testing and the application of regional testing to these four hypotheses in the Rejection-Acceptance Project is available from the Journal Supplement Abstract Service of the American Psychological Association (see Ness and Rohner 1974).

4. Each point on the rejection-acceptance dimension was defined, but only the extremes—i.e., points 1 and 5—were defined for the personality scales (see Appendix One).

5. It is important that these matrices incorporate only uncorrected codes, not corrected codes. Corrected codes may generate artificially high interrater reliability coefficients and could produce a sense of discriminant validity that is more a function of interrater "collusion" than independent measurement by two raters.

6. A forty-page manuscript describing the results and procedures for assessing validity and reliability of data in holocultural research is available from the Journal Supplement Abstract Service of the American Psychological Association (see Rohner and Ness 1975).

REFERENCES

Adams, Francis M., and C. E. Osgood
1973 "A cross-cultural study of the affective meanings of color," *Journal of Cross-Cultural Psychology 4:* 135-56.

Ainsworth, Mary D. Salter
1966 "The effects of maternal deprivation: a review of findings and controversy in the context of research strategy," in Mary D. Ainsworth et al., *Deprivation of Maternal Care: A Reassessment of Its Effects*, New York, Schocken Books: 289-357.
1972 "Attachment and dependency: a comparison," in Jacob L. Gewirtz, ed., *Attachment and Dependency*, Washington D.C., V. H. Winston: 97-137.
1973 "The development of infant-mother attachment," in Bettye M. Caldwell and Henry N. Ricciuti, ed., *Review of Child Development Research. Child Development and Social Policy, Vol. 1*, Chicago, University of Chicago Press: 1-94.

Ainsworth, Mary D. Salter, and B. A. Wittig
1969 "Attachment and exploratory behavior of one-year olds in a strange situation," in B. M. Foss, ed., *Determinants of Infant Behavior, IV*, London, Methuen: 111-36.

Allen, Martin G.
1967 "Childhood experience and adult personality—a cross-cultural study using the concept of ego strength," *Journal of Social Psychology 71:* 53-68.

Apthorp, James S.
1970 "Can we prevent child beating?" *Family Weekly*, February 8: 20.

Ardrey, Robert
1961 *African genesis: a personal investigation into the animal origin and nature of man*, New York, Atheneum.
1966 *The territorial imperative*, New York, Atheneum.
1970 *The social contract*, New York, Atheneum.

Arling, G. L., and H. F. Harlow
1967 "Effects of social deprivation on maternal behavior of rhesus monkeys," *Journal of Comparative Physiological Psychology 64:* 371-77.

273

Ayres, Barbara C.
    1954   *A cross-cultural study of factors relating to pregnancy taboos*, unpublished doctoral dissertation, Cambridge, Radcliffe College.
    1968   "Effects of infantile stimulation on musical behavior," in Alan Lomax, *Folk Song Style and Culture*, Washington D.C., American Association for the Advancement of Science: 211-21.
    1973   "Effects of infant carrying practices on rhythm in music," *Ethos 1*: 387-404.
Bacon, Margaret K., et al.
    1965   *A cross-cultural study of drinking*, New Brunswick, Rutgers University, Center of Alcohol Studies (*Quarterly Journal of Studies on Alcohol, Supplement 3*).
Bacon, Margaret K., Irvin L. Child, and Herbert Barry, III
    1963   "A cross-cultural study of correlates of crime," *Journal of Abnormal and Social Psychology 66*: 291-300.
Bandura, Albert, and Aletha C. Huston
    1961   "Identification as a process of incidental learning," *Journal of Abnormal and Social Psychology 63*: 311-18.
Bandura, Albert, and Richard Walters
    1958   "Dependency conflicts in aggressive delinquents," *Journal of Social Issues 14*: 52-65.
    1963   *Social learning and personality development*, New York, Holt, Rinehart and Winston.
Barkow, Jerome H.
    1973   "Darwinian psychological anthropology: a biosocial approach," *Current Anthropology 14*: 373-87.
Barnett, Homer G.
    1960   *Being a Paluan*, New York, Holt, Rinehart and Winston.
Barry, Herbert, III
    1952   *Influence of socialization on the graphic arts: a cross-cultural study*, unpublished honors thesis, Cambridge, Harvard College, Department of Social Relations.
    1957   "Relationships between child training and the pictorial arts," *Journal of Abnormal and Social Psychology 54*: 380-83.
Barry, Herbert, III, Margaret K. Bacon, and Irvin L. Child
    1957   "A cross-cultural survey of some sex differences in socialization," *Journal of Abnormal and Social Psychology 55*: 327-32.
    1967   "Definitions, ratings, and bibliographic sources for

child-training practices of 110 cultures," in Clellan S. Ford, ed., *Cross-Cultural Approaches,* New Haven, HRAF Press: 293-331.

Barry, Herbert, III, Irvin L. Child, and Margaret K. Bacon
1959 "Relation of child training to subsistence economy," *American Anthropologist 61:* 51-63.

Beaglehole, Ernest, and James E. Ritchie
1961 "Basic personality in a New Zealand Maori community," in Bert Kaplan, ed., *Studying Personality Cross-Culturally,* Evanston, Ill., Row, Peterson: 493-517.

Becker, Wesley C., D. R. Peterson, K. A. Hellmer, D. J. Shoemaker, and H. C. Quoy
1959 "Factors in parental behavior and personality as related to problem behavior in children," *Journal of Consulting Psychology 23:* 107-18.

Bell, R. Q.
1968 "A reinterpretation of the direction of effects in studies of socialization," *Psychological Review 75:* 81-95.

Beller, E. K.
1955 "Dependency and independence in young children," *Journal of Genetic Psychology 87:* 25-35.

Bender, Lauretta, and Alvin E. Grugget, Jr.
1956 "A study of certain epidemiological factors in a group of children with childhood schizophrenia," *American Journal of Orthopsychiatry 26:* 131-43.

Berlin, Brent
1970 "A universalistic-evolutionary approach in ethnographic semantics," in Ann Fischer, ed., *Current Directions in Anthropology, Bulletin of the AAA, Vol. 3, No. 3, Part 2:* 1-18.

Berlin, Brent, Dennis E. Breedlove, and Peter H. Raven
1973 "General principles of classification and nomenclature in folk biology," *American Anthropologist 75:* 214-42.

Berlin, Brent, and Paul Kay
1969 *Basic color terms: their universality and evolution,* Berkeley, University of California Press.

Berry, John W.
1967 "Independence and conformity in subsistence level societies," *Journal of Personality and Social Psychology 7:* 415-18.

Boas, Franz
1943 "Recent anthropology," *Science 98:* 311-14, 334-37.

Boucher, Jerry D.
    1974   "What's in a face?" *East-West Center Magazine, Spring:*
            6-8.
Bowlby, John
    1958   "The nature of the child's tie to his mother," *Interna-
            tional Journal of Psychoanalysis 30:* 350-73.
    1966   *Maternal care and mental health*, New York, Schocken
            Books (originally published in 1952).
    1969   *Attachment, Vol. 1: Attachment and separation*, New
            York, Basic Books.
    1973   *Separation: anxiety and anger, Vol. 2: Attachment and
            loss*, New York, Basic Books.
Brainard, Charles J.
    1969   "Personal worth and perception of one's parents," *Ra-
            tional Living 4:* 17-19.
Brislin, Richard W., Walter J. Lonner, and Robert M. Thorndike
    1973   *Cross-cultural research methods*, New York, Wiley-
            Interscience.
Brody, Grace F.
    1969   "Maternal child-rearing attitudes and child behavior,"
            Developmental Psychology 1: 66.
Brown, Fred
    1937   "Neuroticism of institution vs. non-institution children,"
            Journal of Applied Psychology 21: 379-83.
Campbell, Donald T., and Donald W. Fiske
    1959   "Convergent and discriminant validation by the
            multitrait-multimethod matrix," *Psychological Bulletin
            56:* 81-105.
Carlson, Rae
    1971   "Where is the person in personality research?"
            Psychological Bulletin 75: 203-19.
Carroll, John B.
    1964   *Language and thought*, Englewood Cliffs, New Jersey,
            Prentice-Hall.
Chomsky, Noam
    1965   *Aspects of the theory of syntax*, Cambridge, MIT Press.
    1966   "Topics in the theory of generative grammar," in T.
            Sebeok, ed., *Current Trends in Linguistics, Vol. 3*, The
            Hague, Mouton: 1-60.
    1968   *Language and mind*, New York, Harcourt, Brace and
            World.
    1973   "Introduction," in Adam Schaff, *Language and*

Cognition, New York, McGraw-Hill: v-x.

Chomsky, Noam, and Morris Halle
1968 *Sound patterns of English,* New York, Harper and Row.

Coleman, James C.
1956 *Abnormal psychology and modern life,* 2d ed., New York, Scott, Foresman.

Coopersmith, Stanley
1967 *The antecedents of self-esteem,* San Francisco, W. H. Freeman.

Cox, Samuel H.
1970 "Intrafamily comparison of loving-rejecting child-rearing practices," *Child Development 41:* 437-48.

Crum, Ruth Marie
1972 *The relationship between maternal over-protection and aggressive, anti-social school behavior in middle class adolescent males,* unpublished doctoral dissertation, Wayne State University.

Darwin, Charles
1872 *The expression of the emotions in man and animals,* London, Murray.

Dasen, Pierre R.
1972 "Cross-cultural Piagetian research: a summary," *Journal of Cross-Cultural Psychology 3:* 23-39.

Dawson, John L. M.
1971 "Theory and research in cross-cultural psychology," *British Psychological Society, Bulletin 24:* 291-306.

Denenberg, V. H.
1969 "Animal studies of early experiences: some principles which have implications for human development," in John Hill, ed., *Minnesota Symposium on Child Psychology,* Minneapolis, University of Minnesota Press: 31-45.

DeVore, Irven
1963 "Mother infant relations in free ranging baboons," in H. L. Rheingold, ed., *Maternal Behavior in Mammals,* New York, John Wiley and Sons: 305-35.

DeVos, George A., and Arthur A. Hippler
1969 "Cultural psychology: comparative studies of human behavior," in Gardner Lindzey and Elliot Aronson, eds., *The Handbook of Social Psychology,* Vol. 4, 2d ed., Reading, Mass., Addison-Wesley: 323-417.

Dollard, John, Neal E. Miller, Leonard W. Doob, O. H. Mowrer,

Robert R. Sears, et al.
1939   *Frustration and aggression*, New Haven, Yale University Press.

Dollard, John and Neal E. Miller
1950   *Personality and psychotherapy: an analysis in terms of learning, thinking, and culture*, New York, McGraw-Hill.

DuBois, Cora
1944   *The people of Alor: a social-psychological study of an East Indian island*, Minneapolis, University of Minnesota Press.
1956   "Attitudes toward food and hunger in Alor," in D. G. Haring, ed., *Personal Character and Cultural Milieu*, Syracuse, Syracuse University Press: 241-53.

Earle, A. M., and B. V. Earle
1961   "Early maternal deprivation and later psychiatric illness," *American Journal of Orthopsychiatry 31:* 181-86.

Eisenberg, Leon
1957   "The fathers of autistic children," *American Journal of Orthopsychiatry 27:* 715-24.

Ellison, E. A., and D. M. Hamilton
1949   "The hospital treatment of dementia praecox. Part II," *American Journal of Psychiatry 106:* 454-61.

Elmer, Elizabeth, and Grace Gregg
1967   "Developmental characteristics of abused children," *Pediatrics 40:* 596-602.

Ferenczi, S.
1929   "The unwelcome child and his death instinct," *International Journal of Psychoanalysis 10:* 125-29.

Feshback, Seymour
1970   "Aggression," in Paul Mussen, ed., *Carmichael's Manual of Child Psychology*, *Vol. 2*, New York, John Wiley and Sons: 159-259.

Finney, J. C.
1961   "Some maternal influences in children's personality and character," *Genetic Psychological Monographs 63:* 199-278.

Firth, Raymond
1963   *We, the Tikopia*, Boston, Beacon Press (originally published in London by Allen and Unwin in 1936).

Fischer, John L.
1961   "Art styles as cultural cognitive maps," *American An-*

thropologist 63: 79-93.

Fitz-Simmons, M. J.
1935 "Some parent-child relationships as shown in clinical case studies," *Contributions to Education 643*, Teacher's College, Columbia University.

Fox, Robin
1970 "The cultural animal," *Social Science Information 9:* 7-25.
1973 *Encounter with anthropology*, New York, Harcourt, Brace, Jovanovich.

Frazee, Helen E.
1953 "Children who later become schizophrenic," *Smith College Studies in Social Work 23:* 125-49.

Freedman, Daniel G.
1968 "Personality development in infancy: a biological approach," in S. L. Washburn and Phyllis C. Jay, eds., *Perspectives on Human Evolution*, New York, Holt, Rinehart and Winston: 258-87.

Freeman, Derek
1966 "Social anthropology and the scientific study of human behavior," *Man 1:* 330-42.

Freud, Sigmund
1930 *Civilization and its discontents*, London, Hogarth Press.

Friedlander, Dorothee
1945 "Personality development of twenty-seven children who later became psychotic," *Journal of Abnormal and Social Psychology 40:* 330-35.

Gecas, Viktor
1972 "Parental behavior and contextual variations in adolescent self-esteem," *Sociometry 35:* 332-45.

Gewirtz, Jacob L.
1972 "Deficiency conditions of stimulation and the reversal of their effects via enrichment," in J. Mönks, Willard Hartup, and Jan de Wit, eds., *Determinants of Behavioral Development*, New York, Academic Press: 349-75.

Gil, David G.
1970 *Violence against children: physical child abuse in the United States*, Cambridge, Harvard University Press.

Ginsburg, Benson E., and S. C. Maxson
1974 *The genomic repertoire as an ethological concept*, revised version of a paper presented at the Chairman's

Symposium on Learning Capacities in Neurobiological Perspectives, American Association for the Advancement of Science, Washington, D.C., December 1972.

Goldberg, Steven
1973   *The inevitability of patriarchy: why the biological difference between men and women always produces male domination*, New York, William Morrow.

Goldfarb, William
1943   "Effects of early institutional care on adolescent personality," *Journal of Experimental Education 12:* 106-29.
1945   "Psychological privation in infancy and subsequent adjustment," *American Journal of Orthopsychiatry 15:* 247-55.

Golding, William
1954   *Lord of the flies*, New York, Harcourt, Brace.

Greenberg, Joseph H.
1963   "Introduction," in J. H. Greenberg, ed., *Universals of Language*, Cambridge, MIT Press: xi-xiii.
1966   "Language Universals," in T. Sebeok, ed., *Current Trends in Linguistics*, Vol. 3, The Hague, Mouton: 61-112.

Gunders, Shulamith Marcus, and John W. M. Whiting
1968   "Mother-infant separation and physical growth," *Ethnology 7:* 196-206.

Hallowell, A. Irving
1950   "Personality structure and the evolution of man," *American Anthropologist 52:* 159-74.

Hamburg, David A.
1963   "Emotions in the perspective of human evolution," in P. H. Knapp, ed., *Expression of the Emotions in Man*, New York, International Universities Press: 300-17.
1968   "Evolution of emotional responses: evidence from recent research on non-human primates," *Science and Psychoanalysis 12:* 39-54.

Harlow, Harry F.
1962   "The hetero-sexual affectional system in monkeys," *American Psychologist 17:* 1-9.
1971   *Learning to love*, San Francisco, Albion Publishing Company.

Harlow, Harry F., and M. K. Harlow
1969   "Effects of various mother-infant relationships on rhesus monkey behavior," in B. M. Foss, ed., *Determinants of*

Infant Behavior, Vol. 4, New York, Barnes and Noble: 15-36.

Harper, Lawrence V.
1971 "The young as a source of stimuli controlling caretaker behavior," *Developmental Psychology 4:* 73-88.

Hartup, Willard W., and Albert Yonas
1971 "Developmental psychology," in Paul H. Mussen and Mark R. Rosenzweig, eds., *Annual Review of Psychology, Vol. 22*, Palo Alto, Annual Reviews: 372-73.

Hattwick, Berta W.
1936 "Interrelations between pre-school children's behavior and certain factors in the home," *Child Development 7:* 200-26.

Heathers, G.
1955 "Emotional dependence and independence in nursery school play," *Journal of Genetic Psychology 87:* 37-57.

Heilbrun, Alfred B., Jr.
1973 *Aversive maternal control: a theory of schizophrenic development*, New York, John Wiley and Sons.

Heilbrun, Alfred B., Jr., and Nancy A. Norbert
1970 "Maternal child-rearing experience and self reinforcement effectiveness," *Developmental Psychology 3:* 81-87.

Heilbrun, Alfred B., Jr., and Helen K. Orr
1966 "Perceived maternal childrearing history and subsequent motivational effects of failure," *Journal of Genetic Psychology 109:* 75-89.

Helfer, Ray E., and C. Henry Kempe, eds.
1968 *The battered child*, Chicago, University of Chicago Press.

Henry, Jules
1959 "Culture, personality, and evolution," *American Anthropologist 61:* 221-26.

Herskovits, Melville J.
1956 *Man and his works*, New York, Alfred A. Knopf.

Hinde, R. A., and Y. Spencer-Booth
1970 "Individual differences in the response of rhesus monkeys to a period of separation from their mothers," *Journal of Child Psychology and Psychiatry and Allied Disciplines 11:* 159-76.

Horney, Karen
1937 *The neurotic personality of our time*, New York, W. W.

Norton.

Hostetler, John, and Gertrude E. Huntington
1967   *The Hutterites in North America*, New York, Holt, Rinehart & Winston.

Hurley, John R., and Robert Hohn
1971   "Shifts in child-rearing attitudes linked with parental occupation," *Developmental Psychology 4:* 324-28.

Hutchinson, John W., and John M. Roberts
1972   "Expressive constraints on driver re-education," *Psychological Aspects of Driver Behaviour, Vol. 2 Applied Research. Sec. II.2.C*, Voorburg, The Netherlands, Institute for Road Safety Research SWOV: 1-12.

Ingham, Harrington V.
1949   "A statistical study of family relationships in psychoneurosis," *American Journal of Psychiatry 106:* 91-98.

Jackson, Lydia
1950   "Emotional attitudes towards the family of normal, neurotic, and delinquent children, part 1," *British Journal of Psychology 41:* 35-51.

Jacobs, Martin A., et al.
1972   "Parent-child relationships and illness behavior," *Journal of Consulting and Clinical Psychology 39:* 49-55.

Jahoda, Gustav
1970   "A cross-cultural perspective in psychology," *Advancement of Science 27:* 57-70.
1973   "Psychology and the developing countries: Do they need each other?" Paper presented at the International Seminar on Cross-Cultural Research in Culture Learning. The East-West Center, Honolulu, Hawaii.

Jakobson, Roman
1968   *Child language, aphasia and phonological universals*, New York, Humanities Press.

Jordan, James W.
1968   "Galton's problem as it applies to the Rejection-Acceptance Project," *Rejection-Acceptance Project Holocultural Component: Methodological Working Paper 2*, Storrs, University of Connecticut.

Joseph, Alice, Rosamond B. Spicer, and Jane Chesky
1949   *The Desert People: a study of the Papago Indians*, Chicago, University of Chicago Press.

Jourard, Sidney M., and Richard M. Remy
1955   "Perceived parental attitudes, the self and security,"

Journal of Consulting Psychiatry 19: 364-66.

Kallman, Franz J.
1959 "The genetics of mental illness," in S. Arieti, ed., *American Handbook of Psychology, Vol. 1*, New York, Basic Books: 175-96.

Kanner, Leo
1945 "Autistic disturbances of affective contact," *Nervous Child 2: J*217-50.*
1949 "Problems of nosology and psychodynamics of early infantile autism," *American Journal of Orthopsychiatry 19:* 416-26.

Kaplan, David, and Robert A. Manners
1972 *Culture theory*, Englewood Cliffs, New Jersey, Prentice-Hall.

Kardiner, Abram
1945 *The psychological frontiers of society*, New York, Columbia University Press.

Kaufman, I. C., and L. A. Rosenblum
1967 "The reaction to separation in infant monkeys: anaclitic depression and conservation-withdrawal," *Psychosomatic Medicine 29:* 648-75.

Keesing, Roger M.
1973 "Paradigms lost: the new ethnography and the new linguistics," *Southwestern Journal of Anthropology 28:* 299-332.

Kiesler, S. B.
1966 "Stress, affiliation and performance," *Journal of Experimental Research In Personality 1:* 227-35.

Kohn, Melvin
1973 "Social class and schizophrenia: a critical review and a reformulation," *Schizophrenia 7:* 60-80.

Kuhn, Thomas S.
1970 *The structure of scientific revolutions*, 2d ed., Chicago, University of Chicago Press.

LaBarre, Weston
1955 *The Human Animal*, Chicago, University of Chicago Press.

Lambert, William W., Leigh Minturn Triandis, and Margery Wolf
1959 "Some correlates of beliefs in the malevolence and benevolence of supernatural beings—a cross-cultural study," *Journal of Abnormal and Social Psychology 58:* 162-69.

Landauer, Thomas K.
1973 "Infantile vaccination and the secular trend in stature,"
      Ethos 1: 499-503.
Landauer, Thomas K., and John W. M. Whiting
1964 "Infantile stimulation and adult stature of human males,"
      American Anthropologist 66: 1007-28.
Lenneberg, Eric H.
1964 "A biological perspective of language," in Eric H. Len-
      neberg, ed., *New Directions in the Study of Language,*
      Cambridge, MIT Press: 65-88.
1969 "On explaining language," *Science 164:* 635-43.
Lerner, Isadore M.
1968 *Heredity, evolution, and society,* San Francisco, W. H.
      Freeman.
Levine, Seymore
1960 "Stimulation in Infancy," *Scientific American 205:* 2-8.
Lévi-Strauss, Claude
1966 *The savage mind,* Chicago, University of Chicago Press.
1969 *The raw and the cooked: introduction to the science of
      mythology, Vol. 1,* New York, Harper and Row.
1971 *L'Homme nu,* Paris, Librairie Plon.
Lewis, H.
1954 *Deprived children (the Mersham Experiment),* London,
      Oxford University Press.
Lewis, Michael, and Leonard A. Rosenblum, eds.
1974 *The effect of the infant on its care-giver,* New York, John
      Wiley and Sons.
Lewis, Oscar
1960 *Tepoztlan village in Mexico,* New York, Henry Holt.
Lidz, T., S. Fleck, and A. Cornelison
1965 *Schizophrenia and the family,* New York, International
      University Press.
Lomax, Alan, et al.
1968 "Folk song style and culture," *American Association for
      the Advancement of Science, Special Publication 88,*
      Washington, D.C.
Lorenz, Konrad
1966 *On aggression,* New York, Harcourt, Brace & World.
Maccoby, Eleanor E.
1973 "*Review of* 'The inevitability of patriarchy,' by S. Gold-
      berg," *Science 182:* 469-71.
Maccoby, Eleanor, and John C. Masters

1970 "Attachment and dependency," in Paul H. Mussen, ed., *Carmichael's Manual of Child Psychology*, Vol. 2, New York, John Wiley and Sons: 73-153.

Malinowski, Bronislaw
1961 *Argonauts of the Western Pacific*, New York, E. P. Dutton (first published in 1922).

Mallick, S. K., and B. R. McCandless
1966 "A study of catharsis of aggression," *Journal of Personality and Social Psychology 4:* 591-96.

Manners, Robert A., and David Kaplan, eds.
1968 "Notes on theory and non-theory in anthropology," in their *Theory in Anthropology: A Sourcebook*, Chicago, Aldine: 1-12.

Marshall, Helen R.
1961 "Relations between home experiences and children's use of language in play interactions with peers," *Psychological Monographs 75 (Whole No. 509).*

Marshall, Helen R., and Boyd R. McCandless
1965 "Relationship between dependence on adults and social acceptance by peers," in Paul Mussen, John Conger, and Jerome Kagan, eds., *Readings in Child Development and Personality*, New York, Harper and Row: 367-74.

Maslow, A. H., and B. Mittlemann
1951 *Principles of abnormal psychology*, New York, Harper and Brothers.

McClelland, David
1961 *The achieving society*, Princeton, D. Van Nostrand.

McCord, Joan, and William McCord
1958 "The effects of parental role model on criminality," *Journal of Social Issues 14:* 66-75.

McCord, William, Joan McCord, and A. Howard
1961 "Familial correlates of aggression in non-delinquent male children," *Journal of Abnormal and Social Psychology 62:* 79-83.

McCord, William J., Joan McCord, and P. Verden
1962 "Familial and behavioral correlates of dependency in male children," *Child Development 33:* 313-26.

Mead, Margaret
1928 *Coming of age in Samoa*, New York, William Morrow.
1939 "1925-1939 [Introduction]," in her *From the South Seas; Studies of Adolescence and Sex in Primitive Societies*, New York, William Morrow.

1956 "Some theoretical considerations on the problem of mother-child separation," in D. G. Haring, ed., *Personal Character and Cultural Milieu*, Syracuse, Syracuse University Press: 637-49.

1963 "Socialization and enculturation," *Current Anthropology* 4: 184-88.

Melnick, Barry, and John R. Hurley
1969 "Distinctive personality attributes of child-abusing mothers," *Journal of Consulting and Clinical Psychology* 33: 746-49.

Miller, N. E., and R. Bugelski
1948 "Minor studies in aggression: the influence of frustrations imposed by the in-group on attitudes expressed toward out-groups," *Journal of Psychology* 25: 437-42.

Minturn, Leigh, and William W. Lambert
1964 *Mothers of six cultures: antecedents of child rearing*, New York, John Wiley and Sons.

Montague, Ashley, ed.
1973 *Man and agression*, 2d ed., New York, Oxford University Press.

Morris, Desmond
1967 *The naked ape: a zoologist's study of the human animal*, New York, McGraw-Hill.

1969 *The human zoo*, New York, McGraw-Hill.

Mosher, L. R., J. G. Gunderson, and Sherry Buchsbaum
1973 "Special report on schizophrenia: 1972," *Schizophrenia* 7: 10-52.

Murdock, George Peter
1957 "World ethnographic sample," *American Anthropologist* 59: 664-87.

1965 *Culture and society*, Pittsburgh, University of Pittsburgh Press.

1967 *Ethnographic atlas: a summary*, Pittsburgh, University of Pittsburgh Press.

1971 "Anthropology's mythology" (Huxley Memorial Lecture, 1971), *Royal Anthropological Institute of Great Britain and Ireland, Proceedings for 1971*: 17-24.

Murdock, George Peter, et al.
1962 "Ethnographic atlas," *Ethnology 1*: 113-34.

Mussen, P. H., J. J. Conger, and J. Kagan
1963 *Child development and personality*, New York, Harper and Row.

Mussen, P., and A. Parker
1965 "Mother nurturance and girls' incidental imitation learning," *Journal of Personality and Social Psychology 2:* 94-97.

Naroll, Raoul
1962 *Data quality control—a new research technique: prolegomena to a cross-cultural study of culture stress,* New York, Free Press of Glencoe.
1964 "A fifth solution to Galton's problem," *American Anthropologist 66:* 863-67.

Naroll, Raoul, and Roy G. D'Andrade
1963 "Two further solutions to Galton's problem," *American Anthropologist 65:* 1053-67.

Ness, Robert C., and Ronald P. Rohner
1974 "The logic of regional testing and a modified application of that procedure to four hypotheses in the Rejection-Acceptance Project," *JSAS Catalogue of Selected Documents in Psychology 4:* 121-22 (manuscript 764).

Osgood, Charles E.
1964 "Semantic differential technique in the comparative study of cultures," *American Anthropologist 66:* 171-200.
1969 "On the whys and wherefores of E, P, and A," *Journal of Personality and Social Psychology 12:* 194-99.
1971 "Exploration in semantic space: a personal diary," *Journal of Social Issues 27:* 5-64.

Otterbein, Keith F.
1970 *The evolution of war; a cross-cultural study,* New Haven, HRAF Press.

Pelto, Pertti J.
1970 *Anthropological research: the structure of inquiry,* New York, Harper and Row.

Pike, Kenneth
1967 *Language in relation to a unified theory of the structure of human behavior,* 2d rev. ed., The Hague: Mouton.

Pringle, M. L. K., and V. Bossio
1960 "Early, prolonged separation and emotional maladjustment," *Journal of Child Psychology and Psychiatry 1:* 37-48.

Przeworski, Adam, and Henry Teune
1970 *The logic of comparative social inquiry,* New York, Wiley-Interscience.

Pugh, Meredith

1967 "Two analytic problems in cross-cultural methodology," *Rejection-Acceptance Project, Holocultural Component: Working Paper 1*, Storrs, University of Connecticut.

Radin, Norma
1971 "Maternal warmth, achievement motivation and cognitive functioning in lower-class preschool children," *Child Development 42:* 1560-65.

Reichard, Suzanne, and Carl Tillman
1950 "Patterns of parent-child relationships in schizophrenia," *Psychiatry 13:* 247-57.

Reichel-Dolmatoff, Gerardo, and Alicia Reichel-Dolmatoff
1961 *The people of Aritama: the cultural personality of a Colombian mestizo village*, Chicago, University of Chicago Press.

Rimland, Bernard
1964 *Infantile autism*, New York, Appleton-Century-Crofts.

Robbins, Michael C., P. J. Pelto, and B. R. DeWalt
1972 "Climate and behavior: a biocultural study," *Journal of Cross-Cultural Psychology 3:* 331-44.

Roberts, John M., Malcolm J. Arth, and Robert R. Bush
1959 "Games in culture," *American Anthropologist 61:* 597-605.

Roberts, John M., H. Hoffmann, and Brian Sutton-Smith
1965 "Pattern and competence: a consideration of tick-tacktoe," *El Palacio* (Autumn): 17-30.

Roberts, John M., F. Koenig, and R. B. Stark
1969 "Judged display: a consideration of a craft show," *Journal of Leisure Research 1:* 163-79.

Roberts, John M., and Brian Sutton-Smith
1962 "Child training and game involvement," *Ethnology 1:* 166-85.
1966 "Cross-cultural correlates of games of chance," *Behavior Science Notes 1:* 131-44.

Roberts, John M., Brian Sutton-Smith, and Adam Kendon
1963 "Strategy in games and folk tales," *Journal of Social Psychology 61:* 185-99.

Rohner, Ronald P.
n.d.(a) *The cross-cultural method*, New York, Holt, Rinehart, and Winston (in preparation).
n.d.(b) *Field manual for the study of parental acceptance-rejection* (in preparation).
1969 *The ethnography of Franz Boas*, Chicago, University of

Chicago Press.

1975 "Parental acceptance-rejection and personality develop-
ment: a universalist approach to behavioral science," in
R. W. Brislin, S. Bochner, and W. J. Lonner, eds.,
Cross-Cultural Perspectives on Learning, Beverly Hills,
Sage Publications: 251-69.

Rohner, Ronald P., Billie R. DeWalt, and Robert C. Ness

1973 "Ethnographer bias in cross-cultural research: an empirical study," *Behavior Science Notes* 8: 275-317.

Rohner, Ronald P., and L. Katz

1970 "Testing for validity and reliability in cross-cultural research," *American Anthropologist* 72: 1068-73.

Rohner, Ronald P., and Robert C. Ness

1975 "Procedures for assessing the validity and reliability of
data in cross-cultural research," *JSAS Catalogue of
Selected Documents in Psychology* 5: 190 (manuscript
856).

Rohner, Ronald P., and Evelyn C. Rohner

1969 "Franz Boas and the development of North American
ethnology and ethnography," in Ronald P. Rohner, ed.,
The Ethnography of Franz Boas, Chicago, University of
Chicago Press: xiii-xxx.

Rohner, Ronald P., and Caroline C. Turner

n.d. *Parental acceptance-rejection: an annotated bibliography of research and theory* (in preparation).

Rosenberg, M.

1962 "The association between self-esteem and anxiety,"
Psychiatric Research 1: 135-52.

Rosenthal, M. K.

1965 *The generalization of dependency behaviors from
mother to stranger*, unpublished doctoral dissertation,
Stanford University.

Rousell, Charles H., and Carl N. Edwards

1971 "Some developmental antecedents of psychopathology,"
Journal of Personality 39: 362-77.

Rutter, Michael

1972 *Maternal deprivation reassessed*, Harmondsworth, Mid-
dlesex, England, Penguin Books.

Sears, Robert R.

1961 "Relation of early socialization experiences to aggression
in middle childhood," *Journal of Abnormal and Social
Psychology* 63: 466-92.

1961 "Transcultural variables and conceptual equivalence," in Bert Kaplan, ed., *Studying Personality Cross-Culturally*, Evanston, Ill., Row, Peterson: 445-55.

1970 "Relation of early socialization experiences to self-concepts and gender role in middle childhood," *Child Development 41*: 267-89.

Sears, Robert R., Eleanor Maccoby, and Harry Levin
1957 *Patterns of child rearing*, Evanston, Illinois, Row, Peterson.

Sears, Robert R., John W. M. Whiting, V. Nowlis, and P. S. Sears
1953 "Some child rearing antecedents of aggression and dependency in young children," *Genetic Psychology Monographs 47*: 135-234.

Sears, Robert R., and G. W. Wise
1950 "Relation of cup feeding in infancy to thumb-sucking and the oral drive," *American Journal of Orthopsychiatry 20*: 123-38.

Seay, B., B. K. Alexander, and H. F. Harlow
1964 "Maternal behavior of socially deprived rhesus monkeys," *Journal of Abnormal and Social Psychology 69*: 345-54.

Seay, B., and H. F. Harlow
1965 "Maternal separation in the rhesus monkey," *Journal of Nervous and Mental Disorders 140*: 434-41.

Sebeok, Thomas A.
1968 "Goals and limitations in the study of animal communications," in Thomas A. Sebeok, ed., *Animal Communication*, Bloomington, Indiana University Press: 3-14.

Siegelman, Marvin
1966 "Loving and punishing parental behavior and introversion tendencies in sons," *Child Development 37*: 985-92.

Singer, Margaret, and Lyman Wynne
1963 "Differentiating characteristics of parents of childhood schizophrenics, childhood neurotics and young adult schizophrenics," *American Journal of Psychiatry 120*: 234-43.

Skeels, H. M.
1966 "Adult status of children with contrasting early life experiences," *Monographs of the Society for Research in Child Development Vol. 31, No. 3*.

Slater, Philip E.
1962 "Parental behavior and personality of the child," *Journal*

of Genetic Psychology 101: 53-68.

Smith, H. T. A.
    1958   "A comparison of interview and observation measures of mother behavior," *Journal of Abnormal and Social Psychology 57:* 278-82.

Society for Cross-Cultural Research
    1973   "Constitution and by-laws of the Society for Cross-Cultural Research," *Society for Cross-Cultural Research Newsletter* (Nov. 1973): 5-8.

Spinetta, John J., and David Rigler
    1972   "The child-abusing parent: a psychological review," *Psychological Bulletin 77:* 296-304.

Spiro, Melford E.
    1954   "Human nature and its psychological dimensions," *American Anthropologist 56:* 19-30.

Spiro, Melford E., and Roy D'Andrade
    1958   "A cross-cultural study of some supernatural beliefs," *American Anthropologist 60:* 456-66.

Spitz, René
    1949   "The role of ecological factors in emotional development in infancy," *Child Development 20:* 145-55.

Spitz, René A., and Katherine M. Wolf
    1946   "Anaclytic depression: an inquiry into the genesis of psychiatric conditions in early childhood II," *Psychoanalytic Study of the Child 2:* 313-42.

Stagner, Ross
    1948   *Psychology of personality*, New York, McGraw-Hill.

Storr, Anthony
    1968   *Human aggression*, New York, Atheneum.

Sutton-Smith, Brian, and John M. Roberts
    1964   "Rubrics of competitive behavior," *Journal of Genetic Psychology 105:* 15-37.

Sutton-Smith, Brian, John M. Roberts, and R. M. Kozelka
    1963   "Game involvement in adults," *Journal of Social Psychology 6:* 15-30.

Symonds, Percival H.
    1939   *The psychology of parent-child relationships*, New York, Appleton Century.

Tiger, Lionel
    1969   *Men in groups*, New York, Random House.

Tiger, Lionel, and Robin Fox
    1966   "The zoological perspective in social science," *Man 1:*

75-81.

1971   *The imperial animal*, New York, Holt, Rinehart and Winston.

Triandis, Harry C., Roy S. Malpass, and Andrew R. Davidson
1972   "Cross-cultural psychology," in Bernard J. Siegel, ed., *Biennial Review of Anthropology, 1971*, Stanford, Stanford University Press: 1-84.

Tschopik, Harry, Jr.
1951   "The Aymara of Chucuito, Peru. I Magic," *American Museum of Natural History, Anthropological Papers, Vol. 44, part 2.*

Turnbull, Colin, M.
1972   *The mountain people*, New York, Simon and Schuster.

Tyler, Stephen A.
1969   *Cognitive anthropology*, New York, Holt, Rinehart and Winston.

Wahl, C. W.
1956-   "Some antecedent factors in the family histories of 568
57   male schizophrenics of the United States Navy," *American Journal of Psychiatry 113*: 201-10.

Wallace, Anthony F. C.
1970   "The evolution of culture and the evolution of brain," in his *Culture and Personality*, New York, Random House: 40-73.

Webb, E. J., D. T. Campbell, R. D. Schwartz, and L. Sechrest
1966   *Unobtrusive measures*, Chicago, Rand-McNally.

Whiting, Beatrice B., ed.
1963   *Six cultures: studies of child rearing*, New York, John Wiley and Sons.

Whiting, John W. M.
1941   *Becoming a Kwoma*, New Haven, Yale University Press.
1959   "Sorcery, sin, and superego: a cross-cultural study of some mechanisms of social control," in Marshall R. Jones, ed., *Nebraska Symposium on Motivation 1959*, Lincoln, University of Nebraska Press: 174-95 (reprinted in 1967 in Clellan S. Ford, ed., *Cross-Cultural Approaches*, New Haven, HRAF Press: 147-68).
1961   "Socialization process and personality," in F. L. K. Hsu, ed., *Psychological Anthropology: Approaches to Culture and Personality*, Homewood, Ill., Dorsey Press: 355-80.
1964   "Effects of climate on certain cultural practices," in Ward H. Goodenough, ed., *Explorations in Cultural An-*

thropology: Essays in Honor of George Peter Murdock, New York, McGraw-Hill: 511-44.

1965 "Menarcheal age and infant stress in humans," in Frank A. Beach, ed., *Conference on Sex and Behavior*, New York, John Wiley and Sons: 221-33.

Whiting, John W. M., and Irvin L. Child
1953 *Child training and personality: a cross-cultural study*, New Haven, Yale University Press.

Whiting, John W. M., T. K. Landauer, and T. M. Jones
1968 "Infantile immunization and adult stature," *Child Development 39: 59-67.*

Winder, C. L., and Lucy Rau
1962 "Parental attitudes associated with social deviance in preadolescent boys," *Journal of Abnormal and Social Psychology 64: 418-24.*

Wittenborn, J. R.
1956 "A study of adoptive children: III, Relationship between some aspects of development and some aspects of environment for adoptive children," *Psychological Monographs 70: no. 410.*

Wolberg, Lewis R.
1944 "The character structure of the rejected child," *Nervous Child 3: 74-88.*

Wolf, Eric R.
1964 *Anthropology*, Englewood Cliffs, Prentice-Hall.

Wolins, M.
1970 "Young children in institutions: additional evidence," *Developmental Psychology 6: 99-109.*

Wolman, Benjamin B.
1965 "Schizophrenia and related disorders," in Benjamin B. Wolman, ed., *Handbook of Clinical Psychology*, New York, McGraw-Hill: 976-1029.

Wrong, D.
1961 "The oversocialized concept of man in sociology," *American Sociological Review 26: 184-93.*

Yarrow, L. J.
1964 "Separation from parents during early childhood," in M. L. Hoffman and L. W. Hoffman, eds., *Review of Child Development Research, Vol. 1*, New York, Russell Sage Foundation: 89-136.

Yarrow, Marian R., C. Z. Waxler, and P. M. Scott
1971 "Child effects on adult behavior," *Developmental*

Psychology 5: 300-11.

Zax, Melvin and Emory L. Cowen
    1972 *Abnormal psychology: changing conceptions*, New York, Holt, Rinehart and Winston.

Zucker, Herbert John
    1943 "Affectional identification and delinquency," in R. S. Woodworth, ed., *Archives of Psychology*, No. 286, Vol. 40: 60 pp.

Index